BECOMING ROSIE: MEMOIR OF A GROUPIE

CHRISTINE FOWLER

NORTH STAR CREATIONS PUBLISHING

NORTH STAR CREATIONS PUBLISHING

ISBN: 978-0-578-21932-5

PRINTED IN THE UNITED STATES OF AMERICA

Table of Contents

CHAPTER I

The Seed Is Planted (1955-1969)

"We dance round in a ring and suppose, but the secret sits in the middle and knows..." Robert Frost

As I drive down the road my heart still beats wildly whenever I encounter a tour bus. These days it's probably a family owned recreational vehicle filled with screaming children and tormented parents. Oh wait, that could also describe a rock and roll tour bus: whining rock stars and tour managers trying to wrangle them in. Whatever the actual contents, it's a tour bus to me, occupied by handsome, long-haired musicians and roadies, free from the imbroglios of life at home.

When I see myself in a mirror these days, I notice what the years have done. So many deep wrinkles from puckering my lips around cigarettes, joints, and other things, my hands all knotted up with arthritis, and my beautiful figure with an extra seventy pounds or so on it. My old nose replaced by a different version following an auto accident in 1986. My cellulite-riddled thighs resembling a rippled cloud formation at sunset. At least I have ample breasts now even though gravity has won and they look like the Maxine character in the greeting card. If there was anyone's voice I tried to emulate (besides Stevie Nicks and

Karen Carpenter) it was Linda Ronstadt, I was even mistaken for her once. She had a pitch perfect and tonal quality.

In yoga class, I used to be able to place both legs behind my head. I did Jane Fonda workouts and danced every night, my heart and soul racing. My body was good and my spirit was like a wild mustang waiting to be tamed. I was no beauty in the Cosmopolitan sense, but I was told there was something different and charismatic about me.

I never made the conscious decision to meet famous people or to assimilate into their road warrior culture. Life happens and, sufficed to say, I got caught up in it. It is now some comfort to me and entertaining to my friends when I spin my tales.

When this all began I knew Bob Seger as a local guy from Ann Arbor who had a bar band, but I didn't have any idea I would meet a nice New Jersey guy like Bruce Springsteen, Stephen Stills, the Rolling Stones, or the J. Geils Band, among countless others.

So let me share with you the wild ride of my life during the post-hippie days of the seventies into the disco days of the eighties and then the anything goes era, all while struggling to raise two daughters on my own. I will regale you with my tales of sex, drugs, rock and roll and motherhood, but first I would like to explain how I got there.

To say that one thing could have happened without first something else happening wouldn't be the truth. It was the chaos theory imparting itself on my life. I envisioned my life unraveling like one continuous thread separating from a tapestry. Okay, so perhaps I listened to too much Carole King back then.

What I longed for was a Dadaistic approach to life, a departure from all the traditionalistic crap my parents had shoved down my throat. In the constructs of this period of my life, there was no feeling of selling myself out. I was merely pursuing my adventures. Somehow though, with each unrequited love or shirking of another person's affections, a little piece of my soul was eaten away. I always tried to be honest and loving and kind. I didn't want to use people, and I expected the same in return. Needless to say I was frequently disappointed. When we moved to Plymouth, Michigan in 1958, everything was supposed to be different and wonderful. It was a fairly wealthy ultra-conservative Republican city. We would make new friends, have a new school, and life would be lovely. Were my parents delusional? Who knew? All I ever witnessed was insanity. Several of the women in my mother's family suffered from schizophrenia and depression and had been institutionalized. By the time I was ten years old there was an abundance of fighting between my mother and father. The emotional struggles that saturated our lives with yelling and slapping each other, and my mother running away to the bedroom crying was a bit overwhelming for both my sister and me.

We lived in a modest Cape Cod red brick house on Herald Street. My sisters and I called ourselves the "Herald angels" as in 'Hark the Herald Angels.' It was a very small town, rural by Detroit city standards. We had moved there to escape the trappings of big city life in Detroit and for my father's new job. It was far less dangerous than the Detroit neighborhood where we lived for a time with my Scottish grandmother and French Grandfather. My grandparent's house was positioned a couple houses away from a coal yard and railroad track. The sounds of trains and the clouds of black soot filled our lives and our lungs.

Childhood innocence, what was that? In the 1950's childhood was far from sublime. Childhood evokes a feeling of dread, poverty and fear in me. One time I opened the refrigerator to find a half jar of Miracle Whip and a waxed paper mystery meat wrapped up on the second shelf. I was so hungry I ate a spoonful of the Miracle Whip.

Although my grandparents on my Father's side were well-to-do, we were hungry on a daily basis. This was mainly due to my father's pride I suspect. On paydays there was food on the table and we were instructed to "clean your plate there are people starving in this world." My shrunken stomach could not handle the challenge.

As much as I loved my father I also feared him. My mother was constantly threatening, wait 'til your father gets home, and if he came home in an angry mood my skin would feel the wrath he could unleash. His hugs would be unaffectionate bear hugs that were bone crushing while he gritted his teeth and growled. He waited until he was on his death bed to tell me that he loved me for the first time in my life.

When I was five years old, my German grandmother Irene started to watch me on the weekends in order to lighten my parent's burden She spoke German fluently, was very stern, insistent in her own way, and really could not be bothered with childhood things. It was strange for me to stay with her every weekend and live like a princess, then return to my own despondent mother.

I knew that Grandma Irene adored me. She was a slender woman with big brown eyes, high cheek bones and a small, perfectly pointed nose, a strong jaw, and light brown hair that was always tightly curled with a permanent. Not the typical stereotypical buxom blond German woman. Her voice was kind unless she was spouting something about "shinnies" or "blackies" or making some other racist comment that she never held back..

Grandma Irene liked to dress me up in crisp, blue, chiffon, with lots of satin bows, a fancy dress that would itch horribly with nylon netting in layers to hold it out and up. She would proudly parade me in front of her friends with my hair all curled tightly around my face. Shirley Temple eat your heart out. She would wash me up in the tub, humming a little song. Clean undies on, she would prop me up in front of her dressing table. Carefully separating bits of hair, spit on her hand to run it along the brown strands, and wrap it in a metal curler with a rubber-tipped closure, so tight they hurt my head.

When her masterpiece was complete, we would set off for one of the dowagers whose houses smelled of moth balls, cheap perfume, or stinky Polish food. The rooms were always dark. I was told to sit still in one place with my hands folded in my lap until further instruction.

At home, Grandma Irene gave me beautiful dolls dressed in lace with soft hair, or any toy she could find to occupy me while she smoked Kent cigarettes and chewed Dentyne gum and talked endlessly to her friends on the phone. One of these toys was a primary-colored row of flat wooden squares bound by two rows of woven threads, which ran the length of the toy. These squares hung together in succession and turning them over made the next one fall "click clack" into infinity.

At night, we watched 'The Lawrence Welk Show' and 'Truth or Consequences', while she chewed Dentyne and smoked Kent cigarettes, and drank something in a coffee cup with ice clinking and I sat perched on my little stool next to her with a cup of hot cocoa.

Grandma Irene was the one who insisted I learn to play the piano. There was a Baldwin baby grand at one end of the elite, expansive living room filled with lovely high end furniture, which looked as if Martha Washington had designed it. She would plop me on a little chair next to her and play for hours, singing, sometimes in English sometimes in German. I was only allowed to sing along when I knew the song. Of course I didn't know many of her selections.

At the behest of Grandma Irene every Wednesday my mother dropped me off at the back door of the Smith Music Store on Main Street.

This particular Wednesday it was a blustery, gray, fall day, and it matched my blustery mood.

"I don't want to take piano lessons, I want to take dance lessons with my friends. Lisa's mom teaches in her basement and it wouldn't cost much. I am a good dancer mom," I pleaded.

"We have spent a lot of money on the piano for you girls to take lessons, and that is what you are going to do, now don't be late getting home. Your father will be on time for dinner tonight," she yelled through the still opened car door of our green Ford station wagon.

I trudged up the four large cement stairs struggling to pull the heavy, solid steel, alleyway door open. In my hand was a red beginner's piano book printed lengthwise for the starter musician to turn the pages easily. I had on my favorite little red coat that my grandmother had picked out for me, my best purple pantsuit with an applique of a cat on the shirt and striped pants in various shades of purple.

Smith Music Company always smelled like Johnson's floor wax on a highly polished floor of maroon and black asbestos tiles, coffee brewing somewhere, musty carpeting and wood, wood, and more wood. The Baldwin's, Steinways, and Weber's with their ivory keys from the

Ivory Coast, of the poor elephants who died to make them. The entire front room was a showcase of these gorgeous musical specimens, all shiny and new. Along the hallway were black and white pictures of the great pianists and famous people who had purchased pianos at the store. Mr. Smith was a good family man. What hair he had left was salt and pepper-colored. He wore glasses with black frames, and a little gold metal rim around the bottom of the lens. He was the father of one of my best friends too and so I trusted him completely.

I first saw his assistant Herr Schroeder* in the showroom. He was neatly dressed in a suit, for in those days all men wore suits if they were going to sell you anything. He was busy flirting with a voluptuous, statuesque, blond saleswoman, who seemed much older than he was. She brought to mind Marilyn Monroe or Jane Mansfield. He had a greased down shock of blond hair which made me think of that commercial jingle, "Brylcreem a little dab'll do ya, Brylcreem, you look so debonair, Brylcreem a little dab'll do ya, they'll love to run their fingers through your hair." He spoke with a German accent, a very handsome, slender man. He took a long drag of his cigarette and snuffed it out in an ashtray on the center business desk of the showroom. Mr. Smith took me by the hand and said,

"Christine this is Mr. Schroeder, and he will be your piano teacher." Mr. Schroeder smiled and bent over at the waist and shook my hand. My hand was still small for a ten-year-old girl, and his hand wrapped generously around mine.

"Come this way. We are going in here." He led me to one of five doors leading to small cubicle rooms where a piano, piano bench, and one chair resided. There was a window in the room, but no one could see in because it stared at another brick wall not more than a few feet outside, which would have been Pease paint store.

"Let us start with this song. You look like a little Indian squaw with those braids of yours." He showed me the notes and the keys. Placing my hands on the keyboard, he held his hands over mine and started playing a one-note, tribal-sounding song.

The first several weeks in our secluded stuffy cubicle he would sit in the chair off to the side smoking his cigarette and gazing out the dirty sash window completely disinterested, sometimes correcting me, sometimes giving me advice, but certainly preoccupied with something else. My sister was also taking lessons from him and she never spoke much about how her lessons were going. Slowly she became withdrawn and quiet which was very unusual for her. Every night we would practice for half an hour each before dinner, diligently plunking out our notes on the keys where I had pencil-marked CDEFGAB.

One Wednesday afternoon I sat nervously waiting for Mr. Schroeder alone in the lesson room. It felt like an eternity. Only the upright piano and me. He entered the room and closed the door tightly behind him, usually the door was left open a bit unless there was too much noise in the hallway.

"Come sit next to me and play for me what you have learned this week," he suggested. I sat still opening my little red book through several songs I had mastered. Then I turned to the page that was this week's assignment. I began playing as he moved closer to me on the bench and put his arm around me. This felt very strange and I became uneasy.

"Just keep playing," he ordered as I froze. He proceeded to grope me under the shirt and down the pants. He was becoming aroused. I had no idea what that was all about at my age. It was the most hideous, horrible, heinous, thing that had ever happened to me and I had no idea what to do.

"Just keep playing," he said, as my shaking fingers fumbled for the keys. When I hit the wrong note he would yell, grope me more, and then get quiet again as he tried to calm himself, he continued molesting me. In my life there still has not been a longer frozen moment in time for me.

When the lesson was over I bolted for the door so quickly I left my music book behind, then ran back as fast as I could back to grab it. He yanked me back into the room and closed the door again.

"This is our secret, if you ever tell anyone, terrible things will happen to your parents and sister."

My mother never knew that when she would drop me off at the alleyway back door on Wednesday afternoons I would run right out the front door and wander the streets until she picked me up again on the back stairs. Usually I would have twelve cents in my pocket, and I would go get an ice cream cone at Cloverdale to compensate for my anxiety-ridden thoughts.

Then one day she said to me,

"Smith Music just called me. They said you haven't been going to the lessons. What's going on?"

I couldn't hold it in any longer. I began crying in large sobbing gasps about everything that had happened, and the things that had been said. She held me close for a moment, then flew out to the car in a rage, grabbing her purse and telling me to stay put.

That night when my father got home, my sister and I sat quietly in the living room while my mother took my father into their bedroom. We could hear them whispering behind the closed door. The next thing we heard was the loud exclamation of, "I'm going to kill the son of a bitch!" Then I heard one of the worst things a daughter can ever hear. My father was crying.

In those days when some sensational, shameful subject might bring on gossip and finger pointing, it was the family or victims that would hide away in shame and silence. There was no ambiguity about this. Be quiet. Do not discuss it again. I was violated and I was supposed to shove it under the rug and forget about it.

Later I found out that my little sister was also his prey. Harm was done. We both had trouble in school. I became innocently promiscuous in the woods with a group of boys in my class, and my sister buried it deep in her subconscious. In my assigned family order it was my duty to protect her and I was not able to, nor were my parents able to protect us. It seemed to me the piano teacher had impunity while we suffered. Today it would be a reality TV show. Not long after that, the piano teacher was fired, and Mr. Smith began drinking heavily. It was soon after that the only music store in town closed its doors For me the music had died. My father took to longer evenings in the bars, and my mother became entrenched in her girl scouts.

I became recalcitrant to an extreme, withdrawn and rebellious. Most nights after dinner were spent sitting in solitary, locked in my parent's room listening to my Aunt Amanda's antique radio. It was beautiful with curved Burl wood doors and little brass knobs. Magical music came out of this tremendous box with large tortoise shell accents. All the world was brought my way through those lighted tubes. It was the only retreat where everything felt good.

The music was brought to me by WXYZ. Lee Allen on the horn, with Joel Sebastian who were the main disc jockeys at the time. On the other side of our pond was CKLW in Windsor. These shows introduced me to Motown grooves, and a singing style I had never heard before. I had found my church. I would sing along with Smokey and Stevie, while my parents watched Red Skelton and Jackie Gleason.

When The Beach Boys came along, the California dream was born in me as well. One night as I was listening and singing along, a new group of lads from Liverpool was introduced. I flung myself back on the white chenille bedspread of my parents four poster bed. The beat was a supernatural force that pierced my very being with chills and thrills. My heart pounded wildly. The very next day I ran to the Melody House music store for their album. My life as a rock and roller had begun. Up until that point my musical experiences were singing in the church choir, the school chorus, and doing some solos when called upon by the instructors of music class. In high school I performed in all of the musicals and had the lead in Brigadoon. My senior class voted me most talented, which meant more to me than any competition or trophy. Thank god for singing, it filled the void in my soul.

Along this same time in my life, between puberty and teenage hell, I had the devastating realization of how cruel and violent the world could be. My beloved science teacher Mr. Smock was murdered by a hitchhiker as he was coming home from Kalamazoo late at night. He was found stuffed in his car trunk. The sister of one of my high school friends was murdered by John Norman Collins in Ann Arbor, where she attended college. Then there were my friends Jack Keyes and Susan Radtke who were murdered in their favorite lover's lane parking spot Actually Jack was killed there, and Sue was taken to a lake where she was tortured, murdered, and found later weighed down at the bottom of the lake wrapped in a plastic sheet. The man had disguised himself as a police officer. I found it difficult to trust a man in a police uniform afterward.

I was traumatized to the point of emotional anguish. So much so that I spent each summer night of my 16th year lying awake in fear, trembling. I would eventually fall asleep when the sun began coming up. My mother wondered why I was sleeping so long into the morning. My parents had no concept of what I was going through. My father was rarely in my life unless it was to punish me for smoking, or threatening my newest boyfriend. He had pretty much given up on me. We were two tigers who didn't get along trapped in a cage together. It was my own personal tragic time.

In the fall of that year my boyfriend was sent away for some petty legal problems. His parents shipped him off to military school in Florida, and after spending devoted weekends with his parents to allay my loneliness, I gave up on him and decided to cut loose.

My freak flag flying, hippie persona found the Ann Arbor college culture of the sixties to be the perfect spot to stretch my legs. What an exciting vibrant place. On one corner, people carried signs and marched up and down protesting the cause of the day. On another corner, local folk singers played guitar outside the head shop. All nationalities colors, and creeds were represented there, and I wanted to be part of it. Colorful clothing, head bands and beads were the culture statement of the day. On Main Street, the old Fowler grocery owned by my uncle Elbert, was still called Fowler grocery. Wildly painted Volkswagen vans, or bugs, were the vehicle of choice for hippie folk, very colorful modes of transportation and expression along with "souped up" muscle cars of the that generation.

My favorite corner of State and Huron streets was the location of Discount Records owned and operated by Jeep Holland. Later I found out my friend Jack Ashton also worked there. Jeep was an interesting fellow who had an old white peeling paint house on Division Street. He managed all the bands in town and loved to host local artists in the store, including The Rationals, The Children, The Thyme, Scott Richard Case or SRC, as they were better known. I don't know why every band started with the word "the" but I guess it gave them more entitlement.

Several times a week, I skipped school and headed for Ann Arbor. By then my parents had relinquished the family car to me and I drove myself to school each day. It certainly was not much to look at, but it sure was fun: a beat up red Ford station wagon with fireman lights that flashed on the sides (due to the fact that my father was a fireman). Only two of the doors still worked thanks to the limited driving skills of my under-aged sisterwho had backed the car up into the mailbox totally mushing the side door handle. It was full of dings, and the floor board on the driver's side was Fred Flintstone style. I loved to watch the pavement go by underneath as I drove along. I would drive up to parties, at my friend's houses late at night, lights flashing, and watched them all scattered like a bunch of cockroaches while I laughed my ass off.

Jeep booked his bands in places like the Cavern in Northville which was no more than a community center taken over by local teenagers once a week. Silverbell Hideout (really a ski resort), Mt. Holly, another ski resort, and Eastown, or the Grande Ballroom. The Grande was the best, seedy part of Detroit even in those times, and I wasn't old enough to get in, so I had to borrow my girlfriend's ID when I first started going there. It was an old circa 1909dance hall that a new generation had taken over. The upstairs was cosmic. A huge wooden sunken dance floor was surrounded by small shops around the perimeter. Incense loomed in the air, one would think they had a smoke machine going for all the pot and tobacco floating around. They sold candles, scarves, belts and hats in a boutique. I remember black lights, posters, and yes, a mirror ball. Far out man. Acts like the Cream, the Doors, the Who and a young musician from England who sat on a wooden stool in the middle of the stage with flowing, wavy, long, long red hair, harmonica around his neck, flute leaning on the stool, and a guitar in his lap. He called himself Jethro Tull. Then there was the house band called MC5. They were Rob Tyner, Fred "Sonic" Smith (later to marry Patti Smith), Wayne Kramer, Michael Davis, and Dennis Thompson. Very cool indeed. When Rob would scream "kick out the jams mother fuckers" he would bring down the house. When he tried to do that in Plymouth at a high school dance we arranged, they pulled the plug on him literally. Anti-establishment lyrics were not acceptable in Plymouth. Even John Sinclair was there that night.

John Sinclair was standing off to the side of the performing area, which wasn't even a platform or a stage The audience and the band were all on the same level. John was a poet, and the MC5 manager who promoted the undercurrents of the White Panther movement in Detroit in support of the Black Panthers. His long full beard and shoulder length hair made him stand apart from the brushcut, clean cut, white shirt and tie chaperones that night. He protested at the loss of electricity, as did we all who organized and supported the concert. The chaperones pushed us through the wooden gymnasiums doors one by one as they cleared the masses that had gathered there that night. We stood out in the parking lot and mourned our lost concert as the band loaded out as readily as they had loaded in.

The Northville connection was strong. The Keyes brothers were from Northville. Jack's brother Chris lived with Uncle Russ Gibb who owned the Grande, and another guy from Northville Don Forsythe, helped Gary Grimshaw with the artwork for the posters, ala Filmore San Francisco, very psychedelic. I often hung out with Chris, and he would take me over to Uncle Russ' apartment sometimes. He had a major heroine problem, and to this day I don't know if he made it out of the sixties alive.

My long time romance with the city of Ann Arbor hit a highpoint the night I met Bob Seger and the Last Heard (Herd). It was spring-time in Northville at the Cavern in 1967. I had dragged my sister and cousin Nancy with me in the red station wagon. The place was named after the Cavern in Liverpool, England. We children were ready for an innocent romping stomping night. The hippies had taken over the community center again. Darkness was supplanted by black lights, a lighting method of dropping food coloring in an oil, dish soap, and water mixture in front of a projector to make swirls of lava lamp color on the walls, vendors sold posters and trinkets and we danced until we could not stand up.

I was screaming "Gloria" at the top of my lungs when I noticed a band loading in a side door. The singer was tall with a white satiny shirt with big black pinwheels on it, hip hugger jeans, and a light blue hat like that mailman wore in the Van Gogh painting. It was Bob Seger.

Now my favorite lady at the time was Cher, so my hair was cut just like hers and I ironed it at night to the point of super straightness, bangs covering my eyes with just a nose sticking out. My hair by today's standards would not be considered crazy, but in those days I had a long blond streak down the side, and half of my hair was red and the rest brown. It looked like cutting edge stuff, but it was really just a screw up with a bottle of peroxide. My orange and navy bold-striped jacket, mini skirt, lace stockings, and my Mod shoes on, think Mary Quant, I was all that and sheik too. Five bands played that night of enchantment, mostly local garage guys I knew, and all of them did some version of 'Midnight Hour' or 'House of the Rising Sun'. Even my friend Joel almost made it through the entire drum solo of 'Wipeout' that night. Seger and company were the headliner and they were ready to go. I had never heard such a big sound from a rock band. Pep Perrine on percussion, had a major league set up of bongos and bass drums, enormous cymbals, and tambourines. Karl Lagassa played a mean guitar, Dan Honaker played bass, and Bob was on keyboards. They covered everything from Bob Dylan, to Van Morrison's 'Brown Eyed Girl'. Their original cut at the time was 'Persecution Smith' penned to emulate a Bob Dylan style.

The evening was magnetic, exotic and fun as hell. We were moving and grooving while the smell of Jasmine incense and adolescent sex filled the air.

When all had come to what everyone else perceived as the end of the night, I said to Cathy and Nancy,

"I have to meet this band."

I stomped up the stairs to the stage with my Brownie Starlite camera, the one with the rotating flash cube, and said I was going to take some band photos. I thought I was hot shit all right. My first time back stage. Pep was about to take down his drum kit when Bob jumped behind it and started playing, next photo Mr. Seger stood behind his Korg singing the television commercial " new country corn flakes" he was flakey for sure.

Then the other guys shuffling around the stage handed me some stuff to carry, and now I was a roadie. Cool. I signaled to Cathy and Nancy to come on, and they paraded up the stairs after me.

"We have to get home. Mom is going to kill us, everyone else is gone, and it's after midnight."

I think our curfew had been eleven. Oops. We stood outside while the band all loaded out the equipment into the old Dodge van. Bob was a real motor mouth then, yack yack yacking about playing this town and that town.

"Come see us in Flushing next week," he suggested. "Flushing like in toilets?" I had never heard of it before.

"Yeah, like in toilets," he laughed. Then each band member except Karl grabbed the closest girl to them, and gave us all long wet kisses goodnight. Cathy was with Bob, I was with the drummer, Pep, and Nancy was with Dan.

The next time we saw Seger was not in Flushing like in toilets, but one of the east side Coca-Cola joints for teens. It may have been the Eastown next, I don't really remember. He looked right at me when he sang "Brown Eyed Girl" but he also looked right at me when he sang, "Have you heard about the 'jolly green giant'?" No reference to my height.

I was smitten with the band. I told Bob I couldn't stay around that night because Cathy and Nancy were too antsy. He gave me his number, and said to call anytime. It was far from my Podunk Plymouth corner of the world, but whether it was the Hideout East or Eastown or up north it was always worth the drive for me. We would do the jerk and froog, and gyrate ourselves through the night in our mini-skirts, with long hair flying.

One of both Bob's (and my) favorite bands of the time was 'The Blues Magoos' a Bronx NY rock and psychedelic band who put out songs like "We Ain't Seen Nothin Yet', no we ain't seen nothin' yet, or 'Tobacco Road.' Bob would sing 'Queen of my Night' so beautifully, it made me cry.

I spent many days going over to Bob or Pep's house to hang out. One day I was invited to band rehearsal. I thought that it would be nice to bring Bobby (that's what his mother would call him) a present.

I stopped into a head shop I liked, down the street from the Fifth Dimension club, on Liberty Street. Purple Plum, or one of those crazy type names. It was a rickety old house, and I thought a poster would be just the thing he would love. I walked up the creaky narrow stairs to the top landing, only to be met by a larger than life poster of Frank Zappa on a toilet. That guy has no shame, I love him! Is this a theme? Toilets. Hmm? That was my Zappa introduction. When I met Frank Zappa later, and told him about seeing his poster for the first time, he loved the story.

I found a medium-sized pen and ink picture of our beloved Bob Dylan, and decided to purchase it, along with some long seed beads. Nearly everything I ever wore I sewed by hand. I couldn't afford anything else, and besides, nothing I found on the racks was cool enough. On this particular day I wore a mini skirt, matching jacket with little orange flowers in a paisley design over a ribbed orange tank top. I made my way down Main Street in my red Ford station wagon past the family grocery to Pauline Street and turned right. Bob lived in a charming English Tudor-style home with his mom. When I pulled into his driveway I flashed the fireman lights of the beat up red Ford station wagon.

"Wow that is so cool looking! Man you look nice today." He greeted me in the driveway after dashing out the front door.

"I have something for you," I said, as I handed him the poster.

"That is so groovy, thanks, I can put this in my room. Come on in. I have to play you something!"

His mother's house was neat as a pin and traditional. It was just the two of them, as his brother no longer lived with them. The house always smelled like the homemade apple pie she baked for her "boys." After we met and became friends, I spent many nights when suffering from lonely teenage angst, talking to Bob's mom on the phone. A lovely soft spoken woman, she was missing her sons and I was missing life in general.

The Seger household owned a monaural RCA combination radio and turntable, as many people did in their living rooms in those days.

"Hey I saw you on Club 1270 last Saturday, you looked great, just like American Bandstand, almost," he teased.

Club 1270 was a teen show, which featured a big name artist once a week. Three or four couples would sit at red and white-checkered round tops and pretend to be entertained, dancing to number one hits in between. The show featured artists like Chuck Berry, Little Richard, Little Stevie Wonder, and many others.

"Thanks, I think Bob....it's fun and Jerry my partner is a great dancer," as I looked at Bob sort of sideways.

In my teenage mind Jerry was the only guy tall enough in high school, over six foot tall, to be seen with on television, and man he had a great groovy dance style.

"So what's the big deal? You are so excited," I asked Bob.

"We just cut this last night and wrapped it up, Capitol records is signing us and this is our first single." From a plain brown sleeve, he pulled out a 33rpm record.

"It's the size of an album or my parents old 78's, how is that going to work?"

"Listen!" he said.

The back beat started pounding like a freight train. It was 'Heavy Music' and he sang along.

"It sounds like you're in a jungle. Are you going to play it live, and if so, how?" I was wondering how they would pull off all the noisy African animal screeching parts in the background.

"It is great isn't it?" There were low vocals and screaming vocals, apes and thundering background beats with a long instrumental centerpiece.

"I love it Bob, where is your bathroom?"

"Go upstairs," he pointed down the hall, not paying much attention to me, just getting deeper into his song.

I made my way up the dark-stained wooden stairs to a hallway. On the left was his room, very sparsely furnished, bed unmade, a single mirror hung over a dresser, and white curtains on the double sash windows letting in plenty of light. Certainly not like my room, which was painted purple, with huge, multi-colored paper lanterns and San Francisco Fillmore and Grande Ballroom posters adorning the walls.

I wondered if he was going to stop singing and messing around down there and come upstairs to ravage me on his bed, but he never did. I stepped onto the cold tile floor and dawdled around waiting. After a while, I gave up, flushed the toilet and went back down.

He was still in awe of his recording. He put his arm around me and said, "Isn't that great?"

I told him again and again it was wonderful and I expected him to repay my compliment with a kiss. I think it would have happened if the other band members hadn't barged in the back door.

"Hey anybody here?" Dan yelled.

Our special moment was broken, as it turned out forever.

"Come on downstairs we're all set up," Bob said to Dan and Peppy.

Check this out. Certainly there has never been so much musical equipment in such a small space. Pep Perrine the drummer had three bass drums: two on long pole towers and one on the floor. Kick bongos, snares, high hats, as well as enormous Marshall Amplifiers were stacked all around the edges. They parked me in a tiny folding chair smack against the wall in front of the band. Everything was humming, as they took their places. It was like the Bose advertisement of the guy sitting in the arm chair who gets blasted across the room. There I was creamed against the wall, with the force of the music flattening my face.

They practiced 'Heavy Music' and everything else, and I provided the appropriate applause. After that day I was crushing on Pep. Phillip Edward Perrine from Whitmore Lake. I went to several more gigs, had Sunday dinners at his house with the family, marveled at his pacific ocean blue Malibu SS, and then never saw the band again for many years..

My high school boyfriend was back, and there was going to be trouble. He returned from Miami Military Academy head shaved, and plenty of attitude for his parents. That was the end of my groupie days for a while.

That love interest soon left me broken-hearted and on the re-bound when along came my soon to be husband Curt. He drove a red convertible MG sports car, with his beautiful wavy blonde hair flowing in the breeze.Home is where the heart is, as Elvis sang, so all my young life I searched for a heart like mine. When I found myself pregnant the ripe old age of 18, I gave marriage my all to make a home with my very young, very naive husband.

Curt and I were told by our parents, religion, and society that this is where we must dwell forever. Dictated by the Roman Catholic doctrine of course. On a sunshine filled early October day we were married. It was 86 degrees. We had a high mass, and I was pregnant. This fact was not shared with anyone, not even our closest friends or family knew.

I made my own wedding gown from a brocade linen and some old-fashioned, crocheted lace. My husband's aunt had helped me make the veil. There were possibly sixty relatives and friends in attendance at Our Lady of Victory church in Northville. As the wedding march began to play, I took my father's arm. He walked me up the aisle with a smile on his face, as he gave me over to a boy I had known for three months.

All of the kneeling, and standing began to overwhelm me. I felt dizzy, and I was dripping with sweat. When I looked up at the priest and saw a giant ball of sweat streaming down his face, a black cloud filled my head, and over I went. My soon to be husband placed me on the pew behind us, and they carried on without me. This was of no consequence. By the end of the ceremony I was a married woman.

Curt and I decided to keep our secret and head out to Boulder, Colorado to make a new start. We hit the road right after Christmas and hubby's last shift for Michigan Bell as a splicer. We got as far as Gary, Indiana when our 1964 Dodge Dart broke down in the middle of the night in a snowy blizzard. His parents came to our rescue the next day, and drove us out to Colorado.

We stayed there with friends of my mother's. They were Norwegians and very hospitable. My husband secured at job at Mountain Bell, and we began looking for an apartment. His parents had stayed on with us to make sure we were going to be all right. His mother came to us one day and sat us down.

"I want you two to be honest with me, and tell me why you want to stay out here away from family."

We looked each other in the eye and said we just loved the country and the mountains.

"I know you're pregnant, I heard you throwing up in the bathroom last night. After twelve pregnancies of my own I figured it out. I want you to come home where you have family around and we can help you," his very wise mother explained to us.

After much deliberation and armed only with a Dr. Spock book my mother had given me we agreed, and sadly left our Colorado dream behind to start our little family.

We tried to substitute Colorado for the Upper Peninsula of Michigan for a couple of years after that. We also left our ideals of marriage behind, and found ourselves on rocky ground five years and two children later.

CHAPTER 2

The Cheri Chronicles (1975)

"I like your Christ, I do not like your Christians. Your Christians are so unlike your Christ." Mahatma Gandhi

The projects of Ypsilanti Michigan left much to be desired. Squawking crows flew over the tenement condominiums during the bleak winter. Many welfare moms, like myself, sought housing there. The condos were red brick with white trim and very basic, but clean enough. They were remotely situated on Geddes Road, surrounded by corn fields, so the "projects" would not become a "city" problem.

Cheri was the ex-wife of one of my husband's buddies from work. She was helping me assimilate into single parenthood in the projects. Cheri was epileptic, and did some heavy drugs to maintain equilibrium. Phenobarbital was one of the several medications she was on. She had left her husband Bill, and we were two hippie chicks recently single suddenly living together with a passel of children.

The married household I had left was troubled to say the least. My husband spent his time hanging out with buddies drinking and drugging while I was stuck at home with the children. The only identity I had notched out for myself was that of a church wedding singer and seamstress. The husband would allow me to sing for money at his friends weddings, but nothing more. The odd jobs were few and far between. The small remote town of Wixom, Michigan contained only a Ford factory, so it was not exactly a hot bed of opportunity. When Cheri made me the offer of shelter from my marriage, I leapt at the offer.

Cheri and I spent nearly a month together while she helped me through the transition. The early seventies were an interesting time. Tricky Dick had Watergate, we were living the aftermath of the Arab oil embargo, and the disco era was emerging as classic rock and roll was edged out even though I was not a convert. I had pledged my soul to rock and roll.

At Cheri's house there was constant traffic: fellow hippies, children and friends of various ages. Cheri liked a great deal of flurry around her. An accumulation of lost souls if you will. The earth mother, advisor to all, mentor to the young, and guidance counselor that Cheri thought herself to be, led to many wayward souls grappling for her attention. She was an attractive, black-haired maven with blue eyes. A very kind person, with a short fuse at times.

Cheri had worked as a waitress at the Roostertail on the Detroit River for Jerry Schoeneth. He and his family were the premier boat race people on the river. Later, he bought an interest in the Detroit Playboy Club and Cheri became a Playboy bunny. She told me of her active and open sexual nature, so I was well aware of what I was getting myself into.

On days off she cooked up what she called crystal THC in the oven while she made spaghetti on the stove top. Friends would bring over exotic herb to smoke, as well as an Italian salad. The condominium was decorated with Indian tapestries and beaded curtains. Floor pillows adorned the living space. Cheri insisted on her own slick style.

My religious beliefs were eclectic. I wanted to learn everything I could about all the various religions. There was the ultimate home at the end of life when the black velvet darkness of death, or the bright light, which will lead us to our maker. Soaring onto the next plateau to be reincarnated, reformed, reborn, renewed, or whatever the heck happens to our souls. Belief in the circle of life toward the status of actualization and higher form is the only driving force I live with now, it brings me happiness. I had been reading Deepak Chopra books. Thank you Deepak Chopra for your insight and wisdomCheri wanted me to allow my mind to expand, and be open to her latest philosophy, Zen Buddhism, and whatever she was into on any given day. Isaac Asimov, Carlos Castaneda, Buckminster Fuller, constant conversations running about the universe. Sometimes it was a conversation on Karl Marx, Sigmund Freud, Carl Jung, who was "the greatest man ever", and Foucault. She decided we were all too repressed, and that these theories we conjured up, had far reaching effects from the original thought to create a new genre of social prophecy. Sexuality became the secret of an individual's nature and not the soul. Sex, sex, sex, and more sex was to be discovered.

The only orgasm I had ever had was in my sleep in the middle of the night once when I woke up thinking, "Oh that's what this is all about....wow."

Cheri would entertain a number of interesting people from her college classmates, to old drug dealer friends, to older neighborhood friends she and Bill had together. In a house full of people it was difficult to say the least, to have any privacy for sexual activity.

It all became a bit much when one day, I happened in on Cheri smooching the pooch or rather her German Shepard smooching her pooch. That was a really wild stretch for me.

I had begun experimenting with tetrahydrocannabinol as well. Doing the same things I was accusing my ex-husband of, and didn't that feel like some Catholic guilt and shame. Our collective children were never around when most of this was going down, they were all school age, and in school where they belonged.

The greatest thing Cheri ever gave me was the book 'Essene Gospel of Peace'. Now that, I could relate to. The exact words of Jesus Christ translated from the Dead Sea Scrolls from Aramaic. I did not believe in organized religion at all, and being indoctrinated by the Catholic Church, I had spent most of my church going days hiding in the women's restroom with the pink tile walls and gray metal stalls, writing poetry.

My mother did not understand, nor did she care to listen to anything I would try to have an open conversation about. She even went so far as to take my original copy of the book, as if that would stop me.

"But Mom," I would plead, "This is exactly what Jesus said translated from his own language and not twisted by other writers."

My mother was not listening to any of these ridiculous ideas. What I was trying to convey to her? She considered me a blasphemer. The Our Mother prayer was just as important as the Our Father prayer to me. It became everything. I had been a vegetarian for two years by then, as skinny as I had ever been, and had quit tobacco for cannabis. I thought it was the healthiest state I had ever been in. I was in serious need of affirmation of faith. That was the only thing that would get me through this period of my life. I read that book over and over again. I prayed in private nearly every minute of these trials and tribulations I was going through.

The acculturation of the new me also included new music. There was Roxy Music, the album 'Silk Torpedo', Arthur Brown, King Crimson, Fripp and Eno, and many others including my old pal Bob Seger who had just released 'Beautiful Loser' which I was sure I was. 'Spirit' was streaming through the sound waves on my stereo constantly singing, "It's nature's way of receiving you...." The year was 1975 so whatever was on the airwaves invigorated me, and was a distinct influence.One day Cheri came to me and said, "I want you to meet Johnny, the maintenance man."

Soon I had nicknamed him, Johnny Appleseed. Johnny took me out on "proper dates" on nights my mother kept the girls at her house. He would pick me up in his gold Corvette and treat me like a lady. His skin was as black as ebony, and he stood over six feet tall, with broad shoulders. He was from the Deep South somewhere, and his daddy had been a preacher. Johnny was much older and wiser than I was.

"Would you like to go down by the Michigan Theatre? There's this little club on Bagley by the theatre, and Gil Scott Heron is playing tonight," he suggested. It may have been in the old Adams Theatre.

"I have no idea who that is but, all right, it sounds groovy."

A whole new world opened up to me. The club was dark and smoky with little round tables and chairs clumped together. Afros flying, and everyone wearing caftans, and other African garb. Gil Scott and company sang their songs of protest, and were the wildest thing I had ever seen. Big conga drums, electric guitars, stand-up bass. It was crazy.

As it turned out the club was right next door to the old Michigan Theatre where my ex-husband and I went to see Electric Light Orchestra, after he persuaded me to drop some acid for the first time. They were electric all right.

When we went back to Johnny's place that night, we had some cocktails and he worked his charm on me like no other man had ever done. Smooth as silk. In retrospect I think I was more intrigued than attracted, just to be in my first sexual encounter outside of my marriage, and with a mature black man.

His apartment was furnished in typical super fly fashion, black purple and gold "stuff" everywhere. Tasteful and masculine, but definitely not my mother's early American. He took me up to his round waterbed. It was covered with black fur. In gentle, smooth strokes, he made love to me. Afterward he put me in the shower alone to freshen up. When he saw me rubbing my wet skin with the towel he educated me.

"Girl, you are going to rub off all the natural oils on you, just blot your skin like this," he said as he demonstrated. To this day I think of him whenever I blot. That was our only date, although he did check in on me to make sure my new townhouse suited me. He would sit in the empty townhouse next door and play a piano they had left behind, to serenade me.

Thoughts were flowing through my head now like flashes of white light epiphanies. It was mid-winter in Michigan, and the snow lay sparsely on the ground in a thin white sheet. I left footprints trudging over to peek in the window of my assigned townhouse a couple of blocks away from Cheri's. Johnny popped his head in Cheri's backdoor one day and Cheri said, "Well did you get her place ready?" noticing a big grin on Johnny's face.

"Yeah, it's three blocks over that way."

I was overjoyed to be in my first place. I ran upstairs at Cheri's house, and packed up our meager belongings, rolled up the red sleeping bags from the floor, and waited for school to let out.

Johnny had helped me move in what little I had, and said he hoped I didn't mind the red door. No one else in the complex had a painted door but me. "No, it will be a great help when it's dark," I said.

"Someone might think a hooker lives here," he said.

"Great that's all I need. Children banging on the door constantly and strange men looking for a quickie." We were all moved in. The baby crib and twin bed in one small front room upstairs, and my mattress on the floor in the other room. My Old English sheepdog Tuffy was with us now, and it felt like a home. Downstairs there was a turquoise-colored love seat parked in one corner across from the infamous red front door, and a low rider wooden shelf served as a music center. Strangely enough, I did not miss the television.

It was nearly spring, and Easter would soon be arriving. I had made my little place a home for the kids and myself, sewing curtains, sprinkling live plants around. I decided to add some flair to the place, and painted a mural of brown trees on the living room wall. In the upstairs bathroom, I had created a stained glass window with one of those kits you buy at the craft store. Some sort of black liquid supplanting lead. Peace signs, crosses, flowers, and shapes adorned the window, and primary colors were used to fill in the creations. I was very proud of it.

Strange things had been taking place in my life. Cheri thought it might be my "awakening". I was living my moment with enlightened perception. One night while sitting peacefully on the toilet seat in my rather small half bathroom, next to the kitchen, I had been praying on our existence, and it turned into a form of uncontrollable babbling, in a vocalization I didn't recognize as my own. I later found out this is what people call "talking in tongues". It was as if I had gone to some other astral plane and was communicating in a way unbeknownst to me, a true out of body experience.

When I called my mother to ask her what that meant, she said she had no idea. She now claims to have had the same experience herself some forty years later.

I couldn't even tell Cheri about this as she would think I had gone off the deep end. It was nothing compared to what happened next.

A week or so later after tucking my sweet cherubs into their beds, I sang to them as I often did, some familiar lullabies. "Goodnight my darling girls, I love you very much." I kissed their little cheeks. The dog lay by the bedside watching over them as she was accustomed to, and I, in an exhausted state, made my way downstairs to play some music and relax before finding my own mattress. Life seemed to be going well, the children were happy, they had made friends, and all the family was still a strong presence in their lives.

Flopping down on the love seat opposite the door I slung my legs over the end to dangle while I listened to the Doobie Brothers chanting in celebration,

"Oh, oh, oh, listen to the music."

Trying to embrace the Heavenly Father and the Earthly Mother before falling into a deep reposed sleep, my prayers trailed off. The turntable didn't turn off, and the song played over and over again. I had only smoked one joint all day so I wasn't in any metamorphic state of mind. I glanced over my brown and white wall of trees as I drifted into that natural suspension.

After some time the red door flew open hitting the white wall behind it. At first I was startled by the noise, and then a bright white light appeared and grew stronger and stronger. As the light grew more brilliant, a feeling of peace and serenity came over me. I have never felt anything like it before or since. The feeling was one of security and love. In the white light, stood the silhouette of an angel, no not just an angel, it looked like what people have described as Jesus. The spirit said only one thing to me, "When I come again it will be in the form of a woman." Then, as quickly as the vision appeared, it withdrew, and the light faded away. The door slammed shut again.

The sound of the record playing returned, and I walked slowly over to it, swept the arm off the record and turned off the receiver. In a state of shock, I made my way up the bare wooden stairs to my mattress.

Falling asleep momentarily I awoke to a thundering noise. An enormous storm was beginning to rage outside. Even though it was spring, and should have been rain, we were having a blizzard. The winds howled and screamed. Fear gripped me and I ran to my children. They were still in dreamland undisturbed by the crashing, whistling, blowing storm. There was a beast knocking on my door defying me to answer it, but I stood strong and fought against the tempest with every fiber of my body. I began praying and did not stop until complete enervation ensued. Ice crystals formed rapidly on my bedroom and the bathroom windows. I had to relieve myself and charged for the bathroom. Suddenly the window blew apart from the pressure of the ice formations, covering the floor with my stained glass window. The door slammed shut before I could reach it. It had locked. When I wet my nightgown I began to cry and pray at the same time. The faithful dog standing there with me whimpered too, licking the floor clean. I made my way downstairs to the bathroom, relieved myself, and ran to check on my children. I made certain the children were all right. To my surprise, they were still sleeping in hushed silence within their room not disturbed by the thrashing storm in the least.

The storm was pounding the back of the building more viciously. I knelt on the floor with my head on my mattress, pillow pulled tightly over my head, until the furious weather passed by. As dawn broke I noticed the thick ice on the inside of my window that could not be scraped off with my fingernail. The bathroom door was still locked, I needed help. I got dressed and went out into the knee-deep snow and made my way to Johnny's house.

I pounded on the door until he finally answered.

"You have to help me, there is broken glass and the door locked on me and......" I cried in a panic stricken wavering voice. He grabbed a heavy jacket and followed me as I ran back to my children. I could hear him shouting behind me,

"You did this didn't you?!"

"What the hell do you mean?!" was my response.

"You and your bullshit made this happen, didn't you?"

Running into the house he had tools in hand and I stood by him as he unlocked the frozen door. Broken shards of my stained glass design and snow covered the bathroom floor.

"Pick up what you can, and I will get a new window in, check on your kids. Look in the mirror, what happened to your eyes?"

I looked in the mirror and my eyes were like two saucers, they were dilated and huge. I had no answer for it, but I was not going to fixate on that now. It could have been drugs, or it could have been a night of adrenalin rushing through my veins.

Waking the girls I bundled them up and headed for my mother's house about twenty minutes away. We drove my Volkswagen Beetle slowly through the difficult roads. At one point, I decided to take a wooded shortcut. That car could go anywhere. In the forest which now shone like sparkling diamonds in the sun, there were all manner of birds, birds that I had never seen in Michigan. A bald eagle, a snowy owl swooped in front of the car, and many birds had been blown off course seeking shelter in those woods.

"Someone saved my life tonight," by Elton John played on the radio.

After that night the fear of God ran through me like a sword. I returned to my husband's house, gave up my life in Ypsilanti, and tried to leave the events of that night behind me. No one ever knew why I went back, especially my husband. He simply went on conducting his life in his merry way as if we had never been apart, talk about denial. I never saw Cheri again.

CHAPTER 3

Turn the Page on the Marriage Get a Tatoo (1975)

"When you reach the end of your rope, tie a knot in it and hold on tight...." Thomas Jefferson

It's hard to recall whether I got the tattoo after I left my husband Curt the first time or after the second time. It was plain as the nose on my face that I had left him the irresponsible way the first time, but this time I would get a job. Curt had stamped himself with the head of a Viking to go along with his new Harley, (a gift he got himself for having to come back home with me) so I decided I had to have a tattoo also. Back then, only drunken sailors, truckers, or bikers had tattoos. It was not OK for reputable women or young mothers so, I snuck off to a garage in Plymouth across the street from the Rexall drugstore where I had worked in high school.

"Hi there, Mr. Michael?" I said, banging on the loose screen door.

"Yeah that's me, what do ya need?" he asked in a pleasant enough tone. He was a slightly hunched over older man, with salt and pepper hair, slender build, jeans and a t-shirt.

"Well, my ex-husband got a tattoo done here and I want one too."

He lifted the rattling old garage door. Not a sterile environment, but clean enough I guess. I had no clue about needles, diseases or sterile instruments at that time.

"Which one would you like?" he said as he pointed to a wall of what looked like decals you would stick on a box of keepsakes. I scanned the collection thinking they all look like cheesy guy stickers, skulls and cross bones, "I love MOM" sort of stuff, when my gaze finally fixed on a flower. Not just any flower, but a beautiful red rose.

"Is this going to hurt," I said.

"It might sting a little bit, where do you want it?"

"I don't really want it to be seen by everyone, so my butt I guess," I said, tentatively.

"Okay peel those pants down young lady," he instructed me, not seeming to care whether he got a peek.

The instrument buzzed along and he wiped an alcohol rag over his work as he went about creating his masterpiece. It took all of about thirty minutes to complete the process.

"Here's a mirror what do you think?"

I held the mirror up to get a look at my left butt cheek. I looked at it from different angles and then I realized what it looked like. The inside of the rose was made up of yellows, reds and some other shade that made it look like the head of a circumcised penis.

I handed him $15 cash, thanked him and made my way back to Wixom.

Several weeks into the trial reconciliation I was more miserable than ever, so we figured why not take a 3200 mile trip around the United States with our 8-tracks, a bag of weed, and two small children packed into the back of a Toyota Land Cruiser ? Certainly that would solve all our problems.

Going back a few years before, Cheri was still with Bill and I was still with Curt. In the last five years of married life from 1970-1975 I had only been to one concert: The Steve Miller Band in Detroit at Ford Auditorium. At the time in 1973 I was eight months pregnant and I had just given my husband an ultimatum: either we leave the upper peninsula of Michigan together, or stay in the U.P. without me. He chose to come back to Plymouth with me.

Cheri had gotten us tickets and I was so excited I could have gone into labor right there. Living in the Upper Peninsula there were no radio stations that played anything popular, only old country and western. Steve Miller remained on stage and played to a handful of us until two or three in the morning after his band left, about one a.m. he played acoustic guitar to only us. Cheri and her husband Bill were still married at that time and were with us that night.

The marriage was not destined to survive. The husband stayed out later and later with his buddies, and I felt more and more isolated with two little kids at home. Bruce Springsteen came out with 'Born To Run' and that was all the encouragement I needed. This time I implored him move out of the house in Wixom, and I would stay there with the children until I figured out a better plan.

CHAPTER 4

Leap of Faith: (1976)

"Do not go where the path may lead, go instead where there is no path and leave a trail" Ralph Waldo Emerson

Rocky Balboa had hit the big screen. Ronald Reagan was imbedded in the Sandinistas and Contras. Mary Harris Jones, better known as Mother Jones, continued as an activist for National Progress, and an opponent of child labor. The discovery of DDT and the ozone crisis, along with the onslaught of global warming concerned many of us as the opposition, led by Lyndon LaRouche, founded the Fusion Energy Foundation for nuclear power. Not only that, but he was convinced that rock and roll music was an abhorrent plot by the British Intelligence Agency to infiltrate America. There was so much to be uneasy about.

One bright sunny Saturday in May I decided to pack up my little girls, Chrisanna the oldest one a toe-head, and Damian a strawberry blond, 5 years old, and 2 years respectively, and drove about thirty minutes from our Wixom home to a place I had formerly thought of as a ski lodge, which also apparently had an amphitheater for music. The place was called Pine Knob. The Monkees were playing a matinee there and I knew the girls would love it, since I had raised them on

Monkee reruns. It was the opening of the 1976 season. We sang "take the last train to Clarkston," all the way there, because Pine Knob was in Clarkston, Michigan.

The smells of Pine Knob filled the air, the pine trees cooking in the sun, the food vendor's hot dog aroma, and popcorn. All of it lifted my spirits. We set our seats right up front, and took it all in, ready for the matinee.

Mike Nesmith the founding member of the band was missing from the lineup. We learned he was boycotting the tour for some reason. They looked and sounded fabulous with Davey Jones, my personal favorite, right out there doing his thing.

We strolled down the famous walkway that led into the venue, with depictions of all the artists who had played the Knob displayed in colorful paintings done in a Peter Max fashion: Cher in long white bell bottoms, the Beach Boys, Chicago, and even Bob Dylan were mainstays.

When the show ended and we were leaving, I stopped, looked up at the ski lodge, and clutching their small hands said,

"Come on girls we're going to find a better life."

We hopped in the green VW beetle bug and drove up the hill to the front entrance. The lodge resembled a rustic Swiss chalet with its dark walnut stain rough wood and sloping roof.

The restaurant was called Cloisters on The Knob, I had no idea what that meant. I did not know much about Cloisters or anything else in the world. I had only a high school education and I had led a small town sheltered life, living with my parents and right into my married life at 18 years old. All I knew is I wanted to work at Pine Knob.

The Italian influence in décor was evident. Red plush carpeting and black walls being the prominent colors. A beautiful blonde woman stood at the hostess stand near the main entrance. She was statuesque, and wore a Channel suit. Her face was lit by a gooseneck brass lamp.

"I am here for the job posting and interview," I explained to her. She smiled and pointed toward a sea of round tables covered with white linen. An entire wall of windows looked out over the ski slope and chair lifts.

"Go see Art Ruth over there," she politely instructed me. "Thank you ever so much," I said in my most phony Bette Davis impression..

"You kids stay right here on this bench and stay out of people's way I'll be right back," in my most stern mom voice.

The dining room was bright with a panoramic view out of the floor to ceiling windows. The tables were being set by a tuxedo-clad waiter, who glanced up, but didn't acknowledge me. Art Ruth was a tall, drink of water, skinny as a rail, and constantly sucking on long brown 'More' cigarettes. He was beginning to lose his hair, and had a pleasant enough demeanor. He was the head of Ogden Foods and he ran all the restaurant services and the concessions.

"Hi Mr. Ruth," I said. "I am Christine Olevnic. I am looking for a waitress job." Only after the divorce, did I change my name back to my maiden name.

"Well then," he answered looking me up and down, "Do you have any experience?"

"I worked in a diner for several years."

That diner so to speak, was the lunch counter in the Rexall Drug store where I had worked during high school, and later when I was married and pregnant. There my job was to alternate flipping burgers and running the cash register, while my sister-in-law dispensed medications for the pharmacist, even though she was two years younger than I was. I was envious that they didn't trust me with the drugs.

Through the swinging doors, we heard a great commotion in the kitchen.

"Hold on a minute," Art said, sticking his head through one side of the door. "Hey Joey come here."

"What do you think of her?" Art queried.

"She'll do, we needed someone yesterday!" Joey yelled back as he returned to the kitchen.

"That's it you got the job."

At that time the Italian owners of Pine Knob, the Locchricio's, were deeply entrenched in East Detroit life. There was old Joe, Matt, and little Joey who commanded the day to day business dealings, of their "produce" business, and Pine Knob.

Their very good friends the Giacalone family used to show up for dinner in the main dining room in limousines or Cadillacs. Vito Giacalone (Billy Jack) was a known mobster suspected in the Jimmy Hoffa disappearance. Special attention would be paid by Luigi the maître de, who would personally pour their vino and toss their Caesar salads table side in a large wooden bowl. All waitresses were sent away when they arrived as if a secret society meeting was about to commence.

The Italians seemed to like me because of my rather large French/ Indian nose with the Roman bump. They thought I was a nice Italian girl. Another prominent fixture at the Knob was the bouncer, let's call him Bruno, think "Lucco Brazzi" from the Godfather. Large man, big nose, ugly pitted Scarface-type guy, always nicely dressed in a suit that lent him an air of distinction. He never said two words to me, just grunted in response whenever I said, "Hi Buddy, how ya doin'?"

Under great protest a dark curly haired toothpick-sized man came out with his shirt sleeves rolled up and wiped his brow with a stained white towel. He looked like he had just taken off his tie to start slinging hash in the bustling kitchen.

"What do you think of this girl? She wants to be a waitress?" Art asked the younger Mr. Loccrichio.

"We need someone for the disco buffet; put her in there," Joey said as he stomped back into the kitchen yelling.

"You ever serve cocktails before?" Art asked me.

"Sure I have," I lied. I didn't know a Manhattan from a Martini.

"We are opening the other side for a buffet before the show, and then a disco after the show. You can have that. Show up tomorrow and ask for Donna."

"Oh thank you so much, I won't let you down Mr. Ruth." I turned and found my children playing in the entryway.

"Come on you guys, Mommy got the job," I said to the girls.

"Doing what mom?"

"Serving food and drinks to people," I said, as we got in our little VW bug and took the winding road home through the lakes. My spirit was soaring for the first time in many years, perhaps it was a foreshadowing.

The next day when I arrived at Pine Knob I walked into the disco side of the lodge up twenty or so stairs through the double glass side doors.

"Hi there I'm looking for Donna," I said to the back of a short lady, dressed in a black nylon shift. I had only seen this type of dress on the African American cleaning ladies who came to work for the well-to-do families of Plymouth when I was a child in the fifties.

"I'm Donna who are you?" she said, smiling a rotten tooth grin. Her haggard face was from the school of hard knocks and the varicose veins on her legs were a tell-tale of too many hours spent on her feet.

"You're the new waitress. Well, grab a tray and follow me," she instructed.

Wonderful aromas of food drifted out from behind black curtains and the steam tables were cooking hot, like a sauna. Donna went into an office and came out with a dress on a hanger, "Here this is your uniform, go try it on."

I made my way to the restroom and put on the A-line, halter-top, mini-dress, an orange, polyester double knit. It hung on me like a tent. The skirt dropped down to my knees. I hiked up the brown ties around my neck as far as I could. Still the bust line was made for a well-endowed woman. When I bent over anyone could look straight down the front. This was going to take some guarded moves for my barely B cup cleavage.

"So Donna what do you think?"

"Hum, well it is going to have to do. Here we set the tables this way, we do a country club pour for drinks, that is vodka, gin, rum, wine, beer then soft drinks, you will yell 'one for the money' for pop, and when everything is cleared and tables put away, you can go down and see the shows," Donna informed me in a glib sort of way.

I was over the moon excited. I would get to see the shows, for free! Listening to disco and serving drinks after the show would be fun too. The money wouldn't be anything to write home about, a dollar an hour wage plus tips, which would only be 10% on a buffet service. Better than nothing I thought.

The first show coming up was Neil Diamond.

I believed this would be the way in, someone would hear my voice and have to sing with me, include me in the band. Like some Stephen Sondheim production, I had a need to belong that felt urgent. In some ethereal way it was going to happen. I was running around singing "crackling rose make me smile.....La...La...La...La!" as the days grew longer. Problem was I still had stage fright.

One night Art came to me after the preshow rush and pulled me aside.

"We have Neil Diamond's press conference tonight downstairs and we want you to serve cocktails. Leave the show at nine and come one down for your instructions."

"She's got the way to move me Cherry..." I sang as I ran around preparing tables for the after show.

In all of my naiveté and unworldliness, I bumbled through the night. Not realizing that I was sort of being "offered up" if you will to Mr. Diamond as a token of the Pine Knob appreciation society. His concert was fabulous. He was a real showman with his sparkly, sequined black jumpsuit. People of the press surrounded him and wrote down everything he said. The photographers snapped away. We were all gathered in a small area that in the winter would have been the ski rental and exit to the slopes. The local newspaper and television personalities paid no attention to me as they snatched up every morsel off the tray I was carrying. They ordered drinks from me in a haphazard manner, *hey, bring me this*, and *hey, bring me that*.

The early summer sky was pitch black. The doors flew open with a hot gust of night air, and a whoosh. The mob bouncers preceded Neil, and then, in he walked. He was still wearing his black sequin jumpsuit from the show and he carried himself like a star.

Art came up behind me and said," Hey go ask him what he would like to drink."

"Okay, okay," I responded in a forceful hushed tone. I was star struck. He was shorter than I thought, but other than that exactly as I had imagined.

There was a strong breezy scent of men's cologne, Gucci, Calvin Klein, or Lagerfeld. "Could I bring you anything Mr. Diamond?" was all I could manage.

He smiled and graciously said, "Anything?" and everyone laughed gregariously.

Once again and as usual, I was the brunt of everyone's joke. *Ha, ha,* as Roseann Rosanna Danna used to say. I think he just got a soda or some wine.

Then the commotion began, and the flurry of questions. Flashes, video cameras, shouting over each other, laughter, and tape recorders stuck in his face.

"Mr. Diamond tell us about this album?" "Mr. Diamond how long is this tour?" "Mr. Diamond who does your hair?"

Then just as quickly as he had arrived, he left. One of his entourage came up to me and mentioned they were having a small party at the hotel if I would like to join them.

My first week out in this strange surrounding I had no clue what that meant, or entailed. I had to get home to my children, which happened to be true. Several years later, my good friend Doris would accompany Neil to his hotel for the after party. They called her "Doris Clitoris" although I never asked her how she got that name, nor did I investigate that nickname myself.

She was a sweet, skinny, Jewish girl from Bloomfield Hills. One time it was Neil's birthday, and she took me to the hotel suite celebration for him. The cake was in the shape of his head, and the resemblance was uncanny. They had gotten the hair, the nose, everything right, and we all had a good laugh about it, Neil making fun of himself. Such a pleasant surprise to find underneath all the fame, a nice man.

The next day everyone was madly quizzing me about Neil Diamond and what he was like. Just a regular nice guy was my impression and answer. Guess I was not going to be "discovered" that week.

CHAPTER 5

What Am I Doing Here? (1976)

"Mistakes are the portals to discovery"....James Joyce

There were many things to be learned in my new world, among them, the power of the Italian family I was working for, the motives of Art Ruth, manager of the Ogden Foods hierarchy, and how to deal with raising two daughters alone. Then there was balancing the new job, and my lack of experience. Onward and upward, I decided to take it a day at a time. My new infatuation was a disc jockey named Brian. He worked in the disco on a riser above the small dance floor. He had dual turntables, *ooohhh baby baby, oh baby baby.* He was just out of high school on his way to some preppie college. He was tall with long blond surfer hair and hazel eyes and a distinctive saunter that exuded confidence. Either that or he had a spinal injury. It was hard for me to tell the difference.

There were some sparse nights, income wise, such as the nights the Marshall Tucker Band, and Waylon Jennings played for a crowd who disdained disco. A particularly slow night occurred when Fleetwood Mac, one of my favorite bands, came to town. No one had come up to the buffet for dinner, none of the band members had come up to the lodge, and the after show was deadsville. It was worth it however to see the free show. Stevie Nicks had just started wearing her top hat, and I was so into the music, running all over the venue, singing, dancing like a lunatic. Strains of "Rhiannon" and "Say You Love Me," wafted through the amphitheater. I was in awe of them. I could endure through the rough patch of no money to see them. However the last night they played, I was at my wits end with horrible treatment, and no money, watching all the happy creatures dancing on the lawn.

That particular night at the disco side of Pine Knob not one soul had come up to the after show. "The Rangers" as they were called, a glorified name for grunt help and ushers, all converged on my assigned tables. They wore orange nylon "wind breaker" jackets with the Pine Knob logo on it, and they ordered pitcher after pitcher of beer. Everything drenched in beer stench. Obnoxious, drunk off their asses, they stumbled out after several hours of humiliation, and left me fifty cents. Fifty cents.

As I was cussing them out and clearing the tables, a hot summer wind blew through the open door and a familiar high pitched voice asked,

"Hi there, where can I get something to eat?"

I looked up to see Neil Young staring down my sagging orange polyester halter dress. He had that rugged "Cro-Magnon" man shaggy hair look he was famous for. My little pointed boobs must have looked like his 'Zuma' album cover with the chick flying over it. He was so tall that I was looking directly at his crotch. As my eyes moved slowly up his jeans to his plaid shirt, I said,

"Hi," after an uncomfortable pause.

"Yeah, go right through there." I pointed to the very busy restaurant side of the Pine Knob world. Big mistake.

Segway into my fantasy:

"Oh Neil, stay right here I can get you a burger, it's too crazy over there on the other side," is what I should have said.

Several minutes later I heard a crashing of the restaurant door slamming against the wall and screaming. The bouncers and body guards surrounded Neil, thrusting him through the empty disco to the back door, and down the back stairway to the parking lot. He turned once more to look at me as if to say, "What the fuck were you thinking???" as he was shoved out the door. I yelled,

"I'm sorry."

I was thinking *I hope he isn't high* because I couldn't even walk down those stairs in the daylight without tripping, although I think there was a full moon to guide them. He was the first one of the CSNY troupe I met. All I knew about him at the time was that he was married to one of my favorite actresses Carrie Snodgrass, and they had a son with cerebral palsy.

The next night when I went down to see the Stills Young Band it was magical. I was transported back in time to my friend Lisa's bedroom, where she had shown me the first CSNY album cover where they all looked like Civil War soldiers at Appomattox. Then it happened, Stephen caught my eye with his guitar, his voice (which was gravelly but still solid then) and his blond hair. They played 'Long May You Run' and a chord was struck with me that still resonates till this day. How could they know that would be my anthem?

Soon after on his next LP Neil would sing,

"You are like a hurricane, there's calm in your eye," as he subsequently pulled his fabulous tour bus out of the back gate at Pine Knob. Standing there only steps away, I was awestruck. The diesel stench of all the buses hung in the air so thick it burned my eyes. The summer was in full swing complete with heat. I have never seen anything like that bus before or since. He had an entire cut out Chevy I think it was, as a sky light on top of the flamboyantly decorated home on wheels. It even had a fireplace in the shape of a shell inside, featured on the back cover of 'Decade'. Had I known then what I know now, what a crazy car buff and train enthusiast he is, I never would have let him go to the mirror ball side of the lodge, I would have talked his ear off.

The next weeks droned on working late into the night, not making any money, and getting up early with children. Thankfully all through the girls' childhood my mother took them on the weekends, so they could see their father over in Plymouth, and I could work longer hours. The Lynard Skynard Band oddly followed the Stills-Young Band on the June schedule singing... "I hope Neil Young will remember, southern man don't need him around anyhow."

CHAPTER 6

So It Begins (1976)

"The world is full of magical things waiting for our wits to grow sharper." Bertrand Russell

Next The Band led by Robbie Robertson and Rick Danko came to town. Of course no one came up to the buffet for dinner that night either, not your typical "buffet" crowd. They were the quintessential band of Bob Dylan fame. I really knew nothing about them, but I did know some of their songs and loved the "Annie" one. Ambling my way down to the show, I pulled out a True Blue cigarette and lit up.

Now you have to picture the old Pine Knob theatre, the stripped down version of what it is today, all white walls, cement and orange paint. No nice landscaping and foliage. There were booths of food and t-shirt sales lined up along a walkway. People were arriving for the show late that night, and so I sat in the second row, and watched the "warm-up" band. (Now a days such a crass term isn't used. Instead we say "opening act.")

The warm-up band was Firefall. Their lead singer was intriguing, and their style was unique. I knew of Mike Clark, the drummer from the Byrds, and Rick Roberts was introduced as a former Flying Burrito Brother. Their sound was distinctive: a southern drawl mixed with

Rocky Mountains. "You are the woman I have always dreamed of...."
When the last note was played Rick Roberts jumped right off the stage
and came out to me seated on the edge of the fourth row. Never in
my life have I been as flattered as that night.

"Hi I'm Rick," he said, "what is your name?"

"I'm Christine O."

"I was wondering what you're doing tonight?"

"Well I have to work up there in the lodge...obviously, I don't
dress like this."

He gave me a little snicker and said, "Then come over to my hotel
and have a drink with me later." He was very handsome, thick dark
wavy hair, thick moustache, and eyes deep rich brown that drew me
in.

"Okay, I guess that would be okay, but I have a babysitter tonight
so not too late." I don't think he even asked me about my children. So
it began. That ten-year-long list of one-night-stands, and partying with
rock stars.

Next up that night was The Band, a whole new layer of talent and
decadence. This was Levon Helm, Robbie Robertson, Rick Danko,
famous for certain and out to lure me into their lair.

The crowd was wildly steeped in The Band culture, unlike myself,
and really went crazy when Robbie announced, "It's my birthday!"

I knew the album 'Northern Lights-Southern Cross' and I enjoyed
the concert until I had to go prepare for the after show crowd.

As I ran down the mural laden walkway to get to work, a Latin-
looking man with shoulder length black curly hair, and a white suit,
grabbed my arm, and in a tone that said, "this is your once in a life time
chance" looked me straight in the eye and said,

"Come to Robbie's birthday party tonight at Somerset Inn." He
handed me a written invitation with the room number on it. He must
have been a road manager, producer, or friend. I recall it was still light
outside when all of this happened, and darkness didn't fill the sky until
I made it back up to the lodge. The popcorn smell filled my nose as I
ran, threw open the double doors to the disco world, and was instantly

converted back from Cinderella at the ball, into a schlepping drinks waitress.

In some ubiquitous way I felt I would be missing something of great importance if I didn't make all the stops that night. The evening dragged by and soon I was able to get changed into jeans, and a sexy white blouse, with sandals on my feet.

I made my way to the Sheraton Inn in Pontiac, where Rick was waiting for me. The night air was warm, and sultry, as I motored along in my new used 1963 orange Volkswagen beetle we called "Speedy", because she wasn't.

I knocked on room 347, and Rick opened the door to greet me wearing only blue jeans, and appearing slightly road weary, and as if I had just interrupted his dream.

"Hi there, you weren't kidding you get out late." He handed me a beer and gave me a big kiss on the cheek down to my neck. That was enough, it had been so long since I had gotten laid, I just went for it. In the heated throws of passion we began taking each other clothes off, and fell back to the bed. We made sweet love for all of about twenty minutes when I jumped up and said,

"I have to go. I have a babysitter." I began to get dressed. He made a big attempt at slowing me down, but I had to be somewhere else.

"I'll see you next time around," he said. "I'll look you up.

There were no cell phones, so to call someone they had to be at a stationary place, like home or office, or next to a pay phone. Therefore I didn't bother him for a number, and he never asked for mine either.

I got in my car and sped off to the Somerset Inn in Troy. Again, the hotel was much different from today. It was a very high end hotel for its time. At one end was a quaint English Pub, followed down the hall by a French cuisine restaurant, and then at the front entrance were the desk and lobby areas. At the Inn's south end, were various types of rooms. One of these rooms was a townhouse-style room with a spiral staircase connecting floors and two separate floor entrances.

Of course I entered straight into the bedroom upstairs with the number I had been given. There on a round bed was Robbie en file Grande, surrounded by three naked women, blond, brunette, and redhead, very pretty ladies. Embarrassed as hell, I said hello to all, and scurried toward the spiral staircase on the other side of the room.

"Hey where are you going, come and join us!" Robbie beckoned from the bed.

"What for? It looks like you are all set," I said, as I ran through.

Downstairs there were just a couple of guys drinking and snacking on the spread of birthday food. One poor soul was passed out in a chair in the corner. The room was dark except for the hallway light. One of the stragglers was a handsome black man, in a white suit who greeted me, and offered a beverage. He had a Jamaican or Caribbean accent of some sort,

"You are very late, where have you been?"

"Oh I work at Pine Knob and got out really late."

"Well the important thing is that you made it, but I am afraid you have missed the party, it was a good time. There is some cake left if you would like and help yourself to the food."

A gentle breeze blew the long white shears through the open sliding door and the pool glistened in the nighttime lights. Trying to choose something to eat that was not as ravaged as the women upstairs, I made myself a plate.

"I would like to show you the way we drink this fine tequila in the islands," he said, as he offered up a shot glass of clear liquid.

"We don't use salt, and we chase with a lime."

I took the lime from his hand, and we toasted "cheers" followed by the bitter bite of lime. We made small talk, and I explained that I had to relieve the babysitter. Truth be told, I was a very light weight drinker in those days, and the shot went straight to my head. The room was spinning.

"I had some good Ganja here if you would like?" he offered. He reminded me of the guy who did the "Kola Nut" commercial, same white suit.

I didn't really know what that was, but I pretended I knew and declined anyway. Now the terms, "spleef", "reefer", and "monkey paw", I was familiar with since I had grown some lovely Hawaiian marijuana in my basement when I was married, my husband's entire family being pot connoisseurs. That particular night I just was not into getting my party started at two a.m. so off I went home.

The following week there was a sense of urgency in rudiments of the restaurant, and disco/buffet. Burt Bacharach would be playing for several days and his type of crowd would be very good for business. Even Matt Locchricio seemed on edge and pitched in to help coordinate things usually left up to little Joe. There was no way I could have prepared myself for the onslaught. Throngs of people streamed in first slowly, then filling every single table.

Here's your bank for the night," Donna said, handing over fifty dollars which was to be worn wrapped around my fingers in denominations of ones, fives, and tens.

"Get tables 10 and 15 right now," Donna shouted orders to all the wait staff. The service bar was crowded, the guests wanted two martinis at a time to get primed, to quickly eat, and get out. In a matter of an hour and a half, we had served two hundred people. I was yelling "one for the money" in my sleep that night.

The next night the real Italian restaurant led by Luigi on the other side of the lodge was overwhelmed with demanding people. In an instant the rookie was promoted to fine dining on the other side of the ski lodge.

"Christine, they need more servers, get over there and take some tables," Joey yelled. I had not even been working there a month, and it was the Burt Bacharach crowd, very classy.

It was pitch dark except for the mirror ball dance floor in the center. I grabbed a cocktail tray and went out to take orders. How the heck did that country club pour thing go again? I had not had the opportunity to practice that bit yet. Doc, the bartender, salt and pepper, slicked back hair, with a Frank Sinatra build, was in a foul mood to say the least. He was screaming at girls who were much better than I was, and faster.

I got up there and stammered, "ah, two vodka, three rum, ah..."and with that he took my entire tray of glasses I had set up and through them down the bar sending everything flying, booze and all. I was covered in garbage.

"Come back when you can do it right!" he yelled in a demonic tone.

"Shelly, Shelly what is the call order again? Gin, vodka, rum, specialties, and one for the money," she quickly answered as she ran off.

My personal nightmare continued for at least two hours until people danced and settled in after filtering in from the concert. What a night. I kept stuffing money in my little pocket, hoping I kept the 'bank' around my fingers straight. Getting home that night, and counting my money, it was more than I had ever seen in one place, even though they were mostly mercy tips. There was enough for a security deposit on my own apartment, (my ex-husband could have the house back) and soon after we were living at Dixie highway and Holly road. The one very sad thing was that no pets were allowed, so my Old English sheepdog would have to stay with the ex.

Everything was moving so fast. It had only been a couple of months since I began the separation process. I took only what I had brought into the marriage, my grandmother's antiques, a couch I had refinished, and my orange spinet piano with the antique finish. I found some very good baby sitters a couple of college age young ladies who adored my children, and thought I was set jet (short for suffragette). I would play Elton John on my piano all day with the door wide open, and sing to my heart's content before heading off to work at night. Unbeknownst to me, right across the street on Rattalee Lake Road, was an old blast from the past. It had been nine years since I had seen Bob Seger, and he was living there with his girlfriend Jan, nicely secluded in a little brown house.

Once when I was playing a song from my Elton John song book, and singing away with the door wide open. I saw Bob stop his motorcycle by the side of the road and listen, but when I went to the door to look out, he took off.

Early sometime in my new found freedom I was still having sex with my husband trying to allay some of his pain. I do not recommend doing this. First off, it messes with both of your psyches horribly, you are connecting when instead you should be attempting to disconnect. It gets rather messy.

It was that time of the summer when the Beach Boys rolled into town with their California swagger, white pants and striped shirts. I had a mad crush on Dennis Wilson from the time I was twelve years old. I was his little surfer girl. Every boyfriend I had in high school looked like Dennis with those chiseled features, and a shock of long blonde hair, swooping down over his eyes.

I was sitting in the buffet side of the lodge rolling silverware when in strolled Mike Love and Al Jardine with several of their entourage. Of course I knew who they were, and greeted them with "hello there." They ignored me as they walked on by and into the restaurant. Then Bruce Johnston happened in, and he was friendlier, said said "hello" back. Last but certainly not least was Dennis accompanied by a woman with light brown hair. He had a distinctive walk and as he sauntered by, time stood still. His eyes shown like glittering diamonds (little did I know it was probably drug-induced). I was transfixed for a moment and he gave me that smile. My assumption about his sexiness was to be reaffirmed at a future meeting. He also walked through and into the restaurant. Several moments later he came back in, looked at the buffet, and glanced over at me again. I would have given anything to be his waitress.

"How are you doing on those setups Christine?" Donna shouted from the kitchen.

"Oh, great, nearly done," I snapped out of my trance.

Then the strangest people paraded through. They looked sort of Italian, maybe friends of Matt's or Joey's. They definitely looked east side, wearing suits of dark brown, hair slicked back, Cuban heels clacking across the linoleum floor. Black leather, sort of warm for a Michigan summer. There was one guy who had protruding eyes who appeared to be the mouthpiece of the gang. He spoke with a strange accent. Definitely east siders. I later learned it was the opening act for the night: Billy Joel and his band.

When I went down to watch the show that night, Mr. Joel sat on a piano bench in front of his upright piano, and got a case of the giggles. He laughed so hard, and long, that he fell off the bench to the amusement of a full audience. For a significant amount of time he kept that up, about ten minutes or so. They were very honky tonk, and in my opinion, didn't fit the summer of fun theme of the Beach Boys with their beach balls flying around. I wondered who had booked them.

When the beach balls were flying, and all was right with the world again, strains of 'California Girls', and 'Caroline No' lilted through the air. After the show was a dud, however, no money that night. So Brian, the seventeen-year-old disc jockey and I made the most of the performance, singing along through the open back doors.

I spent the best part of the night dancing around as Brian played what he wanted to play for music. He always started the night with Steve Miller, who was one of our favorites: 'Take the Money and Run', 'Fly Like an Eagle' or 'Dream Weaver' and of course I loved Queen's 'Bohemian Rhapsody'. The rock and roll songs of the summer were Kiss 'Rock and Roll All Night' and Foghat's 'Slow Ride'. Afterward, we would have mad passionate sex outdoors, and go our separate ways. Sometimes we would go to his parent's house on the lake, moonlight shining being the only light, keeping library quiet. His house was on my way home, and we would go skinny dipping, love making, and sharing the summer from their walkout basement. I was the original cougar being twenty-six to his edge of seventeen. A regular woman of the world.

There was very little consideration from me about what I was doing, where I would be going in life, or who the heck I was going to have sex with. Just being free, or having the feeling of freedom, for the first time in my life was liberating. I flew from one sexual encounter to the next with reckless abandon, my spirit soaring most of the time. The emancipation of me.

My summer job was nearly half over. On July 16,1976, Harry Belafonte brought in a classier crowd of concert goers, which translated into good money. The Dixie highway apartments that I lived in seemed to be working out all right, affordable, secluded, and there were several children for my daughters to play with. Still, it was a strange place. Just a privately owned strip of six apartments in a row. Up the hill, the owners lived in a southern style, antebellum white mansion.

One day I got a call from Cheri's ex-husband Bill that he wanted to "stop by" now that my marriage was over too. It sounded like a friendly enough thing to do, which of course turned into a hop into bed for a quickie. I learned that day that almost anything you fantasize about, rarely lives up to the fantasy when it comes to reality. The expectations are way too high, the time, and place may be wrong, the reasons that you are in that moment may be erroneous.

So Bill and I parted as friends, and I never saw him again. In the words of Khalil Gibran whom I was reading at the time, "friendship is always a sweet responsibility, never an opportunity."

CHAPTER 7

Sound and the Soul
(1976-1977)

"The true delight is in the finding out rather than the knowing."
Isaac Asimov

In the archival history of rock and roll music in Detroit, one has to re-member the radio stations, and disc jockeys. They were delivering the gospel according to rock and roll. They partied like they were rock stars, and could always be found back stage hobnobbing and promising air play, and obtaining sought after coveted merchandise. Girls who had been cast off by the musicians were great perks.

"The Riff" WRIF head master, Arthur Penthollow, schooled the rest of Detroit on what a truly great DJ should be. His howl "Baby!" became an anthem. Ken Calvert "the casual one," Jim Johnson and Karen Sevelli, the token woman of the group. She held her own with the boys.

The radical station, and my personal favorite was WABX or the "X." ZZ Top sang, "I heard it, I heard it I heard it on the X!!" The celebration of "hump day" became big at this time with all the stations jumping in on Wednesdays. The DJs at the time were Dave Dixon and Mark Parentou, and several other founding members.

Then there was the troubled WWWW or W4 in Detroit where Howard Stern was working. They could not decide on their format, rock and roll or country, and after going country Howard Stern said good-bye to Detroit for the BIG APPLE. One night listening to WABX a new disc jockey named Steve Machevich, came on late night and I loved his voice. He invited people to call up and I did. Before I knew what was happening I had a date with him and he was on his way to my house after his late night broadcast. Spontaneous, desperate, very radical and intriguing.

The girls were away with their father that evening, and I was just plain lonely. Filling a void with a stranger. I heard his car pull up in front of the apartments crunching loose gravel under his Goodyear's. He knocked at the door, and I answered sporting only my old bell bottom jeans and a knit shirt.

"Hi I'm Steve, you must be Chris," he said staring into my dumbfounded look. The face certainly didn't match the voice, silky smooth, erotic voice. He resembled the hunchback of Notre Dame played by Lon Chaney without the hump.

"Hi there, Steve, come on in. I really like your radio show and your format."

"Well I'm just filling in for John O'Leary. He didn't show tonight or there was some confusion on vacations, or something, so I got my debut," he explained. John was a new-comer to ABX then, and he loved making the "scene" the local music. I would run into him everywhere in the clubs around Detroit.

"Would you like a drink? I have beer?" inviting conversation, and whatever else might happen. Let me tell you the whatever part. We got pretty inebriated and smoked some weed, played some rock and roll on my little speaker/turntable, and then he pulled out a Polaroid camera and began shooting. It started out innocent enough, and then he began to undress me, while taking a few more pictures. Pretty soon the line was crossed, and the shots were pornographic. Showing my dance moves in the nude, and displaying what the good lord gave me. I told him I had acquired a rather irritating disease several weeks ago thanks to my buddy James G from Detroit Management Agency.

"It wasn't active at all right now,"I added and he didn't care what I had. At that time I didn't know anything about this virus, and neither did anyone else, except that it was a kin to a cold sore on your mouth, and since when did a cold sore kill anyone?

When he left that night little did I know that Pandora's box had been opened, and everyone who came through that radio station would enjoy the exhibition of that night. Every rock band that visited the radio station, which is how it was done in those days, got a glimpse of "the Rose".

CHAPTER 8

Season of the Which Way Do I Go? (1976)

"It is better to keep your mouth closed and let people think you are a fool than to open it and remove all doubt..." Mark Twain

Off to work I went. The group Sha Na Na was airing one of my favorite TV shows at the time. They were a retro throw back to what, the Sharks and the Jets? Greasers and Frats? Who knew, but that's when I met Jocko. Jocko Marcellino. He saw me in the audience that night, and came looking for me in the lodge after the show, escorted by their manager, a gray haired, very refined British gentleman who always sported an ascot and was called Mr. Reginald. Mr. Reginald was all about finding women for his entourage, and he invited me to come to Ohio and see them play in a week or so. It sounded good to me. The kids could visit Cedar Pointe for our usual vacation spot, and I could do something I enjoyed as well. Fabulous!

Next day July 21st was to be two days of James Taylor or J.T. as everyone called him. The first time I heard 'Fire and Rain,' I was living in the upper peninsula of Michigan. It sounded like home when he sang. It still sounds like home to this day, he could be singing some AC/DC song, and his voice would still sound like home to me. Why?

"Hey Donna this is one of my favorite bands, do you think I could wrap up early from dinner shift and head down?" I beseeched her.

"Sure it should be a light night, we only have fifty or so reservations." It was a steamy, hot, end of July evening as I made my way down to the show where cars were still crawling into Pine Knob off the back road.

J.T. had a full band with Leland Skylar on bass, Russell Kunkel on drums, Clarence MacDonald on keyboards, David Sanborn on sax, Danny Kortchmar (Kooch) on guitar, and my soon to be friend and lover David Lindley on violin and slide.

David was an adorable, extremely talented man small in stature, big in heart. These musicians were the core of L.A. henchmen. They would circle back around in various forms with Jackson Browne, Crosby, Stills, and Nash, and Dan Fogelberg, among others.

The show was filled with old hippies and new fans, as he played all the old standard favorites and closed with "rock a bye sweet baby James" as per usual. Great show, great musicianship, and no income that night, nor after from the show crowd in the lodge.

Brian, the DJ, was on his little stage spinning records to an empty dance floor, and I was twirling around singing out the open doors as usual, when in walked JT. He sat all by himself at a bare table, begging to have drinks spilled onto it. All of the other fancy schmancy people who came from the show had already made their way to the main restaurant.

"You go wait on him, you're the big fan," one of the other girls said to me. He was enjoying the music tapping his hand on the table. He wore a long-sleeved white shirt and blue jeans. His hair was long and brown, and his eyes were azure sparkling pools, and they could certainly melt a popsicle.

"Hi there Mr. Taylor, what can I get for you?" I approached in my orange polyester, nightmare of a dress, uniform.

"I'll just have a coke right now, thanks," he said. The Carly Simon song 'You Belong To Me', was echoing around in my brain as I was thinking about how dashing and handsome he was.

When I returned with his drink, we made small talk for a while, not really flirtatious, just friendly, about what bands I liked and who we had coming up for the remainder of the summer. He asked if I could sit down with him, and I said I better not if I wanted to keep my job. He then said, "I'll put you on the guest list for tomorrow." I turned to wait on another table and when I turned back to JT he was gone. I implored the other waitress saying,

"You know it is really slow tonight and I better let the babysitter go while I can still afford her, would you mind closing tonight?"

"No problem kid take off," she said with a grin on her face that said, I know where YOU are going. It wasn't true though. James had told me where they were staying, but there had been no invitation that night. He was very married to one of my favorite singers, Carly Simon, so there was no way I would have anything to do with him in that circumstance. As far as their marriage goes, it would have had to be an open marriage arrangement of sorts.

Making my way home in "Speedy" the Volkswagen beetle, my wallet empty, I found my little sweethearts sleeping soundly in their bunk beds. How was I going to buy them school clothes in the fall, or put food on the table?

Next up at the Knob was Johnny Mathis, thank goodness, good crowd, good money.

There isn't anything eventful that I recall for Johnny M. except, as I predicted, really good money. It was the busiest preshow dinner crowd to date. That night I hung out with Brian afterward, and he told me he was going away to college in a couple of weeks. Well that was bound to happen. So long, summer romance.

The next afternoon at work, we were setting up the tables for the ZZ Top concert when some guy came running in, "I'll pay anyone $75 who can take me to metro airport, or this show is not going to happen!" exclaimed the long haired blond, surfer-type guy.

"Oh Donna, please let me take him that would be two night's tips for me at least," I pleaded.

She contemplated the idea for a minute or two, pensively going about what she was doing, then turned to me, saying, "Okay that's fine, come back up here and get to work as soon as you get back though."

"What's your name and what are you driving?" he asked. "Ah you can call me Rosie, and that's my car," I said, pointing to Speedy.

"Oh man that is going to be tight, but I think we can make it work. We have a blown amplifier part and they are sending it rush FedEx to be picked up at Metro in one hour."

Now I had heard that ZZ Top was travelling with live animal stock, which they brought out on stage, so we talked about that, and he said his name was Zeek Ranuchi (couldn't get away from those Italians) from Miami. He said he owned an aquarium shop down there and was just doing this gig for a friend as a favor. He was a quirky sort of nervous guy,short in stature big in personality, with a great tan and curly light brown hair.

Traffic was getting thick as a swarm of bees after someone hit their nest, as we made the hour long drive down I-75, then I-94 to Merriman Rd. He seemed to know right where to go, which was odd, since I had no idea where he was directing me to a part of the airport I had never seen before. We stopped outside a group of garage buildings,

"Wait here I'll be right out," he said, frantically. A few minutes later, he reappeared carrying a large Marshall amp box of some sort, which we barely squeezed into the flattened front seat. He jumped in behind me.

"Okay let's go, pronto!"

"Okay Tonto, pronto!" We made it back by 6:45 pm and I dropped him off at the back gate entrance.

"Thanks, Christine, I'll see you later," he said, as he struggled with the amp part liberating it from the car.

Back to work I went in time to wrap up several diners checks, and help with after dinner clean up.

"So did the low life pay you?" quipped Donna.

"Ya, he did, cash and $80 instead of $75, pretty good preshow income I'd say."

That was nearly my rent money for the month. I tried to get down to the show, but it was too crowded and way too rowdy for me and my little orange dress

Afterward Zeek came up to find me, "Hey I brought you a little something for being so nice. Come on outside."

We walked over to my car and got in. He pulled out a brown paper bag that looked like a sack lunch, and some sort of little tray.

"Do you like blow?"

"Sure, yeah, of course," I said, not wanting to appear ignorant. I had never done it before. I assumed it was cocaine, but not knowing any better could have been disastrous. He could have given me any substance on the planet and I wouldn't have known the difference.

He laid out about four lines and handed me a rolled up hundred dollar bill. I snorted up those lines like I knew what I was doing. That was my virgin tryst at cocaine.

"Oh my god, girl, you are some kind of Hoover!" Zeek cried out in a shockingly high pitched voice for a guy.

"What does that mean?"

"That is brown Peruvian, a little bit goes a long way, that was supposed to be for both of us," he explained calmly.

"Oh sorry, I didn't realize that," not knowing anything about cocaine etiquette. My head heated up, it burned my nostrils, and it felt as if I could feel my blood coursing through my veins. I began talking exceptionally fast.

"Okay just a taste more, then I have to get going." He gave me a kiss goodnight. That was the last I saw of Zeek. It had not occurred to me until later that perhaps the amplifier was not the only thing smuggled through the back gates, god was I naïve.

The Doobie Brothers rounded out the month, and that was my first backstage pass experience. Their roadies were exceptional. Really great bunch of people and staff, who had been working for them for some time, and were just plain, nice guys. They were the San Francisco area people, and I think of all the Californians I met they are the ones I became closest to. They were playing three nights, so that meant they were in town for at least four nights in a row. One of the guys came up to the lodge, invited me to come backstage, and gave me a stick-on patch, which said Pine Knob on it, nothing special just an ink stamp that said Doobie Brothers and the date. Most bands went on to have their own special pictured passes, and the ever coveted laminated pass, on lariats around the neck.

There I was standing in the wings, ten feet away from Michael McDonald playing keyboards singing, "Taking it to the streets." When they played 'Listen to the Music' I was telepathically sent back in time to that night of the great storm in the townhouse with the red door. That song had played over and over again on the turntable that night.

Heart had been the opening band that night, and it was the first time I met Howard Leese the guitar player. We only exchanged glances, slight conversation, and a few opinions before they had to leave. It was mystical, exhilarating, and I soon got a taste for being in the action on stage and singing along with the band. Acquiring that pass was going to be my goal from now on.

Meanwhile back at the ranch, my ex-husband had shown up with my Old English sheepdog Tuffy and insisted,

"Listen you have to take care of your dog, she is too much for me, I got rid of all the puppies, and now I have plans that don't fit with her for the weekend," he stated bluntly.

"Okay, I will try to sneak her in, but I will get evicted if I get caught, the girls and I will be out on our ears, do you understand that?" I took hold of the leash reluctantly.

My daughters were jumping all over him, and pleading with him not to go, and he shook them off fighting back tears. Very painful stuff for two 26-year-olds to be going through. I never wanted to perpetuate this hurt and anguish. As predicted, the next day someone complained about the dog after only one night, and there came a knock at the door.

"Okay you know no pets are allowed here Mrs. O, and the noise complaints are coming in, I am afraid that you are out of here!" my landlord said in a harsh tone.

I chased him all the way up the hill to the antebellum house earnestly appealing my situation,

"We have nowhere else to go....it was only overnight, not to stay.... we will be quieter, I promise."

Devastated by this news and his severe treatment, I cried as I stumbled all the way down the gravely dirt road back down the hill unable to see the ruts through my tears. My thoughts were, that son of a bitch, doesn't he know his karma is ruined for a good long time evicting a single mom and two little girls?

I walked down to the mailboxes to pick up a newspaper. At my age, I didn't realize the wisdom of the common assertion that "when one door closes another one opens." In the paper I found a condominium in Lake Orion, with two bedrooms and 876 square feet, rent with option to buy. I called, went to see it, and by the weekend we were moving in.

Art Ruth had given me a couple of days off to get settled in, so of course I thought about getting out of town. Mr. Reginald* had called me, and said that Sha Na Na was coming back to Pine Knob on July 31st, to play another show and then off to Blossom amphitheater in Ohio, and I was invited to come to both shows.

The upcoming shows at the Knob were lackluster. The Lettermen and Mac Davis, were playing so there was a great opportunity to take my girls and have an adventure.

After the Sha Na Na show we kicked August off with a bang. Cedar Pointe and the Holiday Inn water park, and the Blossom concert. Following the show at Blossom, we were invited back to the hotel to visit before the band had to take off. Due to the fact that I had two kids in tow for all of this, not much sex was happening, like none at all with Jocko, at that time. He was still so nice meeting me after the shows and buying us beverages, adult for me, coca cola for the girls. Jocko introduced us to all the guys, including Bowser and Chico, who came down to the bar, and of course I was sitting with Mr. Reginald in his ascot and Christian Dior suit, charming me with his British accent.

The kids were super excited, and really were having trouble making the connection amongst television, the stage, and real life.

"Well we have to get on the bus and head out, this is where we say good-night my dear," announced Mr. Reginald.

"Oh that's fine, we are staying just down the road in the Holiday Inn," just down the road was about twenty miles or so, maybe even farther. "Are you going to be all right to drive?" inquired Mr. Reginald, skeptically assessing my speech pattern.

"Oh we're good, I'll get a cup of coffee for the road," I assured him as we said our farewell to everyone.

Now in those days of no GPS, no cell phones, we had to rely on maps and memory.

"Mom, do you know where you're going?" Chrisanna asked.

"Yes we came east so we will go back west, very simple," easy for me to say.

After driving for way too long up and down highway 2, Damian had fallen asleep, and Chrisanna my co-pilot said,

"Mom we missed the exit....we have gone too far....turn around," she directed.

"Okay, you're right, what the heck exit are we looking for?" I said, as I turned the car around and pulled over to look at the map. That was before I realized that all exits have numbers, or what mile markers meant. I was navigating by street name, and city.

I had thought it would be all lit up around Sandusky, but the city had gone to sleep at one o'clock in the morning. Once I had made several turns, spun around once or twice, I was lost.

"Okay I am lost, now what should we do?" I said, expecting a sign of brilliance from my six year old.

"I remember a car dealership, let's drive up on the regular road and look for that," she stated in a Yoda sort of way. She was even the size of Yoda.

"Oh my god, this map is for shit, I'm just getting off here," I literally cried.

"Mom that's what I remember!" she exclaimed pointing far down the road.

"Thank God, good job Chrisanna you got us home. There's the road to the Holiday Inn!" I was exhausted, panicky and at my wits end.

The remainder of the weekend was really fun and splashy in the wave pool for the girls and me. By Sunday evening we made our way back to reality, winding around Lake Erie, and back up I-75, to our new little condo in Lake Orion. Back to work the following day was a far thought as our heads hit the pillows that night.

CHAPTER 9

Endless Summer Ends (1976)

"Summer ends, and autumn comes, and he who would have it Otherwise would have high tide always and a full moon every Night"....Hal Borland

Elsewhere in the world there is a Michigan man in the white house thanks to tricky Dick, it is an election year, and we are celebrating 200 years of freedom from British rule. Gas prices are $.59 per gallon, a house costs approximately $35,000 and people might begin carrying pictures of Chairman Mao because he has just died. Earthquakes in China, tidal wave in the Philippines, and the Son of Sam terrorizes NYC starting his rampage on July 29th. Being a huge movie freak, I watched, 'One Flew Over the Cuckoo's Nest.' Then there was 'The Omen' which brought a barrage of teasing upon my youngest daughter due to her name. I felt so bad and kept reassuring her she was named after Saint Damian and her grandmother, and she was not the evil demon as depicted in the movie "The Omen". The new home was a distraction for all of us, getting to make friends, learning our neighbor's habits, and thinking about a new school in the fall.I never wanted that summer, that magical summer to end. On August 8th and 9th of that year it was the soulful funk of Earth, Wind, and Fire led by Maurice

White, and Philip Bailey, Verdine White, Ralph Johnson, Larry Dun, Al McKay, Johnny Graham, and Andrew Woolfolk all rounding out the group from Chicago. Their afros the prominent feature of their look the sound unmatched by anyone else. They could do it all, funk, soul, R&B, disco, gospel, and anything else they wanted to do. Their stage presence was electric with the horn section and those fabulous stage clothes with the crazy colors and textures.

"Bet this is going to draw a great crowd," said one of the other wait staff to me.

"What do you mean? There are all kinds of people who come out to see them, we will make great money and be super busy. We won't be able to go down to the show tonight, way too crowded and busy."

To this day I still have not been able to see one of my favorite live performance bands, Earth, Wind, and Fire. My fellow waitperson was right. We made money hand over fist. People partied late into the night. The following week brought back memories of being with my husband, all the albums I owned and would play endlessly dreaming my life away: the Carpenters songs, me trying desperately to emulate Karen Carpenter's solid, steady, unwavering voice, when I would sing 'We've Only Just Begun' at weddings. Did I mention I was a wedding singer? Not the Adam Sandler type, but the aria type. My big claim to fame was 'Ave Maria.'

Up next at Pine Knob were Seals and Crofts with "diamond girl, sure do shine..." and Loggins and Messina sent me into a post marital depression. Then Quincy Jones came into Pine Knob, and all I knew was that he was a great music producer who was married to the Mod Squad starlet, Peggy Lipton.

A night off in between, and a nondescript Janis Ian show gave me time to regroup with my little family. Daughters duo were doing fairly well adjusting to the new condo, making friends, attending an outstanding school, which to this day receives academic excellence awards. They were almost always in sight from the upper story windows of our home, while they played at the swing sets. Oh my god, I had done something right. Jump back Jack. Still spending weekends at my mother's house and visiting with their father, who had a very strained relationship with me. This enabled me to work late, and not pay the babysitter. Blessings were flowing.

Back to work the following week for two nights with Crosby and Nash. Their estrangement that season from Stephen Stills and Neil Young had them following up a duet album, 'Whistling Down the Wire'. They were staying at the Somerset Inn in Troy. I recall seeing a limousine pulling in the back gate around time for sound check, which was not characteristic of them at all, but transportation is transportation after all. There was time to wander down to the amphitheater before the dinner hour. Doo, da doo, doo, doo, da doo running through my head as I sauntered down to the orange seats to hear the tenor thrills of Graham Nash. That must have been the moment when someone invited me to come to the bar that night. There were usually sound people at the mixing board, or road managers wandering from backstage to front to hear the sound quality. It was Joel Bernstein who took me into the fold. That was the real beginning of my relationship with CSN.

It was my Damian's birthday, which we were going to celebrate the following weekend. With my family situation taken care of, I was given license to party that night.

The restaurant at the Somerset was much like a European pub, dark heavy wood and beams, heavy wooden tables in a sunken area around the curved horseshoe-shaped bar. Plaques of family crests filled the walls along with some art. The lighting resembled candlelight. It smelled of stale beer and woman's perfume. I walked in having been to a wedding, I was wearing a bright blue, sleek and silky long evening gown that tied around my neck in a halter style. I sat along the bright side of the bar where I could be spotted by whomever had invited me. The entire room was Crosby, Nash and crew, sans David Crosby who now that I know him, was probably off getting rip roaring blind high on a crack pipe. Up walked Graham excusing himself to order a drink saying to the bartender, "I'll have a Dubonnet on the rocks with a twist please," and he said "doobonnie" with a lovely British accent.

He glanced at me and smiled, took his drink and said "have a good night," to me.

Moments later Joel walked up and said,

"Hey come on over and join the party, don't sit up here alone." That was all I needed to hear and I joined in the merriment. We were telling jokes, singing songs, Graham entertaining us with something that happened on the road, and the drinks were flowing. When the bar closed down Kootch, David, Russell, and several of the crew went up to one of their rooms to do some lines. I was tagging along with one of the roadies as usual. Danny Kortchmar was whispering and cooking up something when one of the guys jumped up on the bed behind me and with one move untied and dropped my gown to the floor. I was only wearing panties, and instead of going for it and do-ing a dance, or laughing it off, I was mortified. I grabbed my dress and started yelling obscenities at the guy amidst the laughter Kootch was generating. Feeling sorry for me David Lindley took me by the hand and said come with me. We went across the hall to his room where he was being apologetic.

"They just a little crazed on the road trying to have fun."

"Yes at my expense, I should leave."

"No please stay, it is safe with me."

We fell into each other's arms and I spent the night in his embrace.

The following days at Pine Knob one of the mainstay "house" bands rolled into town for a week. Chicago was comprised of mem-bers, Peter Cetera, Terry Kath, James Pankow, Walter Parazaider, Robert Lamm, Lee Loughnane, Danny Seraphine, Laudir de Oliveira. It was one of my favorite bands. They were following up the Chicago album with the picture of paint scaffolding being cut down by an obese old lady in hair rollers with a cop behind her, whilst they all dangled in painters pants splattered with primary colors. (a theme the J. Geils Band would later capitalize on)

Art Ruth came to me that day saying,

"How would you like to work a lunch shift tomorrow instead of dinner. There is some good money to be made."

"Heck yes, private party, who is it?"

"The band Chicago and their management, record label people, big party of about twenty-five."

"I'm your girl, Art."

"Good, do you own anything to wear like a white shirt and black pants? You could wear a little scarf or something too."

"Sure, I could come up with something."

The following day we set up two long tables together near the windows overlooking the ski slope. Linens in place, bread plates, full six piece silverware service, centerpieces, water and wine glasses, check.

In they came from separate entrances in the building, with very weighty discussions going on, business stuff. Now this was the first time I got a look at the real restaurant menu. Table side Caesar salads to order, hors d'oeuvres I had never heard of, and lavish entrees. Wine was being served by young Joey playing the Sommelier of the day, and I took drink orders as quickly as I could. They were all very polite, well mannered, and preoccupied with the reason for the event.

I felt overwhelmed, terribly inept, and rather foolish. One of the band members Danny Serphine sensed by the quizzical look on my face that I didn't know what the hell I was doing. Placing a dish of escargot in front of him he said,

"Do you know what that is?"

"No, not really, could you tell?" I whispered.

He chuckled, "They are snails."

"You mean slimy creatures with shells?"

"Yes they are a delicacy."

"Ugh."

He found my expressions very humorous, and so went the rest of the service, me serving things I had never served before, and trying to serve from the left and clear from the right, except for drinks.

Jimmy Pankow, always the most exuberant, and fun guy of the group asked me if I was coming down to the show sometime. Of course I would and he made certain I got a backstage pass. This was the beginning of our longtime acquaintance.

What a great week I had, great crowds, good money, and a whole lot of fun. They were also staying at the Somerset Inn, and I found myself with one of the crew skinny dipping in the pool. There were lots of people staying at the hotel peeking out at us through their drapes so I did my best Esther Williams imitation. The pool was central to the rooms then, and could also be seen through the main lobby, so when we saw the deskman making a fast paced walk toward the pool area with an angry look on his face, we went scrambling for our clothes laughing our asses off.

That was my introduction to the band Chicago who were always a class act and sharp dressed. Now Danny Seraphine is my Facebook friend.

After a week of Chicago, I was exhausted and partied out. I had some serious parental reckoning to do. Get the kids enrolled in school and do some clothes shopping. The summer was coming to an abrupt halt. The pinnacle show of the season for any good Italian person was about to happen.

Frank Sinatra had two nights at Pine Knob. The chairman of the board, Mr. New York New York was coming, and you would have thought the pope, or Queen of England was going to make an appearance the way everyone was in such a dither. Everything had to be "just so" including me. They moved me into the large restaurant, the real restaurant for two days, no more little orange dress, a real tuxedo look. It was monetarily the highlight of the summer for me, which meant I could afford that school shopping trip and make the rent. Of course Frank never came into the lodge, he was too important for that. I am certain they went to Lelli's or the Roma Café or even Somerset banquets for some lavish, swanky, revelry on the east side where all the good Italians in Detroit lived.

The rest of the shows at Pine Knob were fairly blasé. I always enjoyed Linda Ronstadt's unwavering voice.

The low point of the season happened that week too. Poor Rita Coolidge was singing with her then husband Kris Kristofferson. He was so inebriated he had to be carried off of the stage. Leaving her to finish the remainder of the show solo, which she did. I felt so sorry for her that night. That had to be true love, true stupidity, or a little of both.

Near this time Art Ruth came to me one day and said,

"Hey kid have you thought about what you are going to do when the season ends?"

"No not really, I thought I would just work in the dining room for the winter."

"There is not enough work to go around, Luigi takes care of whoever is in there. However, there is this great restaurant opening up in Troy and they are interviewing right now, would you be interested?"

"Of course I would what sort of place is it? Would I do all right?"

"Well it is a Chuck Muer restaurant called Charley's Crab and it will be the flag ship restaurant of his whole chain. Very upper class, connected to the Northfield Hilton. I have already given them your recommendation, and you are to go down for an interview day after tomorrow."

"Thank you so much Art....you know I hardly know what I am doing out here in the real world, thanks," and I gave him a hug and kiss on the cheek.

Holy shit now what? I had to make a suit to interview in, I had no clothes that were presentable. Good thing I was a seamstress, and made all my own clothes.

On the day of the interview I had a mauve gabardine skirt suit on with a floral silky shirt underneath, my hair was curled and coiffed and I was looking good. Parking my car, I walked around a manmade hill or island, which led to the front door and valet hut.

There in the driveway were two men wearing suits on this hot sunshiny day, at a table doing the interviews right out in the open. It was explained to me that there was too much heavy construction and toxic danger going on inside. It would have been a huge liability.

"Hello, I am Christine O, Art Ruth sent me," I said, introducing myself to one of the men.

"Oh yes you came highly recommended," he responded.

"So can you sing?" asked the man interviewing me.

"I'm a great singer, I have always sung with the church choir, in school in chorus, glee club, solos, and done all the musicals," I exhausted my resume in one breath.

"Well you are going to have to sing the happy birthday song each time a cake is delivered which is one of our signature draws here at Charley's."

"Great I happen to know that one."

Following the interview he informed me that they would be calling people the following week. What did that mean? Were they are giving me the brush off, or what?

I went about the task of being a good mom and getting my girls ready for school to keep my mind off of my unemployment situation. Being twenty- six years old, I had no idea about the future, I was trying to get through each day and do the best I could not to kill anybody. Baking cupcakes for school when I was called on to do so, making clothes for the girls instead of buying in order to save money, putting a decent meal on the table for all of us. So, thank god, the call came to start at Charley's Crab the next week.

The training session was so exciting. There must have been 80-100 people in the dining room seated on the brand new tapestry high back chairs which would fill the main room, while artisans hammered, sawed, and we learned the Muer way to the smell of sawdust and carpet glue.

"Only about half of you are going to make the cut here," said one of the four corporate executives who worked with a chef named Larry Pagliara. All dishes were referred to as Chef Larry "this" and Chef Larry's "that".

We were told about our benefits, including profit sharing. The executives pointed out how fortunate we were to be there. They said we were the cream of the crop. This was all very exciting to me, and I made a few friends rather quickly, several are still my best friends to this day. We studied the menu, we attended wine seminars and tastings, we learned about table settings and serving properly.

Opening night for the Detroit area upper echelons was to be next week, and hopefully all the smells would be different then. It was the most successful and chaotic situation I have ever been in. All 75 servers trying to serve drinks and food to people who were getting whatever they wanted for free. Chef Larry was expediting, and through the open kitchen he could be heard screaming at the back of the main dining room. It was a very drunken, face down in the Paella night, for one elderly lady, and many others.

I grew up in a family where my father was constantly "yelling" about something, and usually the yelling was directed at me, but I have never experienced anything like this angry chef. The mind set and temperament are only matched by the surgeons I have to work with now. The demand for perfection and the disparaging remarks were very frightening. Thank god I wasn't on the firing line for that first tirade. From the Caesar salad to the marinated lamb rack, and every piece of fish that left that kitchen, the chef got it right. Unfortunately he died a very young man on the ski slopes of Colorado suffering a massive heart attack, which rumor had it was cocaine-induced along with a lot of liquor.

The guests that night were people like the automotive big three execs, Lee Iacocca, the Fords, the Chrysler executives, old Detroit money, the Kresges, and the MacAulay's, and the nouveau riche, mostly pizza people. All the dining room areas were full and bustling.

Very successful night, and as a fund raiser, I believe they did very well. The place was happening with bright lights, great smells, piano playing by Bob Seeley who specialized in boogie woogie jams, and fine looking well-dressed crowd. It made my heart soar to be a part of this. I had known of Bob Seeley for a long time. He and my father, a drummer, grew up together on Detroit's fine west side. They would hop freight trains to Chicago together to hear great blues and jazz. They would hang outside of Baker's keyboard lounge at night to listen to the artists, and maybe get a chance to sit in on some jam sessions. It was so wonderful to be able to reunite my father and Mr. Seeley after so many years.

The next few months flew by, as the process of elimination dwindled down our worker bee numbers at the Crab. We went from 80 to around 37 people serving the restaurant. I had learned so much. My German grandmother had taught me fortitude. I still had not yet learned what it would take to be the perfect mother. I was partying, living the restaurant high life and night life. I was busy meeting famous people, and keeping my personal life at a distance. My mother god bless her, still taking my children on busy money making weekends.

Christmas was approaching and the money was great. I cannot recall how I got involved with Punch and Colleen Andrews, but I did. Eddie (Punch) Andrews is and was Bob Seger's manager and long-time friend. It may have been the DMA guy James, or it may have been some other meeting, but I was invited to a Christmas party in their home.

My couture that evening was burgundy and forest green velvet. A printed dark green jumpsuit with a cropped dark red velvet top that tied in the front that I had made the day before. There was a full moon that night as the tires of my blue Rambler sedan crunched in the snowy driveway. It was bitter cold and my nerves were adding to the tremors I was experiencing.

Arriving early to the party at around 8pm, I headed straight into the kitchen where I always felt at home. Colleen was there with her sleeves rolled up preparing food trays.

"Hey Col what can I do, let me help," I said rolling up my sleeves when I noticed her frantic demeanor.

"Oh thanks, put these cold cuts on this platter...then this sauce in the center," she said. I could not believe that someone with that kind of money wouldn't have their party catered. Then I heard through the grapevine what a tightwad miser Punch really was.

Their house was an old circa 1930's large bungalow country home on a great enormous lot in Birmingham, Michigan. All the rooms were traditionally separate and crammed full of lovely antiques, tasteful traditional décor, along with Punch's collection of antique clocks. Each wall held some treasure. There was a banjo clock identical to the one that resided in my parent's house, which had belonged to my grand-mother. She also had a twin clock in her dining room. They both made the most wonderful tick tock sound, with George Washington at Mt. Vernon on it, and it was actually made in the USA not Switzerland or Germany.

There were so many tick tocks and chimes that the house sound-ed like a clock shop. Except for the massive stereo system that piped through the home, the clocks were all you heard. In the back room study was a state of the art sound equipment that filled one whole wall.

People were beginning to arrive. I was working away in the kitchen when in walked Charlie Allen Martin, the Silver Bullet Band drummer, in a three piece baby blue suit. He was shorter than I was in my Elton John style platform shoes, but I walked right up to speak with him.

"Hello Charlie, I'm Christine and I understand that you are a per-vert," was my opening line.

"Yes, some people think I am," he smiled and put on that soft and sexy voice in response to my daring introduction.

We made flirtatious small talk for several minutes then he said, "Hey I'm with someone tonight, my girlfriend Lenaya, but why don't you give me your number and I'll give you a call sometime?"

"That would be just fine," I set my drink down, and under the phone on the wall I found a pad of paper, and scrawled my number down for him,

"Here you go, I'll talk to ya later," and I gave him a kiss on the cheek.

Making my way down to the basement, there was a nice seating area, and against the wall was a Wurlitzer jukebox in pristine condi-tion. It was filled with every Motown song I knew and then some other 50's and 60's music on 45 RPMs vinyl records. Several people I didn't know were milling around and greeting each other. I went to the oth-er side of the stairway and there was Joe Walsh playing ping pong.

"Hey you wanna play some ping pong?" he asked me in that

distinctive Joe drawl of his.

"Sure, I haven't played since I was a kid. We had a ping pong table, but it was mostly used for my Barbie doll city," I quipped.

Joe was funny and friendly and we attempted one set of ping pong before I decided I had had too much to drink, and would prefer to be a spectator. After a while I went back upstairs to find Colleen with coats in one arm, and a platter of food in the other.

"Here let me help you," I said taking the pile of coats from her arm.

"Just put those on the bed in the little bedroom, okay? Thanks Chris."

I poked my head into each room until I found one with a pile of coats on the bed. The room had two entries, and as soon as I placed the coats on the bed and turned around, there was Bob coming in the other doorway.

"Hey remember me?" I exclaimed.

He was shocked, flustered, nervous in response, "My girlfriend is here tonight, shhhh," and as quickly as he came in, he went out. That long dark hair flying.

Bob looked great. He seemed shorter, but again that must have been my shoes, and he had lost weight since I knew him. Nearly ten years had passed since I used to hang out on Pauline Street. I was crushed. He didn't have to fucking date me, he only had to be nice to an old friend.

Making my way into the dimly lit living room to socialize, I found Glenn Fry, Don Henley, and the rest of the Eagles band, and Tom Weschler whom I got to know that night. He had one messed up eye, whether or not he was legally blind or not, I have no idea, but he was a cool cat who worked at the Birmingham Camera store. Tom was Bob Seger's "go to" photographer for most of his albums. Other music industry people were packed into that house exchanging stories, drinking, certainly doing some recreational substances in a back room, which I wasn't part of that night. Alto Reed was always a flamboyant life of the party guy. I was also reacquainted with my old Plymouth friend, Chris Campbell, and his wife, Chris Blagus. I knew them from high school, from hanging out around our home town, and from the Rexall Drug store where I worked during high school.

Several minutes later, I realized Bob did recognize me when a song blasted through the house. Punch was playing 'Ivory' from the Ramblin' Gamblin' album. (Cue 'Ivory') "She was born with a face that would let her get her way....you had everything you wanted child that is until today..." There was no other reason to play that old ghost unless it was for my benefit.

Slightly humiliated, slightly uneasy, and slightly drunk, I ran from the party like Cinderella from the ball. The only difference was no one was chasing after me.

CHAPTER 10

Entrenched in Detroit Music (Early winter 1977)

"I'd probably be famous now if I wasn't such a good waitress..."
Jane Siberry

The next morning "Cinderella" woke up to prepare for another work week, and off to Plymouth to pick up the girls. Thank goodness for my mother or I would have completely lost my mind. However there were those in the condominium who did not appreciate that I was a working single mother, who made life even more difficult for me.

One night I got a phone call at work from my oldest daughter saying the babysitter didn't show up. There was a lady from social services there in the house, and she just sort of let herself in.

I was angry, crying, driving like a mad woman up I-75 in the blackness of a no moon night believing that someone was in my house, going to take my children away. In a matter of fifteen minutes I was there, half the time it usually took me.

I flung open the door and ran up the stairs to find a rather large black woman dressed like Madea, or the church lady from *Saturday Night Live*, sitting in my living room chair flanked by my daughters sitting absolutely silent.

"What is going on here?" I said, out of breath.

"Are you Christine Olevnik?" she inquired.

"Well yes I am."

"There was a complaint filed by one of your neighbors about your children running wild."

"Which neighbor, they are all my friends, and I know them fairly well?"

"I am not at liberty to say, but your house looks very nice and clean, and well decorated, and I can see by your uniform you are working," she stated in an overtly calm manner.

"Get yourself a babysitter for several more years, your oldest needs to be 13-years-old before they can be left alone," she informed me.

"No problem, ours just didn't show up tonight, I'm afraid," I said, fear subsiding.

She had been writing on a tablet this entire time, nodding and saying, "uh huh," a lot, before she turned and left. As I watched her car pull away, I turned to the children,

"What the heck happened tonight? And what the hell did you let any stranger in our house for?!" I was angry, but subdued.

They both began chattering at once.

"Well the dog got out and we were chasing her....and....and," they tried to make up some tall tale.

"I am missing a night's pay, that is our grocery money for the week, and now I am forced to pay a sitter a whole bunch of money. Okay we'll figure this out, I am just so happy she didn't take you away, you know she could, this is a very tough thing we are dealing with here. I need you to know we have to stick together on this and don't get the neighbors involved," I reiterated. They nodded in agreement and life went on. To be legal for the next several years I made certain we had a babysitter whenever I had my girls.

The remainder of that winter was spent working at the Crab, and establishing close lifelong friendships. Raising my children, now seven and four years old. It was always a juggling act. Chuck Muer the chairman of the board of C.A. Muer Corporation had singled me out to take care of his family whenever they dined at the restaurant, I loved his children, and Mr. Muer made certain he took care of my little family.

One weekend we had a cocktail and press party for the employees to celebrate our first Travelers Award from AAA and Diner's Club. Chuck was running around snapping photos of my daughter and another waitress' son, and some other still moments while the Detroit Free Press photographer took a group photo from the upstairs balcony. A week later Chuck was in for dinner and someone came running up to me,

"Hey Chris O., Mr. Muer is requesting you come back to his table..." said an envious fellow employee, in shocked disbelief.

I made my way to the back of the main dining room nervously. I could see my reflection in the full wall mirror that hung behind his table as I approached.

"Hello Mr. Muer, someone said that you wanted to see me?" I said.

"Yes, I have something for you," he said, as he raised a large brown paper wrapped rectangular frame from underneath the table.

"Oh thank you so much," I said, and I started to walk away.

"Wait...go ahead and open it," he laughed.

I smiled and tore at the paper. Inside was a silver frame with two pictures of my daughter and the little boy playing together at the award party. The other three people sitting with Chuck admired his photographic prowess, and I was very grateful. That was the sort of person he was. Generous, creative, and just a great human being.

Other exciting accomplishments were unfolding that winter. Not only were the musicians from Pine Knob, Meadowbrook Theatre, and Royal Oak Theatre staying at the Northfield Hilton, but the sports figures also came to town. Then aside from all the frivolity of the work environment there were always local bands to go see after work on the weekends. Next door at the Northfield Hilton was a club called Hurley's. Each night they had a live band and especially on weekends, I got to know some of the local standard henchmen, jazz and pop musicians including Ron English.

It was during this time in 1977, that I heard the bad news. Charlie Allen Martin of the Silver Bullet Band had been hit by a car on the Southfield Freeway service drive one evening while walking back to his abandoned car with a gas can. He had just come from band practice at A2 Studios in Ann Arbor and as he was driving back to Rosedale Park, he had run out of gas. He became paraplegic when a blood clot moved in his spine several days after his operation.

I had gotten fairly entrenched in the underground club scene. Bookies was a big one, clubs on Six Mile Road West Side Six, where the left over Herman's Hermits band would play, or Mitch Ryder. Groups like the Look, Barooga Bandit, later known only as Barooga. They were managed by Punch Andrews, also Seger's manager. Martha and the Motels would come to town and play sometimes in Ann Arbor at the 'Chances Are' club.

I also went to the Patti Smith performance at 'Chances Are', the night she met Fred "Sonic" Smith from the MC5, who would later become her husband. She was the quintessential New York poetess/performer who I idolized. I sat at my little table mesmerized by her. When she had finished her performance and left the stage, suddenly she came running back in a furious rage screaming, "Some mother fucker here stole my coat!" This was her tattered brown signature coat she always wore. She was beyond anger, but she left with a husband, so I call that an even trade.

Work at Charley's Crab was fun and stressful. Often, I was so far in "the weeds" I couldn't see straight or figure out what to do next. In my estimation though I was becoming a top notch wine specialist and a pretty good server. One busy Friday night I was waiting on table #80, a lovely, long oak booth overlooking the downstairs foyer and front door, with plants on a ledge just below. The two couples at the table were sparing no expense, and were obviously upper middle class by their dress and jewelry. Halfway through the service, one of the women mowing through her plate of lobster, fingers full of butter, exclaimed, "Oh my god, my diamond flew off my finger and fell down there," pointing to the plant below.

The men were out of the booth looking over the edge, and I thought I would come to the rescue, "Here I think I can get it," I offered in a 'Bridget Jones' sort of way. Now the wall between the table and the ledge was constructed of horizontal planks of solid wood. I barely managed to get on the floor, crawl underneath the table, and force my head and right arm through the opening in

the planks. The audience of people had grown now and people were even looking up from the foyer. I groped around with my right hand, and finally felt the ring.

"I've got it," I bragged. This was followed by gasps and cheers from people around me, but when I attempted to pull myself back out of the wood planks, I was stuck. Something had swollen. I had very large post earrings on that could not fit through again going back the other way. It was at this point that the tragic ring rescue turned into a farce, and everyone started laughing. The woman had her ring back, and the men were on the floor now trying to rescue me. Another server Luanne came over and asked,

"What is going on?"

Another server next to her said, "Oh Chris O has her head stuck in the railing."

"I'll get someone, and maybe some ice, hang in there."

"Here, take the earring out and I think I can fit," I suggested.

One of the men did just that and with a tug and a pop, out came my head and arm all intact. This was still amusing to everyone who had now turned to go back to their seats, I was laughing so hard I was crying.

One of the gentlemen offered,

"That was more entertainment than we thought we were getting tonight, could we buy you a drink?"

"Oh no thanks, not allowed to drink on the job," and off to serve the other guests I went.

CHAPTER 11

Dream of Future Past (Spring 1977)

"I dwell in possibility..." **Emily Dickinson**

It was now springtime in Troy, Michigan and that meant Pine Knob season was opening for 1977. I was so excited, all the people I had become acquainted with the previous year would be back in some form with some group or another.

The stable of waitresses at Charley's Crab were considered higher class than most by the standards of that era. One of the early servers in our original training group was named Joan. She had met Teddy Kennedy on a trip to Washington, DC several weeks before, and he would have his secretary announce to her he was going to call, then he would call. He had a certain "type" and she fit the bill to a tee. She shared all her stories of him with us, and later that year she moved to DC to be near him.

There were some shows I wanted to work at Pine Knob in order to get in for free. I arranged to work both jobs for the summer. My bosses at Pine Knob, Joey Locchricio and Art Ruth, had decided that since I was working for Chuck Muer I must be good enough to work in the fine dining side of the lodge with Luigi. That was fine, because

Brian, the disc jockey, had gone away to college now, and would no longer be my other summer fling.

One early evening at Charley's Crab before the restaurant was really open for business, the brass curved raw bar was filled with oysters and clams packed in crushed ice, and the bottles were clanging with stock being replaced, when a lovely black woman looking like Easter Sunday, dressed in a suit and large fancy hat came in followed by three very fly looking black gentlemen, and was escorted to table 22 in my station. The table was in the center of the main dining room. Sunlight streamed in through the leaded glass bay window casting rainbows of light across the white linen.

"Hello there, my name is Chris. I will be your server tonight. May I add you look wonderful, like Gladys Knight and the Pips, or someone," I exclaimed meaning it in a good way, but then wondering if it came out right.

One of the men turned to me as they all laughed, "Sweetheart, we are Gladys Knight and the Pips." I felt like such a ditz. They introduced themselves as William Guest and Edward Patton, who were cousins and Gladys and Merald "Bubba" Knight, who were brother and sister.

I was thrilled. "Are you playing somewhere?" I said.

"Yes tonight at Pine Knob."

"I've been listening to you ever since you were at Motown Records, I just love your music. Now let me tell you what is really good tonight," and the salesperson in me busted out. They laughed and enjoyed what was nearly a private dining room experience.

The following week was one of the highlights of my life. Crosby, Stills and Nash were in town for at least four days. I chose to work at Pine Knob for the first show and then took the other nights off. Joel Bernstein and several of the road crew were back with them again, so getting passes would be no problem. The band at this time included George "Chocolate" Perry on bass, and Joe Vitale on percussion, both of which I would get to know better several years later.

The tour was to promote the CSN album pictured with the "three musketeers" seated on Crosby's yacht. Later, the songs from this album, including, "Dark Star, "Shadow Captain," and Nash's dauntingly spiritual "Cathedral" carried me through some very tough times, but the album had not been released nationally yet. Their busses pulled into Pine Knob early on June 2nd, one for each of them and then a crew bus. They were so great together on stage, but compatibility was challenging off stage. Each one had his own demons to wrestle with, but mostly Crosby and Stills butted heads, while Graham did his best to quell the tempest.

The concert featured all of their old standards and their new music, which absolutely wowed the crowd who had followed them from the Woodstock days. David Crosby's beautiful tone has always been one of my favorites. Graham's harmonies are second to none, and the magnificent guitar work and raspy voice of Stephen had me captivated.

After the show and following my work obligation, I made my way back to Troy and the Somerset Inn where we were all meeting for drinks. My perpetual need to hang out with musicians was overwhelming, but the need for acceptance was even stronger. I knew I wasn't beautiful, but I was pretty enough, and fairly charismatic with (what has been described) as an effervescence about me.

Somerset lounge was fairly empty until we arrived. I was sitting at a table with the crew enjoying a beverage when Graham came in first, very friendly and greeting everyone. He was slender, handsome, and for all intents and purposes, alone. I made my way up to the bar to order another drink. Graham followed and ordered, saying, "I'll have a 'Dubonnie' (Dubonnet) on the rocks with a twist." He smiled and I reintroduced myself. All the pleasantry aside we returned to the table to join the others who were discussing who screwed up what, which song was the best, things that may need some refinement, etc. All the shop talk grew boring and I went up to sit at the bar next to Joel and see if I could get passes for the next evening.

"Hello Joel, Rosie, I met you last year. You probably don't remember me, but..."

Being the diplomat he replied, "Of course I do...how have you been?"

As we were chatting, in walked Stephen. He went straight for the table of crew members, and had a drink while staring relentlessly at me. Now his escapades were fairly well known. He had been married to Judy Collins and then to a French woman, and then rumors always filled the tabloids about him, always with blondes up until this point.

He must have gotten some liquid courage, because he came straight up to me and whispered in my left ear, "I would like you to come up to my room and see me, I'm in 243." Then he turned and made a hasty exit. So as they say, curiosity killed the cat, *meow*.

It was one of the same suites Robbie Robertson had booked with one number for the downstairs and another number for the upstairs. Stephen had given me the upstairs number, but I knew better. I wanted to get to know the man first. I went to the lower door of the townhouse suite with its spiral staircase and beautifully furnished sitting area with kitchen area, frig and fully stocked bar. I knocked on the door timidly at first, then realizing I could not be heard, I hit the door with a more robust pounding. On one of my down beats, the door swung open, and I nearly fell inside.

"Well hello I didn't think you were going to come," Stephen said.

"I was making so much noise out here I about woke up all of Troy," was my answer in my own defense.

"Would you like a drink?" he offered in a good host way.

"I think I have had enough really..."

"Perrier?"

Stephen always had Jack Daniels, Perrier, and Marlboro reds nearby...as well as lots of cocaine.

"Sure that sounds good, thanks." I had never heard of Perrier before. We had not put that on our menu yet at the Crab. I took a swig and laughed like a child.

"Woe that is bubbly. It tickled my nose."

This got a laugh out of him and we were off to a good start. Moonlight streamed through the sliding wall of windows out to the courtyard as I tried to make small talk attempting to harness the mounting sexual tension that was growing between us. There was no background music, no soundtrack being played out except some-where off in the distance I heard a violin. Stephen took me by the hand and led me slowly up the spiral staircase. He had on a white shirt, jeans and bare feet so I could see him quite easily in the darkened room, with only a bit of light from the bathroom. We set our drinks on a nearby table, and began to slowly undress each other, me unbuttoning his shirt, he lifting my dress over my head. That was enough resistance, we madly embraced each other in a passionate kiss. Stephen was clean shaven and I could feel the curve of his lips. The kiss was like coming home, it was so perfect. We tumbled naked on the plush bed, my mind was soaring into ecstasy. He was taking me to a place I had never ex-plored. He kissed my neck tenderly, then moved south to my breasts, and palming them like two fragile objects planted kisses on my nipples. Moving erotically down my belly with his lips, he found the sweet spot on both sides of my waist, sending chills throughout my being. Placing his mouth over my clitoris he began to suck on me softly, then lick my lips with his mouth. I had never experienced this sort of love mak-ing before, he was exploring untraveled regions of my body with his mouth. We were not speaking, we didn't need to, our bodies were speaking for us. Just before I peaked, he moved on top of me and slid inside of me. We gasped in utter joy and excitement, then collapsed in the pure exhaustion of the moment.

Seconds later we were both sleeping. During the night or shortly afterward he got up and left the suite, probably to go burn the mid-night oil with the crew and do some blow. When I awoke in the morning he was by my side.

"Hey I'm starving let's get some breakfast," I suggested.

"I'll just order something up I want to do some reading," as he pointed to a large stack of hard cover books. It seemed to me that Stephen was always trying to prove his intelligence to people. He had nothing to prove to me, but we got room service. I had my usual eggs and bacon, and as I came to know him he was having his usual club sandwich. We drank our coffee. Stephen always put his pinky up when he drank from a cup. I read somewhere that it was pretentious and not necessary etiquette, and so I had broken myself of that habit.

We sat reading in bed all morning the covers pulled up around us. I was trying to find something that interested me by title, but they were all beyond my comprehension, and perhaps even above Stephen's, but I still gave it a shot, and found a book that described the stage and acting. I was reading along when something struck me funny and I began to laugh,

"What is it?" Stephen wanted to know. "Oh nothing this is just humorous," I answered.

Silence again and we continued reading. Again something struck me funny.

"What is it now?" he demanded.

"Just something funny." I shook my head at him. It was then that the books and our bodies flew into a flurry of pages and sex. I forget who attacked whom, but it was a great morning.

"I have to run downstairs to the gift shop for a moment," I exclaimed and threw on a pair of his jeans and a large red shirt. I was down the stairs and out the door before he could stop me.

I walked through the lobby greeting people along the way, some crew members who were staring blankly at my apparel. I purchased what I needed and as I left the gift shop I was met by Stephen.

"Hello love what is going on?" I asked.

"You left with my CCCP shirt, given to me by the Russian hockey team, I thought you were taking it," he admitted. Little did I know what a huge sports fiend Stephen was and apparently how much that jersey meant to him.

"What? Listen, I wouldn't take your bloody clothes buddy," and I marched off back to the room with him following me.

"I'm sorry, that just means a lot to me," Stephen offered up an explanation.

"Obviously more than I do!" I quickly undressed and got into my own clothes, grabbed my purse and headed for the door.

"Wait, don't be angry, listen we have a baseball game this afternoon against the Rangers and I want you to come," he said holding onto my shoulders. CSN vs the Pine Knob Rangers, that would be interesting. So I proceeded to go home and regroup, call my mom and see how the kids were doing.

The game was being played close to my house at a Clarkston elementary school. I arrived in my orange VW bug just in time for the game to commence. David and Stephen were actually, physically, playing, and of course all their crew. Graham was standing on the sideline because of course it wasn't cricket. The Rangers were all in their orange jackets or t-shirts, and there was a great deal of trash talk being tossed around by the teams. "You are going down, Stills!" shouted one of the Rangers. "We'll see about tha. Put your money where your mouth is," he retorted.

Stephen was up to bat and hit a fairly lofty double. The problem was he had a gimpy leg, and he was not exactly motoring around the bases. The ball was well fielded and Stephen took a slide a bit early into second base. Somehow he managed to acquire a very large gash, and tore open a pair of brand new blue jeans. After that, he was benched.

Running madly over to see if he was all right, I said, "Oh my god how did that happen? Don't move I'll be right back." The Rangers were already helping him into the back of their equipment van.

I jumped in Speedy and took off for the drug store. I raced in grabbing hydrogen peroxide, dressing and tape, and raced back to the field. When I showed up with my bag of supplies, he said, "Hey someone found a first aid kit here and patched me up already, but that was sweet. These are my favorite jeans though."

"Good thing it wasn't your hockey shirt," I said in a smart mouthed response.

"Maybe you can fix these jeans for me?" he said, perhaps trying to make me feel useful.

The Rangers handily beat the CSN crew, although since their ringer Stephen was out of commission it was almost by default. There was a show to do and the show must go on. I cruised home, checked in with my girls, who would be home the next day and got ready for the show. I lugged my sewing machine out to the car. I would go to the hotel first and repair his jeans. Never fear the quintessential seamstress is here. I had chosen a blue print dress to wear, onto which I had sewn some clay glazed beads, ever the hippy chick. When I got to his room he was lying on the bed, "Here help me get out of these," he grimaced and dangled his boots off the end of the bed. I tugged vigorously with all my might.

"Jesus, cowboy, you got tight boots!" I exclaimed as I fell backward awkwardly holding on to the right foot. He laughed at me once again. He got into an affectionate mood, and we tumbled on the bed. Somehow the mending of the jeans never took place, and I left when he got into the shower.

A backstage pass was waiting for me at the trailer, and I walked down the sloped back road, glancing up at the abandoned chair lift on the ski hill halted by the soft summer breeze. Their cars arrived not too long after I had gotten there.

Once again the show was fantastic, flawless, and fun. Stephen and I spent another amorous night in each other's arms, and early the next morning I quietly got dressed and whispered, "I'll see you later at the show tonight," in his ear as he slept. I was unaware at the time that rock and roll noise had taken a toll on his ability to hear. He moaned and turned over.

My mother had brought the girls home early that Sunday and I announced,

"Girls we are going to see Crosby, Stills, and Nash tonight, and we will be backstage, so be on good behavior okay, I really love these guys," I meant one guy in particular, but they got the message. Before I would take my daughters to a show we would play the album on our living room turntable, and dance around the room together for a little warm up session. Oh, how we loved to sing and dance.

"Ready girls, let's go... did you feed the dog? Did she get out?" doing the last minute check of lights and electrical appliances.

"Yes mom we got it," in unison as they raced each other down the stairs and jumped into Speedy.

"Now when we get there, just stand where I tell you to stand and no running all over the place, okay? I can get you pop and stuff from the backstage room, so don't beg for that all right, and be polite to people." I really didn't need to coach them because they were well-behaved children.

People were already packing the parking lots to tailgate. The limousines were pulling in as we parked, each in his own separate car. Heaven forbid they should travel anywhere together.

We got our passes, and walked down the driveway where white semis were lined up for the load out. We made our way through the usual orange backstage door.

"Sorry you can't come in this way tonight, honey, go to the other side and the crew will direct you," stated a big bouncer type guy.

Okay, fine, what was the big deal? Curious to find out, we went on to the other stage door and were greeted by familiar faces of the crew guys making last minute adjustments, running cable, testing microphones, and tuning guitars. We made our way to a room set up with Heineken beer in iced tubs, soda pop, Perrier of course, bottles of Jack Daniels and cartons of Marlboros. I grabbed the girls a soda and cracked a beer for myself.

"Help yourself. This is Stephen's room," one of the guys instructed, so we did. The dressing room assignments had changed for that night for some reason. Hearing the introduction of the band we made our way out to stage left to stand for the show. In back of the black stage curtain there was a little toe headed, blonde kid climbing all over the amp and storage trunks. He saw my girls and ran over to them,

"Hey come and play with me," he exclaimed.

"Can we mom?" asked the girls looking up to me for approval.

"Sure go ahead," I smiled shaking my head, hoping we weren't about to get kicked off the stage.

They were going crazy having so much fun, it looked like the Led Zeppelin album cover for 'Houses of the Holy' all those blonde children scaling the trunks. Then CSN took the stage and the crowd was on their feet cheering. I went over to one of the crew and said,

"So who is that little boy playing with my daughters?"

"Oh that's Zeek, Neil Young's kid, he's here tonight."

It suddenly became clear why there had been such a hubbub. Neil probably had one of the main dressing rooms for his family and friends.

"Is he going to sit in with the guys?" That would be a dream come true for me.

"I don't know. I don't think so, there's too much crap going on," was the answer and educated guess.

By that, I assumed the politics of the personalities. The show went on with 'Suite Judy Blue Eyes' and then they played 'Dark Star' to a relatively quiet audience because no one was familiar with it yet. My heart just sank. I was in love, but the closer I got to Stephen, the more he seemed to distance himself. That night the load out was inevitable, on to the next gig, and we parted ways. I had his record label phone number, but no personal numbers were exchanged. If you wanted to reach someone in those days, you had to write a letter. There was the usual after party on one side of the stage, and Stephen came over to say good-bye to his side of the stage. Slowly and sadly, the Stevie Nicks song filled my head, "thunder only happens when it's raining, players only love you when they are playing." It should have been getting through my thick skull at that point. There was a whole lot of summer to go and I wasn't going to be bogged down in this melancholia.

CHAPTER 12

Life in My Groupie Land Dream Continued (1977)

"They who dream by day are cognizant of many things which escape those who dream only by night," **Edgar Allan Poe**

Working only at the Crab for the next week kept me busy, and my mind off of the great CSN week.

It so happened that Hall and Oates were playing three nights at Pine Knob that week. I loved their music, had two of their albums, and I was going to the WABX live interview at the radio station that week and hoped to meet them. That would be the highlight of my week, or so I thought.

I was serving another table when in walked John Oates with another man. They were seated in a little booth for two next to my station. When their server approached the table, I could hear John complaining, I don't think he liked the table, and I heard something about "chowder". That was it, just as quickly as he sat down, he turned around and stormed out, without even having a chance to greet him or say hello.

I asked Susan his server, "What got into him?" "Guess he didn't like the chowder, he wanted New England clam and we only have fish," was her answer. I did go to the radio station anyway and never got to meet Hall and Oates, one of the mainstay bands of Pine Knob.

The rest of the week was uneventful, Gordon Lightfoot nearly put me to sleep with his same sound to every song, one man band act. Dan Fogelberg I missed seeing that year, but then I got to see Glen Campbell. Now my preconception was this country-folk singer who did 'Lineman For the County', but little did I know what a showman he was.

The show was going to start in 30 minutes or so, as people filed into the venue. The pavilion was filling up rapidly when out of nowhere dark clouds swarmed in the sky, and a violent sideways rain began swirling into the seats. It had to be a tornado.

Normally, in the worst weather, the people in the seats were protected from the elements, but not this night. The wind acted like a tornado, sweeping sheets of stormy rain right down over the stage. The stage hands scrambled to cover the equipment, electrical cables were sparking and everyone in the entire 5,000 arena got soaked. Everything up to the lights was drenched. As quickly as it had come into the theatre, it left. Crew ran around with towels, shop vacs, anything that could get the show up and running again. They ran out, checked, checked, double checked, uncovered instruments, and out came Glen Campbell.

"Good evenin' everybody....thanks for stickin' around!" He began singing and doing this little striptease thing until he was shirtless and telling jokes and had the entire crowd laughing and forgetting their discomfort. He then demonstrated how he could bounce his pectoral muscles back and forth and made some reference to Elvis. He was so entertaining. Who knew?

Every summer the girls and I would go to an amusement park on Lake Erie in Sandusky, Ohio called Cedar Pointe as previously mentioned. That summer, right after Captain and Tennille's show we took off. We always stayed in the Holiday Inn with the water park and all of the mildew/chlorine smelling rooms surrounding the pool area. We had a blast riding the daredevil thrills by day and splashing around by night. That was in keeping metaphorically with the way I was living my life in those days anyway. It did mean that I missed the Kinks, Spinners, and Boz Scaggs, who had the disco hit of the decade going for him 'Lido Shuffle', and even America as well.

Meanwhile back at work, things were very busy, the golf pros always came in for the Buick open. People like Arnold Palmer or Lee Trevino would be there. I got to wait on Jack Nicholas and Lee Trevino that year, Lee carrying on with the smack down he was famous for.

Not only Pine Knob but Meadowbrook Theatre would always bring people into the restaurant. One night Helen Hayes, Rosemary Clooney, and Rose Marie came in after their show 'Three Girls Three'. There were only a few straggling diners left in the main Glancy-MacCauley dining room. After greeting them and realizing who they were, I was so excited. I grew up watching the 'Dick Van Dyke' show with Rose Marie, and loved the brashness of all the ladies.

"Bring me a JB rocks with a twist," Miss Clooney ordered. It must have been a rough night, she was rather gruff, but that is the way she had always come across in her movies too. Then there was Helen Hayes, delicate and demure, one of my favorite stars of stage and screen, very much the polite ladylike icon I always thought she was. Rose Marie must have been just trying to reign in the other personalities, and was fairly sedate until she got a drink in her then I got to experience that wonderful big laugh of hers. Of course she was wearing that bow in her hair. The dining room was empty when they decided to leave, probably after midnight, but I didn't mind, I was thrilled, and they left me enough of a tip to pay the babysitter extra.

The band, Chicago, was in town doing their usual five or six day stay in lovely Troy, Michigan. This would be the last year that I saw founding member, Terry Kath, play with them. He would be sorely missed, as he had been influenced by Ray Charles and had that same sound to his vocals, the deep gravel and raspy growl. In the past Chicago had always stayed at Somerset Inn, but following Terry Kath's death, they stayed at the Northfield Hilton. Perhaps the memories were too strong and a change of scenery was called for.

Hurley's lounge in the Northfield Hilton was always where I would find Jimmy Pankow and hang out with him. Given a sufficient number of cocktails he always turned into an Irishman complete with brogue and all. He was a lot of fun, always in a good mood when I would see him. One night several years later he would take me up to Robert Lamm's room where several friends had gathered to party. Bobby was laying out some lines for everyone, booze was flowing freely, and then for some reason we started singing songs. I chimed in with my old standard, 'Me and My Bobbie McGee' and the room got quiet. Bobby Lamm exclaimed,

"Oh my god you sound just like Janis."

"Wow thanks....that's quite a compliment."

"No I mean it, do you sing anywhere, with a band or anything?"

"No not right now, I used to be a wedding singer, you know 'Ave Maria' music, that sort of thing."

"Well you really should think about doing some session work or something you sound great."

I think he was just high, but I was hoping he meant it. My whole reason for being backstage was to be off stage in the wings singing along, as if I was a real band member, creating my own harmonies, supporting the lower weaker notes, and just feeling part of the cast.

That week was also Englebert Humperdinck, whose odd name certainly did not match his handsome features. He came into Charley's Crab, sat in the main dining room on table 2 and ordered a broiled fish.

We cooked our fish on pewter plates that could be placed directly into the broiler, and then onto a wooden base to be served. His server came running into the kitchen throwing the fish plate on the counter,

"Mr. Humperd-i-c-k won't eat this fish, he doesn't want any metal touching his food."

The kitchen manager responded with anger, "Then he can't eat Caesar salad either, because that is made individually in a large metal bowl, and he can't have a cappuccino because that comes out of a metal spigot, and he can't have cream in his coffee because that is in a metal pitcher!"

It was challenging to be his server to say the least. I never heard his performance, although I believe he is still on the music circuit, perhaps only for the blue-haired ladies now.

It was during this part of the season, mid-July that I was dreaming of getting away. Everything was beginning to exasperate me: working two jobs, the children, the broken down car I was patching together. My dream was answered when the Doobie Brothers came to town. All my old roadie friends were still with the band, a British guy named Bill was their road manager and we became close. We proceeded to have some good fun partying back stage for the shows, then back at the hotel afterwards.

One night after the show back at the Northfield Hilton in Hurley's lounge, Ron English's band was playing and Willie Weeks and Michael McDonald came down from their rooms to check out the scene. They were going to sit in for a few songs. Ron said to me,

"Come on Chris you can sing backup for us, we're just doin' some old Motown stuff," so they gave me a microphone and told me to stand on the opposite side of the stage from Michael McDonald, and Willie Weeks. It was the best jam session I was ever in. We played a rousing rendition of 'Funky Town', followed by 'Mustang Sally', 'Heard It Through the Grapevine' and 'Dancin' In the Street'. It was the highlight of my month to say the least, and the closest I ever got to singing with someone famous.

Several of the same girls from town followed the Doobies around, and I began to make a circle of "groupie" Detroit area friends. There was an older African American fellow who was the fraternity father of the Doobie Brothers road crew, I shall call him Ben (simply because I cannot recall his real name) and there was Mike, and I called one of the guys Rowdy.

"Hey what are you doing in the next couple of days?" Ben asked.

"Not much I have some time off, why?" "Well we are playing at this place up north in Charlevoix called Castle Farms and we have plenty of motel rooms, do you wanna go?"

"Of course but I need to drive separately and get my kids on the way back, if my wreck of a car will make it."

The next morning, as we left the Northfield Hilton, the weather started out bright and sunny, but as the day went on it became over-cast, and much cooler. We headed up to Charlevoix in the northern lower peninsula of Michigan, caravan style several tour busses, several rental cars, and Speedy, with 'Hotel California' blasting on the radio. It was approximately a four hour drive, and we arrived early for the next day's performance. We stayed in some mom and pop motel with an office, a couple of special suite cabin rooms, and then a strip of single rooms around the back of the circular driveway. The suites were log cabin style, and the rest of the motel was painted white. Michael McDonald and the band members were staying in the suites, and the rest of us were in the line of smaller rooms. They were clean and adequate, and we started out jumping on the beds to "test them out" for the real up and down that would happen later.

We ordered several pizzas with various toppings, had a twelve pack of Budweiser, and I went outside to peruse the surroundings. There was nothing but woods all around the motel. The air was won-derful, crisp, clear, and pine-saturated. I noticed Michael McDonald walking out toward the back woods. I followed him far enough behind that he wouldn't see me. When he stopped by a creek that ran along the trail in back of the motel, I stopped following him. I just stared, he was so handsome. His hair was still black and becoming a little salt and pepper, he wore a white shirt long and untucked with blue jeans, and sandals. His blazing blue eyes were hypnotic. I could hardly talk to him, I admired him so much. Michael was such a subdued quiet person he did not speak to me. I made my way back to the room to find Mike and Debbie under the covers.

"Hey Rosie coitus interruptus!" shouted Mike, "go find Rowdy. He's next door."

So Rowdy and I smoked some weed and I sang, "Dooby dooby doo."

Later that night as we lay in bed watching television with our bellies full of pizza and beer, Ben came knocking at the door,

"Hey Michael wants us to come up to his cabin and party." That didn't take much coaxing and we all jumped up and followed.

We brought our six packs of beer, and some wine, and of course someone had some weed and blow. I walked over to Michael sitting on a couch,

"Hi there Mr. McDonald, my name is Christine but you can call me Rosie that's my rock and roll moniker." I extended my hand and he took it.

"Well hello Rosie have a seat and welcome to my cabin." He had a little head start on us by the looks of him, but he didn't have to play that night, so what the heck.

The cabin was solid log with a stone fireplace blazing embers, and other than that no light. There was a double bed and a nicely furnished seating area that we all plunked down on and made ourselves at home. No other band members were present that night. We played some music, talked about the show and did our drugs.

Several hours went by of this, and with no one giving a big sex show, Michael invited us all to leave, he had to get some sleep. We all retired to our respective rooms, I had sex with someone I'm sure, maybe Rowdy.

The next morning there was a brisk chill in the air. Northern Michigan is pretty cold at night, even in July. I grabbed my jeans, a gauze shirt I had made, and a sweater, and we headed to Castle Farms. The load in of equipment had begun. It was several miles out of town, but as we approached my jaw dropped and I was in awe of this magnificent place, a fairy tale castle, built in the Normandy region of France style. The towering turrets, six of them, were large rounded edifices with conical spires on top, made of large rectangular blocks of stone that were rough as if hand hone. The entry was a large stone archway and our procession drove through it and over to the stage, which was to the right. The audience was actually outside of the building on the front of the grounds. Mr. Loeb, the president of Sears and Roebuck, built Castle Farms in 1918. Rumor had it, his son had been kidnapped by the mob and the story did not have a happy ending, much like the Lindberg baby. This story was still circling around the building in 1977. While the guys set up, I decided to explore all the rooms that were down a walkway flanked by stone archways. They were set up as dressing rooms, reception area for backstage guests and it was going to be a good party.

If I'm remembering correctly, the band members that year were Patrick Simmons, Jeff "Skunk" Baxter (from Steely Dan), Keith Knudsen, Tiran Porter and Michael McDonald. They were fairly friendly and would say hello, but really each had their own thing going with girlfriends, wives, and entourage, and mainly stayed to themselves, which was fine with me. After all, they were the northern California band associated with Hell's Angels and Hell's Angels were one badass biker bunch of crazies from what I had heard. I was never much of a biker type chick since I lived with Harley Davidson parts in my living room most of my married life. My husband loved to take things apart, he just wasn't very good at putting them back together, metaphorically and literally. ha ha!

The concert that night was fabulous, except some of the sound played out into a double lane highway, with a thick woods behind it; the acoustics left something to be desired. Still and all, the old standards held up just fine, 'China Grove', 'Listen to the Music', 'Jesus Is Just Alright' and 'Black Water' streamed through the Michigan night sky and up to the stars. The after show party was nice enough with strange broadcasters and up north people surrounding the "stars" who all were in attendance. The food was great and the beverages were very nice, even champagne was being passed around at one point. It doesn't get better than this I thought, dreamlike surroundings, fabulous music, good friends to party with, and I got away for the weekend.

The following week it was back to work and business as usual at the Crab. Our uniforms were, white blouse, black pants, black vest and any sort of scarf we liked. I could tie a scarf in twenty or more different configurations and embellish them with pins and buttons. I had long, square, rectangular, but always colorful scarves, mostly hand-made by me and not Gucci or Hermes. The wait staff was as diverse and colorful as my scarves. Some were the owner's children, some were from the old Charley's Crab on Pine Lake in Bloomfield Hills, Michigan, some were upper middle class women who didn't need to work because their husbands had perfectly good jobs, and some were like me.

We were struggling to make a living, either students, want-to-be restaurateurs or single parents. The divorcees were considered the most dependable, because they had to pay babysitters and the rent. I was always there to work and on time. I would take extra tables that others didn't want, and I would always cater to the V.I.P.s that frequented the Crab. They were called the "Marching Chowder Society" members and carried little cards that afforded the patrons a discount for each time they dined. Some of the waitresses had bought their own chowder cards and were making money on the side punching their cards and pocketing the extra money. I was not clever enough to dream up that scheme, nor would I stoop so low to do that. If I couldn't make money on tips then so be it. Several people who had these cards for their own profit were soon found out and fired. It must have been painful for Chuck to find this out, since some of them were his favorites.

Some of my best work friends were Darlene, Dee, and Cheryl. Darlene we called Zsa Zsa because she was a cute as a Barbie doll complete with long blonde ponytail. Dee was the most talkative person I had ever met, she would just talk right over you in mid-sentence. Then there was Cheryl. She was demure and petite with blue-green eyes and perfectly sculpted features.

"Come on let's go smoke a doob, I just cashed out my last table," Cheryl would say to Dee and out the back door of the kitchen they would go. Walking the full circle around the Hilton getting high, they would roll in the front door, hit the restroom and hidden in the cupboard under the sink would be Visine, mouthwash, and spray perfume to cover their sins. No one was the wiser and back to work they went.

After work we would all go to Hurley's for an after work drink and see what kind of mischief we could get into. If nothing else, we would dance to the local band and then go to the cars, smoke another joint, and drag ourselves home.

Sammy Davis Jr. played Pine Knob after the Doobie Brothers that year and I had to work there, the money was supposed to be really great those nights. I had already missed the first couple of nights going up to Castle Farms, so I caught the last few shows and raked in a good chunk of change.

I missed Harry Chapin, but got to experience Fleetwood Mac who had just put out their album, 'Rumors'. It was climbing the charts like a bullet. Stevie Nicks in her top hat, and all the band in their energetic prime were something to behold.

CHAPTER 13

Some Loves Last Forever
(1977-1978)

"Wherever you go, go with all your heart," Confucius

James Taylor came to town next that year, and my knight in shining armor, David Lindley, was with him. It was so wonderful to see him again, that face right out of a Charles Dickens novel.

David was a fun, calm soul and an extremely talented musician. Also very fashionable. He always called himself "the claw", and could be found lurking about in some strange places leaving mysterious notes stuck on crew member's doors.

David had a British or maybe Scottish "look" about him. He was about my height, with long black, wavy hair, and lovely eyes. He was always very kind to me, and unpretentious. When he played a slide guitar, or a violin, he captured my heart hook, line, and sinker. That was the beginning of a great friendship.

Of course I had a backstage pass from the crew I had gotten to know the previous year, and I was determined to be with this talented musician again. He played the concerts to perfection. The James Taylor concert in those days was a pretty big production, with some of the finest talent in Los Angeles.

Afterward we all retreated to the Somerset Inn in Troy for some drinks in the lounge. That is where David and I became reacquainted. His humor and casual demeanor was very attractive to me, coupled with his quirkiness, and love for colorful clothing. We made our way to his room at closing time, and there we made love to each other in a very traditional, but affectionate sort of way. He treated me with great kindness. We had a lot of, fun together.

In the mornings he would practice Tai Chi, and try to teach me some moves, and I would tap dance on the bathroom floor, and sing in the shower. When I came out he said,

"You have a good voice. You should come out to L.A. and get some session work."

"Where would I live?"

"I live outside of L.A. near the desert it isn't that pricey out there," he coaxed.

"I don't think I could uproot my children just yet, they are still trying to get over my separation situation."

"Well let me know if you change your mind," he smiled at me and in some odd way I didn't doubt his sincerity.

We spent two lovely days together, and then it was off down the road for J.T. and company, and back to work for me. My daughters were around all week after that. They loved music as much as I did, and when I asked them if they wanted to go see Bob Seger that week at Pine Knob they were excited. I called Punch up and asked for some tickets. He seemed reluctant, but obliged anyway. The fact that I had my children with me was probably why he wanted to keep us apart from the other frivolity.

"Come on girls, let's get going I don't want to be late," I prodded them out the door. They were wearing their best gear and big hair, and Damian had about ten bangle bracelets on. She was the fashion conscious one, and Chrisanna was more blue and plain Jane, nothing frilly for her.

We always took the back road into Pine Knob since we lived right on Waldon near Clarkston Road about fifteen minutes away. July was coming to a close, which meant one more month until "back to school" happened.

"Hey Mom can we get a T-shirt?" Chrisanna wanted to know.

"Sure let's see where our seats are first, okay?"

We made our way to the white trailer near the back gate where all business transacted. I asked about our tickets, and was handed an envelope. Inside were three lawn tickets. I wasn't prepared for the lawn at all. No blanket, no cooler, and we were all dressed up with our big Farrah Fawcett hair and our jewelry.

"Mom I thought you said we had seats and passes....and..."

"Well what can I say, I thought that was what was going to happen, I'm sorry, we'll have fun anyway." We made our way to the back hill and found a spot.

Bob and the band hit the stage to a roaring crowd. Local boy makes good, I thought. Man, he has come a very long way. His long hair was tossing with each move as he rambled and gambled his way through the sets.

I noticed Punch walking through the crowd and he squinted his eyes in the setting sun looking up toward the lawn. The man really needed glasses. He saw me finally and came up to say hello.

"Sorry about the lawn tickets that was all that I could get, and some people didn't want children backstage before or after the show," Punch explained.

"That is child discrimination you know," I said.

"Well sorry, it is kind of a rule of ours, but hope you have fun," he said, and off he went.

Bob Seger played Pine Knob twice that summer, but the second time around I didn't even try to get in. I was a spoiled pissed off brat about the whole thing. Like my father used to say,

"A bird could sit on that lip," my pout was so huge. Money was going to be good at Pine Knob the next three days, so I arranged to work there instead of the Crab for Neil Sedaka. He was an old crooner, but everyone loved the old songs and the crowd would bring their wallets. Another highlight of that week was meeting Gabriel Kaplan, who was in town doing, 'Up Your Nose With a Rubber Hose' stand up at a local club. He sat all by himself way upstairs on the last table in the Crab, number 85. Perhaps he was just tired, or just being a New Yorker, but he was very short and rude to me. Even when plied with humor, he wasn't going for it. Very disappointing for me as I thought I was being funny. Possibly he was just being "New Yorker".

To my surprise the following week David Lindley was back in town. He called me up and we arranged to meet. He had jumped on the Jackson Browne tour, and they were staying at the Somerset Inn. I had to work, so I wasn't able to go out to the show, but I met David afterward and stayed the night with him. We fell into each other's arms as the moon shone over the pool, and the breeze blew in the balcony window, like a siren song through the shear drapes. We made love again, becoming more familiar with each other. The following morning we got up and made our way down to the restaurant in the hotel with its French theme and brightly colored yellow and white tables. We had just received our menus, when David said, "Hey they have French fried ice cream, let's get some."

"Okay I have never had that for breakfast before."

We were enjoying our deliciously sinful breakfast when Jackson Browne came walking in with a handful of flyers he was passing out. He wore his uniform white t-shirt and faded jeans, to go with his shaggy brown hair.

"You guys have to read this. The nuclear power plants they are building in this country are a travesty and must be stopped," he voiced with a great deal of authority.

"Jack this is Christine, Christine, Jackson Browne," David introduced us.

"Nice to meet you, what do you know about nuclear power?"

"Nothing really, but I have a feeling you are going to tell us everything you know," I said.

He pulled up a chair and proceeded to expound on the efforts of the government to end this threatening menace to our planet. This was one serious man. Not since I had met John Sinclair had I heard such radical rhetoric. Very captivating speech though. Our morning ended when the bus pulled up out in front of the hotel, and away David went again.

Later in 1977 a fairly new band on the rock scene played at Pine Knob. Tom Petty and the Heartbreakers rolled into the Northfield Hilton and walked into the Farragut dining room. Yes the Admiral Farragut who said, "Damn the torpedoes full speed ahead." I had them seated in my station.

They were on the tour promoting their first LP, simply titled 'Tom Petty and the Heartbreakers'. It contained such great standards as, 'American Girl' and 'Breakdown' which were becoming big hits.

After work that night I went over to Hurley's to meet up with some of the crew. It was a week night, so Hurley's was fairly slow and closing early. One of the crew guys had been chatting me up and suggested, "Hey let's go up to T.P.'s room and keep this party going, the guys are all up there." Indian said to me, his name was Indian for real. I never asked how he got that name, because he didn't appear to be a Native American.

"I'm up for that, it's early enough I have a babysitter for a couple of hours still," I responded. Off we went for the long walk around the horseshoe to room 332.

When we arrived the Indian guy wrapped on the door loudly and an eye appeared in the peep hole, "Hey come on in....you have some smoke?" T.P. inquired of his roadie.

"Ya I've got a couple J's of some pretty good Hawaiian," Indian lit them up and we all sat on one of the double beds together to make our circle tight.

I was flanked by Ben Tench and T.P. Their legs went one way off the bed and I was sitting with my legs the other way. We all introduced ourselves. There were some other ladies sitting on the bed and some crew members. I had a bit of an alcohol buzz going, so that was a nice night cap. We were all chit chatting making small talk. Ben was very sweet and friendly, T.P. with that slow, low sultry voice of his was saying they were going to Castle Farms next stop. Before I could say oh I was just there a few weeks ago, Indian jumped up, headed for the door, and turned out the light on his way, and pulled the door shut. It was pitch black not even moonlight from the window when someone leaned into me, holding my face, and gave me a kiss I remember to this day. It was perfect, sweet, and the man smelled good to me. I couldn't tell who had pulled me down. The way I was sitting and how stoned I had gotten it was hard to tell, but I believe it was Benmont.

We were all laughing, and giggling, and when the lights went back on everyone was sort of tangled on the bed making out, except the man who had kissed me. It was time for me to get going home, but the weekend would be idyllic for another trip up north to Castle Farms.

Again it was a weekend and the girls were with my mom. I jumped in my car and headed up I-75 for Charlevoix. The morning was already sultry heading upward to 90 degrees. It would be cooler up north, so I brought a jean jacket to throw over my black and white striped shirt, and my faux leather pants. I thought I was smokin' hot.

The radio playlist went something like this, 'Hotel California' by the Eagles, 'Tonight's The Night' by Rod Stewart, 'Margarita Ville' by Jimmy Buffet, 'Rich Girl' by Hall and Oates, 'Rocky's Theme' from the new movie about a boxer in Philadelphia, 'Fly Like an Eagle' by Steve Miller Band, 'Blinded By The Light' Manfred Mann, 'Night Moves' by Bob Seger and the Silver Bullet Band, 'Give a Little Bit' by Supertramp, and 'Nobody Does It Better' by Carly Simon, of course written for James Taylor begging the question, does he do it best? Then the airwaves waved good-bye and there was the end of civilization as I knew it. Nothing but country western music the rest of the way. There were only a few cool radio stations back then, and they were in the major cities. Once I got near to Traverse City there might be something decent to listen to, in the meantime I had my cassette tapes ready to make the miles fly by.

The traffic back in the seventies was nothing like it is today. Once in a while a semi would blow by, or a station wagon with a family going up north for their yearly vacation. No road rage, or anxiety-ridden idiots on the road, for the most part. Everyone knew what the muscle cars were, and stayed out of their way. The Chargers, the GTO's, the Mustangs. They all were souped up with hemi engines, and mag wheels making Detroit proud.

I recalled the directions to Castle Farms and got there just in time for the concert after driving nearly four hours. I pulled up to the familiar gate and a security guard stopped me,

"Who are you here to see," he inquired.

"My name is Christine Olevnik and I should be on the guest list," I answered.

He looked over the clipboard in his hand, "Oh yes, I have you right here, go park over there, and wear this tonight," he said, handing me a stick-on pass. It was already growing dark and a good size crowd had gathered in front of the stage, and lots of people on the grassy hillside between the road and the standing area, with their coolers and blankets spread in an array of colors. The smell of cannabis was floating through the air.

The sign on the roadside said Tom Petty and the Heartbreakers. I strolled around the grounds making certain nothing had changed from the last time I was there with the Doobie Brothers. No, nothing had changed, same castle feeling with the austere grey stone and heavy dark wood, making me feel like a princess in fairytale land. Oh wake up Christine, you are a single mother, party animal, groupie, up here to shag a band member, or a band's member, whichever the case may be. Just then, Ben popped out from the dressing room area.

"Hey glad you could make it, go grab a drink in the hospitality room, we are just about to go on," he waved and I complied.

I was thinking this might be a good time for me to let them hear my voice I had been practicing their songs and thought I might fit in, so as soon as they paraded, single file, walking very briskly, out of the dressing room toward the stage, I followed. Up the stairs to the stage I went, then suddenly a bouncer said,

"Hold it right there where do you think you are going?"

"I was just going to stand on the side to watch," I said.

"Oh no you don't. Band members only."

The band broke into 'I Need To Know' followed by 'Refugee' and 'American Girl'. I sulked away and found a spot in back of the stage to listen. Once briefly during the show I caught a glimpse of one of them moving around on the stage, but for all intents and purposes I missed the whole concert.

One of the crew who I had come to know from the hotel party invited me out into the crowd to watch the show and handed me a beer. "You're missing the show, come on out here and stand." He dragged me by the arm to what I affectionately called the orchestra pit.

It was Ben's side of the stage,

"Yeah, you're right this is much better," I said and I stopped pouting, feeling much better after slugging down a beer. Then, after the show, this crew guy and I popped into the bus for a little slap and tickle before going to the after show party. There was a part of me that really wanted to be a part of the band, and there was an alterego that really wanted to have sex with musicians, but I usually had to go through the roadies to get to the main attraction. In most cases the roadies were better lovers.

The rooms were set up with an array of the usual party standards, Budweiser and Heineken beer, Perrier bottle water, some food and bags of chips. A cool northern Michigan breeze was flowing through the building refreshing the night air with the scent of pines. I walked over to Ben and told him the usual things all band members want to hear about how wonderful they were. I was having a major melt down crush on T.P.'s long blond hair, puppy dog eyes, and especially his bucked teeth. For some reason I always loved big teeth. I just said hello to Mr. Petty, went out, got in my car and made the arduous trip home, by myself along the pitch dark highway a four hour drive As usual I was feeling the cowardice of being insanely attracted to someone and unable to act upon it. I cried all the way home feeling sorry for myself that what I wanted to happen didn't.

By this time there were some realizations I was coming to.

First of all, I had always thought that if a person was famous then they were a wonderful person who deserved it. Wrong. For some reason it was meeting Dicky Betts that taught

me that lesson. Can't remember precisely why that is, but that's how I remember it. He was probably being a jerk, but I probably deserved it.

The next valuable lesson I learned was: the roadies are the best in bed, not the stars. The crew guys are out there away from any other entanglements they may have, and for the most part they are lonely, wanting to sew some wild oats, and very willing to try to please the ladies. I knew guys who would spend their entire per diem in one night on some girl, and have to borrow the rest of the week to survive. The stars, on the other hand, just act shy, aloof, and go come on baby "do me", and that is that. I know I am generalizing, but I have quite a bit of experience to back this theory up.

CHAPTER 14

Not Just Rock and Roll
(1978-1982 the sports years)

"Just play. Have fun. Enjoy the game," Michael Jordan

In the fall the major sports teams arrived in town. The Lions played at the Pontiac Silverdome, the Pistons played at the Palace. We even had a soccer team briefly who played in the Silverdome. Somehow the Detroit Tiger baseball players found their way out to Troy. Dave Rozema and Kirk Gibson were often seen having themselves a good old time in the bar listening to Bob Seele wail on the piano. Pat Riley, coach of the Lakers, would sit at the sidebar all by himself and enjoy a bowl of fish chowder. Ever the gentleman and fine dresser, I think he was friendly to me because his wife's name was Chris. One time he set me up with a friend of his, whom I dated for a couple of years, whenever he was in town. His friend would stand over by my tables or station it was called, in his Armani suit, and watch me work. Then he would buy my patrons drinks in the lounge if they would leave my table, so he could take me out. He always got his way.

Mike Abdenour was a trainer for the Pistons who always had an entourage of women with him hanging out on table 40, his favorite. He would call out,

"Hey Chris...whatcha doin' tonight? We're having a party next door."

"No thanks Mike not tonight you look like you have your hands full," I would laugh in response.

Charles Barclay was often seen in the restaurant because he was dating one of the managers, Cheryl at the time. He was a lot of fun and always friendly, saying hello as he passed by. So there I was in a sea of men whose belt buckles were right at about my face level. I always wondered if I seemed like a child to them.

Then I encountered Larry Byrd and Kevin McHale from the Boston Celtics. They were young and wild guys then, let me tell you. Larry just as corn pone as can be, and Kevin just acted like he didn't really care about much, but I loved that baby face of his. I would let them take turns cuddling up to me, while they were away from home.

Larry would yell from his table in the Farragut dining room, "Hey Chris, ya spankin' it?!"

I had no idea what the hell he meant so I would retort in a snarky sort of way,

"Oh ya Lar I'm spankin' it," and he and Kevin would bust out laughing. I have several ideas as to what they were eluding to, but I still don't know exactly what that meant. Then by the end of the meal they would invite me to their room. Now there was no courting or having cocktails first, just go to the room and wham bam thank you mam in a Byrd vs. McHale tag team. I would go with Larry first, most of the time. He would walk ahead of me in long strides. Reaching his suite around the horseshoe shaped hallway, he said to me not forfeiting any time,

"So let's lose these clothes Christine and get down to it."

The room was dark. Only the bathroom light was casting shadows around the suite. Neither romantic nor satisfying in any way shape or form, missionary style always, and basic. Next Kevin would come knocking on the door, and take my hand leading me down the hall to his room. He had a cute sexy little grin and I was much more attracted to him than Larry. The same atmosphere was created in his room. He left his white t-shirt on and exposed himself to me. He was erect, he shoved my naked body back on the bed and climbed on top of me. In somewhat of an urgent effort he climaxed quickly before I could even become aroused, and sent me packing.

So that went on for the early part of autumn each year.

The fall brought new cold weather recipes to the Crab. The steamy smell of fish chowder drifting through the air, the sweet spices of cappuccino, the smells of pumpkin cheesecakes and squash dishes with the aromatic spices that lifted them, became a standard for the time of year. Colder breezes would fly through the heavy wooden front doors, and swoop into the restaurant, as guests arrived in the brick paver foyer. It was a beautiful entry with an ornate antique buffet and mirror, high two story ceiling, leaded stained glass windows, and fresh flowers greeting the patrons next to the bowl of pastel colored mints. The theme song from the movie 'The Sting' began each night on the piano in the lounge with Seele tickling the ivories. It was my favorite time of year to be in the restaurant, and when Halloween arrived we got to wear costumes.

Being the consummate seamstress I would always come up with something elaborate I created myself. This particular year I was The Rose. I made my body the green stem wrapped in satin, then my upper body and head was the flower itself. I included layers upon layers of red satin pedals all around my waist. The main dining room was filled with businessmen that night, Kmart headquarters was huge then and headquartered in Troy, as well as EDS, and the big three always had people on expense accounts staying there. That night men were plastered, yelling across the room.

"Hey send the rose over here I want to smell her."

"Hey sing us a song with rose in it," and so on. I usually accommodated their requests, but mostly men on business trips on the road were just plain obnoxious.

One time the Lakers were in town, and Jack Nicholson and Rob Lowe came walking in early one evening. The dining room was packed and noisy, and it was immediately before the Pistons game, so diners were mostly men going out to the Palace. They sat in the main dining room at table 12 which was center of the room near the Captain's table. Sunlight was still streaming through the leaded glass window, so it was an early game. Jack was being his usual boisterous self, goofing off, while Rob Lowe with those piercing, "Frank Sinatra" blue eyes of his, kept asking me for things, "Where's the restroom?"... "Are you going to the game?"...etc. Of course I had to work, so I had to decline, besides it was a night when I had to pick up the kids at grandma's house. Let's just say I appreciate the Rob Lowe of today rather than the wreckless scandalous rogue he used to be at that time.

Most of the time I didn't have the opportunity to meet any of the Lion's players because on game day they were coming from home, or some other nearby place. However when the Lions were pursuing Barry Sanders they brought him to Charley's Crab for dinner. It was early in the evening and the young football player, and a sharp dressed businessman sat at table 22 in the main dining room. It seemed like a Saturday afternoon, not many people had arrived yet, and Mr. Sanders and his manager were expecting more people in their party. The man with Barry was slick, salesman type and they were both wearing finely tailored suits. Mr. Sander's suit was much more modest and home-spun than the big talker. Nothing flashy about him.

The third man was pitching the Lions organization to Barry. He was so young, extremely shy and polite. The night was spent over much debating, fine food, and very little alcohol. Whenever I approached the table it became unusually quiet, and strictly ordering from a waitress.

We all know the outcome of that meeting. Barry Sanders spent many years following in the footsteps of Lem Barney and Billy Simms, making his own mark until late 1998.

Also during the eighties at the Crab, Rodney Peete came in quite frequently. He was strikingly handsome with a smile that could melt ice. One night he came into the restaurant with a gorgeous actress that I knew as Holly Robinson. They were seated in my station next to the Wanderer table in the front of the restaurant at table 10. I approached the table in my usual happy go lucky manner.

"Hi Mr. Peete nice to see you again, what could I start you off with tonight?"

"Hi there," Rodney said and motioned for me to follow him a few steps away from the table.

"We are having a very special night together, will you help me out?" he inquired.

"Sure I'll be glad to just tell me what you would like."

"I just want to start with some nice wine, then appetizers for a while, then later dinner, and some nice cognac at the end and maybe share dessert. We want lobsters and steaks and you fix us up all right? Just a nice romantic dinner, and to be left alone," he suggested.

They stayed on my table the entire evening, tipped me very generously, and at the end he handed me a napkin that said, "Thanks. She said yes." I had never seen a more adorable couple, and Holly was a very sweet person as well.

One of my most memorable sports weekends when everyone came to town was the week of Super bowl XVI. It was to be held at the Pontiac Silverdome on January 24, 1982. The San Francisco 49'ers versus the Cincinnati Bengals were a great match and to this day the game remains the highest rated sporting event in history. It was the first, and nearly the last cold weather climate "bowl" ever played.

The weather that week was some of the worst in Detroit's history. Even when Detroit is surrounded by constant lake effect snow, it's nothing like what we were experiencing that week. The snow was deep, the ice storms were devastating, and the temperatures dipped as low as 13 degrees below freezing with wind chills of 21 below.

Poor CBS crews and other reporters were numbering over 2,000 that week, so they were cramming into every major hotel in the surrounding area, over in Southfield, and even down to Detroit, some twenty miles away.

Being snowed into Troy in those days was no fun. There were no 200 channels on television, no video games, no computers, there was a Pacman game and one other pinball game or something of that nature in the hotel, and that was it. No theatres to get to, no arcades, or any other forms of entertainment existed out there. Everyday some would straggle in before the restaurant opened for the evening.

"What's there to do here?" the crew would ask.

"Some of the local pubs have dart boards, and there is always Trivial Pursuit or cards," was my idea of fun for them. The poor big city guys were beside themselves, Pat Summerall and John Madden being some of the biggest and loudest complainers. Madden didn't like it one night when I walked into Hurley's and said, "Hey John you holdin' down the fort over here?" He gave me a glare that could have socked me in the jaw. Michael Jackson's 'Thriller' album was out that year and his songs were always playing in the background throughout the Hurley's disco, and 'The Girl Is Mine,' played the back ground theme for the night, as Madden huffed off in disgust.

The Monday before the game I had gotten up early and was trying to coax the girls out of their beds.

"Come on girls we have to get going. It's horrible outside and we need extra time," I cajoled. They had three alarm clocks each one farther from their beds and set minutes apart.

"Three alarms already, let's go."

"Okay, okay we're up," answered the older of the two. "Are we going to grandma's this weekend?" inquired the younger daughter.

"Yes, as a matter of fact, grandma is coming out early because the big football game is this weekend and I will be 'super' bowl busy."

"Ha ha mom, we want to go to Pontiac and see everything at the Mardi Gras."

"There isn't anything there for kids, it's all just a drunken strolling party, no family stuff, and besides grandma is going to take you skating at the ice arena in Plymouth so bring your skates."

After seeing them off to school, I readied myself for work. I had done a fresh batch of laundry and needed to iron all of my bow ties. We had gone for a new sophisticated look at the Crab. Mr. Muer decided that his signature bow tie would look good on the rest of us, so our uniform went to a black vest and bow tie. I quickly made an array of brightly colored ties to color coordinate with earrings. Just as it was time for me to leave for work, we were being bombarded by another few inches of snow. I implored my mother not to drive out to my house that night. I was an opener for the restaurant so I left earlier than usual. The babysitter would be coming early too due to the weather, so the girls were fine, and I left a macaroni casserole for dinner.

When I arrived at the restaurant I was greeted by one of the managers,

"We have very few reservations tonight, and I would like you to work just the seventies upstairs by yourself. There won't be a bartender so you'll have to go downstairs for cocktails, I'll open the wine cooler for you though, so sell wine if you get the chance."

It was the Monday night before the game. By six o'clock the restaurant was sparsely seated, at best one or two tables, and I had a remote balcony section upstairs, very likely to be sent home for all my struggle getting there that night through the snow and ice in my little white Nissan.

I had no money in my pockets and the prospects were dim. Just as things were looking bad for the night, two or three busses pulled up outside. One of my managers came running upstairs,

"Get ready, we are about to get hit, there are three busses filled with San Francisco 49er's outside and they are all coming in to eat!" She ran back downstairs.

I bent over the wrought iron railing and there they were, all men, reporters, CBS people, coaches, trainers, etc. converging on the Crab. It was as beautiful as New Year's Eve. Thank the football gods, my financial picture was looking up. I ran down to help seat and was met by throngs of people coming up toward me. I ran and iced mugs, got wine buckets filled, found all the glassware I could, got the ice bin filled, and got myself ready for the rush. They were all on expense accounts and all there to spend money and have a great time.

Some of the wait staff had already been called off or sent home, I picked up as many tables as I could, three four-tops along the balcony, then two or three others. It was complete and utter madness. We had sent home the upstairs bartender, so the manager jumped behind the bar and started pouring as quickly as possible. Corks were flying, limes were squeezed, and lobsters were cracked.

Now I knew who the key players were, I followed football to some extent. When things calmed down somewhat, one of my friends came running up to me in an excited frenzy, then gathering herself, in a subdued manner said,

"I have Joe Montana and Dwight Clark on table 2."

I composed myself, checked my look in the mirror, straightened my bow tie, the song 'Maneater' running through my head, "Woo here she comes, watch out boys, watch out boys," and I made my way slowly and seductively downstairs toward table 2. Joe was so handsome and I had a propensity for blond haired men at that time, and when he looked at me with those beautiful blue eyes of his, I was quite smitten. Dwight Clark was very easy on the eyes too.

"Hello you guys welcome to Detroit," I said. "I am very sorry to bother your meal...."

"Hey no bother we're done eating," Dwight offered courteously.

"Hi there, who are you?" Joe asked.

"Well people call me Rosie, and you're Joe and you're Dwight?" was my answer.

"I love to watch you guys play, you are so good together."

"Thanks Rosie," Joe said. "I never ask for autographs, but I have a feeling you guys are going to win this game on Sunday, so would you mind signing this menu, it's all I have for paper?"

"Sure no problem, what are you going to give us?" Joe said laughing as he took the menu from me and signed it.

"How about some chocolates?" and I ran back to the kitchen and came out with something I could get free. The restaurant was so busy the only available plates were hot, and by the time I got back to the table the chocolate had melted.

"Sorry we are so busy..." and I swiped a finger full of melted chocolate and placed it in my mouth slowly licking it off, humming, then looking around to see if anyone saw me, Joe and Dwight were about falling off their chairs laughing.

"Well all right then," was Joe's response. Just then John Madden came running through the dining room yelling "yahoo" with glittery footballs on springs on his head bouncing around wildly.

He got the attention of everyone, they were all shouting after him egging him on.

"I have to go check on my tables upstairs, I'll be back," I said, and I ran off.

By the time I had wrapped things up with Dick Vitale and the others in my section, the dining room was emptying out. It seemed so early for me, but being the night owl I am, 10pm seems early. I ran after Joe just as he was entering the foyer. We were alone standing there, as I offered him a mint from the candy jar on the antique bureau.

"Hey how come you are all leaving so early?" I wondered.

"We all have curfew this week. It is in bed by 10 or 11pm all week," Joe said.

"Oh that's too bad I was going to ask if you wanted to have a drink with me after work next door," I said, boldly going where I hadn't gone before.

"Listen I'm staying at the Westin in Southfield, why don't you come and see me, room 547," he said.

"Okay I'll try. If I get stuck here late though, it is either due to bad weather or a long night, but not for lack of trying, all right?"

"It's all right. Whatever time you show up is fine," Joe smiled that beautiful grin of his, and turned to get on the bus as the reminder of the nasty weather bombarded his face through the door opening.

By the time all the side work and clean up was done it was after midnight. I was exhausted and smelled of fish chowder, I had no change of clothes, and I certainly wasn't going to risk life and limb going all the way to Lake Orion to change clothes, and then try to make it to Southfield, even if it was for Joe Montana. The weather was so treacherous that it took me an extra half hour to get home. Ice on the four lane highway was so thick that in second gear my car slid sideways across the road and slammed into another motorist both of us unable to control the situation.

It remains one of the biggest regrets of my life not keeping my date with Joe Montana that night. After the super bowl week I found out' he and his wife were either divorced or getting a divorce a couple of years later. Really kicked myself in the ass over that one.

The rest of the week business was very good. Pontiac Michigan had Saginaw Street dressed up like Bourbon Street in New Orleans, and 26 extra liquor licenses were issued. The parking at the Silverdome was at a premium because 2,000 parking spaces were kept for George H.W. Bush's secret service. Busses (1200 of them) were bringing in people from all over the metro area, and 81,270 seats of the 82,000 in the Silverdome were filled. The San Francisco 49'ers would go on to win the game against the Cincinnati Bengals, 26-21 that Sunday, with "Joe cool" himself being named MVP. Joe even went so far as to be the holder on field goal attempts. It was a very exciting time in Detroit that week to be certain.

CHAPTER 15

(Fall 1978)

"Life's greatest happiness is to be convinced that we are loved..." Victor Hugo

In the fall of 1978 I received a phone call that would change my life.

"Hello is this Christine?" An unfamiliar man's voice came from the other end of the line.

"Yes this is, who is this?"

"This is Charles Allen Martin calling. I found your number the other day, and thought I would try to see if you were still at the same place." Since his automobile accident he said he had been in rehab at the Detroit Medical Center.

"Charlie Martin the drummer from the Silver Bullet Band?" I asked.

"The one and only. I was wondering if you would be free some time to go out to dinner with me?"

Since no one had been beating down my door for a date recently I accepted readily.

"I can go out next Wednesday night if I can get a babysitter," was my answer.

"Okay, you have kids?"

"Yes two girls, 8 and 5 years old."

There was a pause and then we started a dialogue that would last about an hour, was I married before, where did I come from, and so on.

"So I live in Farmington Hills right now in an apartment, would you be able to meet me over here?" Charlie said, not wanting to go too far from his comfort zone at the time.

"That sounds great, I'll be over by seven or so next Wednesday."

I hung up the phone and considered what impression he had just made on me. With my innocence slipping away day by day, lay by lay, I thought he seemed to need someone. Perhaps I could trade some promiscuity for grace by helping Charlie out. Maybe I should consider settling down a little bit. Much had changed since I met the rascal drummer in the blue satin suit at Punch and Colleen's Christmas party.

It was a chilly fall day and a cold rain fell as I jumped into Speedy the orange Volkswagen beetle that wasn't, and headed for Farmington Hills. Charlie lived on the ground floor. I pushed the buzzer, and he answered in his sexiest voice, "Hi there, come on in."

I smiled at this atrophied version of the man I had met. I hadn't remembered that his eyes were so close together in his head that I almost had to look at him cross-eyed.

The apartment was down a dark, carpeted hall, a Spartan residence. He was living very sparsely with a wheelchair path winding through still packed boxes. All the furniture was up against the wall, and the pathways were not so appealing to the eye. Weird. Then the kitchen did not even work for Charlie. He could pull into it one way but could not turn around or do much of anything else. I felt horrible for the poor guy. The bedroom down the hall was better, and the second bedroom was empty except for some unpacked boxes of stuff and a keyboard that was inside the closet. You had to open bi-fold doors to access the keyboard. The whole set-up seemed very strange to me.

Charlie had taught himself to play the piano plunking out chords, and playing by ear. We would have closet sing along time. Let me explain, his keyboard was kept in a narrow closet in his spare bedroom filled with boxes. One of his favorite songs at the time, was Toto's

'Love Isn't Always On Time'. He could spend hours on end playing keyboards in that closet staring at the back wall He also had a practice drum pad that I would hit on. He taught me paradiddles, and other beats and I would play accompaniment to his closet piano. Amid all the boxes in that bedroom that were left unpacked there were platinum and gold records sticking out from one labeled Capitol Record Company. I couldn't hold back my inquisition any longer.

"So what happened to the girlfriend, Lanaya, Linda, Lydia, or whatever her name was?"

"She took all my belongings, my baby blue Continental, and headed for New York City."

"A baby blue Continental, really? Isn't that sort of a boat for you?" was my response, not that she took the car but that he was driving THAT car. All the other band members had beamers, Mercedes, or Rolls Royces, but Charlie had a Lincoln boat.

"Oh man that really sucks, I'm sorry, that must have been a tough pill to swallow," I back tracked.

"Ya, I sort of expected it though. Let's go and get something to eat," he changed the subject.

That night I didn't stay, we had a nice Italian dinner at a small restaurant, and I thought we got along pretty well. He was very easy to talk to, an outgoing, gregarious sort of guy. Just my type.

He wasn't much to look at with his poker straight, stringy hair, his small frame and boney atrophied legs knocking together at the knees in the wheelchair, but there was something about him. The pheromones were flying. He certainly was the most intelligent guy I had ever gone out with. He boasted that he had a 145 IQ, whatever that meant. Mine had never been tested that I knew of but I felt smart most of the time. I would say some three to five syllable word and Charlie would go, "That's not a word, you mean blah blah blah," and set me in my place on the intellectual pyramid.

The following weekend he wanted to surprise me. He knew what a huge Bruce Springsteen fan I was, and asked me to go to the Masonic Temple to see him. I had to work that night, but I "wheeled and dealed", gave away tables, and got myself out of there. We were meeting each other there since I was driving from work in Troy and he was coming from Farmington Hills.

I jumped into my car with my work clothes on, smelling of fish chowder, and as I flew down I-75 piece by piece of clothing came off, and others went back on. This took skill since I had peeled everything off down to my underwear. Thankfully Volkswagen beetles have high side doors to hide behind. In the end, I was decked out. Tight jeans, striped shirt, a red corduroy vest, and a beret.

Running late to the box office I could hear the band going on stage in the background. The Masonic Temple was familiar to me, my father had been a Shriner and a Mason for years, and childhood memories flooded back as I ran past the marble pillars and carved English walnut doors.

An usher escorted me to a prime seat on the aisle where Charlie's wheelchair was parked. He beamed when he saw me, grabbed my face and gave me a big kiss.

Baby, I was born to run. The E Street Band set the stage on fire, Clarence Clemons on sax, the big man always dressed to a tee in a fine suit, little Steven, the motley one of the bunch sporting his signature bandana, Garry Tallent, Roy Bittan, and Max Weinberg all played their hearts out that night, and naturally "the Boss" took command.

It was magical, as if they knew about Charlie's accident and they were playing right to him. We were close enough to make out distinct features of their faces.

The temple that night was in the smaller stage forum that they sometimes used for smaller crowds. The E Street Band and Bruce played every song I knew, and Charlie and I were of course dancing and singing along. Charlie would do this thing where he would bump up out of this chair and shake his hips, and he was a great singer. During the encore, Bruce pointed right at us and yelled, "This is for you."

That was the night I fell in love with Charlie Allen Martin. He was not letting his handicap get him down, he was courageous and fiery, and the first time he kissed me it worked.

I spent the night the following weekend after sending the kids off to my mother's house. Charlie hit on all my points of rapture. He knew the spot on my neck, he knew the place down my belly that made me tingle, he just already knew the right things to do. I had never been with such a man, familiar with the female body like he was with me, or that at least cared about pleasing me to that degree.

He had admirable tenacity and I was out to prove to him he was still a desirable sexual being. He was as skilled at maneuvering the wheelchair through and around anything. He could still maneuver a Pearl drum kit, and me.

"So how many guys have you slept with?" was his question over breakfast the next morning.

"Maybe a hundred or two," I answered, "let's see, there were four or five before I got married, then a couple while I was married, and then I lost track after I left the marriage, so who knows, a great deal and one woman in a threesome one night."

"How about you?" I said.

"Well just about one in every city we ever played in including 'sweet Connie' out in Washington," he offered.

"You mean sweet Connie in the song?"

"Ya she had the whole show and that's a natural fact," he laughed.

"Who's the most famous person you've been with?" thinking that there must be someone he has met.

"I watched Joan Jett lick an ice cream cone once and she was the only one," he answered.

"And you, who have you been with Miss Pine Knob?" "Well I guess most famous is Stephen Stills."

"Wow that's pretty impressive."

We got so excited talking about past loves and lays that we made our way to the bedroom straight away and made mad passionate love "our style" for several hours. Charlie was able to do for me what no other man had done before. Help me have an orgasm. I had many orgasms before, but only alone in the intimacy of my shower, or the subconscious of a dream. Maybe it was the thought that the end all be all, would not be him sticking his dick in me. He was unable to have an erection. I don't know, but everything was working just fine for me.

Now Charlie had some royalty checks coming in, but no other income to speak of, so he decided to start a t-shirt company. He made 'Detroit Rock and Roll Capitol of Earth' shirts with a globe on them. Okay, not just rock and roll capitol, not just of the United States or Michigan, but of the earth. Quite a thought.

So we would go out every weekend promoting the shirts at record shops such as Full Moon Records, and Harmony House, and had some decent sales, but Charlie didn't really have any business acumen to speak of and needed some soldiers working for his cause. We had stock piled up in every crevasse of the apartment living room. Carmen Harlan at the television station WDIV heard about Charlie's endeavor and asked to interview him.

This was very exciting stuff for Charlie. He didn't think there was much notoriety beyond the Silver Bullet Band, but Carmen was willing to help him out. Besides he had an enormous crush on the freckled beauty. Now my memory may be failing me but I do believe the television station was in Detroit at that time. We made our way downtown and into the studio.

"Hi Charlie, welcome," Carmen greeted us herself that morning and told us how we were to proceed. It was all quite fast paced, we walked into a large room filled with typewriters and people frantically working and talking over each other, and I suppose that was the copy room where all the creativity happened. Carmen grabbed some papers and led us out into the studio scene in front of the large television cameras and production people mulling around.

I was no stranger to television, being on 'Club 1270' and 'Swingin' Time' before, not to mention 'Milky's Party Time' when I was ten years old. I had gotten to see George Perrot's set at that time, very exciting stuff for me, and probably the first time I caught the world travelling bug.

"This is my girlfriend Christine by the way Carmen," as Charlie wheeled a couple of feet behind her.

"Okay, Christine, you can have a seat over here and watch the show," she smiled, and in 10, 9, 8... etc. the show commenced.

Carmen explained how Charlie had been in an accident and was now promoting his t-shirts and to call a number to order.

This was the era before computers and online ordering, so each shirt had to be ordered with a paper check by mail, then packaged by Charlie, taken to the post office, and sent back to the customer, so his inventory had to be fairly vast.

After the interview, the weather had taking a turn for the worse and snow and slush kept us downtown for a while hoping the plows would clear a path for us. We celebrated our success at a revolving restaurant on top of the Renaissance Center. After several glasses of wine it became quite an event finding the table when I returned from the bathroomOn my way back from one such excursion, I called out, "Charlie, Charlie, where are we?" as I walked the perimeter of the tables.

A kind waiter guided me back to my table on the opposite side of the circle, and all was well. We had a lovely dinner and the roads had cleared. Upon leaving Detroit that crisp cold winter night, we had the smell of success stinging our noses.

Sometime in the early winter I developed a severe illness. My attributed it to taking birth control pills. I had gone to my gynecologist, who was the only doctor that I ever saw, and was diagnosed with ovarian cysts, only this one was the size of a baseball and surgery was in order. I was to be admitted the following Monday for preparation and then the procedure. Calling Charlie with the news, he said he had scored Alice Cooper tickets, a Belkin production. Maybe it will make you feel better before you go under the knife," he said in his charming Charlie way.

"Thanks, going under the knife, you had to say that.....okay, I'll come over to your house and we can go down there, maybe I will feel better with some rock and roll."

The following night I put on my best rocker garb and my fake chinchilla coat, beret, and red heels, and off I went to Charlie's apartment. We made our way downtown, went to the Cobo back door and were welcomed with open arms by all the stage hands and security guys. Charlie beamed and started spinning in his chair just to show he was BACK.

We took a spot at the side of the stage, I was sitting across Charlie's withered legs, turning some shade of ashen gray, and feeling just as awful as can be. Alice and his theatrical ensemble took the stage and put on a show the likes of which I had never seen before. It was a story, a play, rock and roll opera style with dancers, and singers, and stage sets. Incredible. I decided there and then that is what I wanted to be, the female version of Alice Cooper. Afterward, I was too sick to stay around for the afterglow backstage scene, so Charlie took me back home, and that Monday I entered the hospital in Pontiac.

My family was all present as I was prepped, drugged, and whisked away to the surgical suite, and when I woke up I had a huge incision across my belly with staples across the reddened line. I had given birth to two children naturally, resulting in a perfectly flat stomach, and now there was a big swollen pooch. The three day hospital stay which left me with one ovary was only tolerable because of the visits from Charlie and my family.

Charlie decided that before Christmas he should meet my family because we would be spending some time together with them and he wanted to make sure he could get around the house and so forth. It had only been a couple of months, but I guess he was ready. Once family gets involved it's a whole new ball game.

Charles, as his family calls him, had already taken me to his boyhood home in Rosedale Park a section of Detroit with lovely old homes. We had driven around several blocks to showcase the area and he had pointed out Ted Nugent's house.

"Yeah Nuge would sit up in that window and wail on that guitar so the whole neighborhood could hear it," Charlie explained pointing to an upstairs, leaded glass window of a brown brick colonial.

We made our way around the block, Charlie driving his silver

Chevy sedan which had been customized for handicapped people.

We pulled into the driveway of a very cold looking, two story, rather enormous, home.

"How many people live here?" I wondered.

"Well Aunt Dot used to live here until she got married, and my mother, grandmother and aunts all lived together."

"So you were raised by a houseful of women?"

"That would be the picture."

"So you're the little prince and I am sure they doted on you continuously," I said.

"That's about it, but before you meet my mother I have to tell you something. She is a bit 'off' shall we say. She is a schizophrenic who got pregnant with me on one of her fugitive episodes in Buffalo New York. At least that is where they found her."

"Oh I should fit right in, I have two schizophrenic aunts, one of whom is living with my parents right now."

"She took off so many times, they would find her months later in Texas or somewhere," Charlie explained.

"So your grandmother raised you?"

"Aunt Dorothy was more like my mother to me, you'll meet them sometime, well let's go in," Charlie invited as he pulled the wheelchair out from behind his driver's seat and hopped into it.

There was no ramp so we had to pull the chair up the front cement stairs onto the porch. We rang the old fashioned doorbell. It was round brass with a button in the middle, that was a buzzer, not a chime. A frail gray-haired lady in a fifties house dress answered the door.

"Hello Charles. Good to see you...come on in, oh and you brought a friend," the woman said.

"This is my aunt Shirley."

"Hello, nice to meet you." I gazed around the expansive living room with the antique decor.

An old television was on with some soap opera in one corner, his Grandmother was intent on watching her show, completely ignored us, so we made our way around the room, Charlie approached a very tiny, skinny woman with salt and pepper hair who looked just like him, except for the wire rimmed glasses from the depression era.

"This is my mother," he said.

"Hello, there it is nice to meet you." I extended my hand but she didn't take it.

"Hi," was all she could manage and then she went back into her catatonic state. They may have offered us something to eat, I don't remember, but sufficed to say we didn't stay long.

"Well that's the old biddies club, Aunt Dot and her husband live downtown, we'll see them later, they are more normal and cordial," Charlie sort of apologized for his grandmother and mother.

"Don't worry, I take people for what they are, I am certainly not judging anyone. She is your mother and you take good care of them, which I really admire."

"They used to let me practice my drums in the house all hours of the day without saying a thing, so I have to thank them for that."

Later we went out for dinner, then back to the apartment, made love, and watched movies all night on Charlie's Beta eight track player. This monstrous cassette player consumed most of a double dresser top, and when the eject button was pushed it was like listening to a garage door open, a huge receptacle came out of the garage on top to accept the tape. Crunching with industrial audio, back in the receptacle went, and we were living life large watching a movie in a bedroom. In the morning we were going to pick up the girls at my mother's, and I was going to introduce Charlie to my family.

CHAPTER 16

(1979-1980)

"The course of true love never did run smooth"
.....William Shakespeare

The next morning a fresh coat of snow covered the ground and we made our way to Plymouth, to the red brick bungalow I grew up in. I was very nervous. I had not brought a man around since my husband and I parted ways. The ex was always still around the house, since he and my father worked together, and he would see his girls there for visitation.

We pulled into the driveway and Charlie pulled out the wheelchair while I ran ahead into the house announcing our arrival. Everyone clambered to the window or the door to help and greet. Now there was another Charlie in the family so my Charlie became "Charlie with the wheels" to everyone. The whole family was enamored by him and thoroughly entertained. We were a family of singers and Charlie fit right in.

That year we all bonded over Christmas cheer and Charlie's antics, pulling wheelies in the little living room while we all danced around him. My girls loved the attention he paid them. He called them "the gorillas" and would hug and kiss them, and call them Sanna and DaDa, his pet names for them. He was proving to be possible father material.

Now Charlie's affection for women was not just for a special few, but for all women he came into contact with. He would swoon over pretty women going down the street, he would blatantly approach pregnant women in the grocery store and assume he was irresistible to them, and ask to rub their bellies. Who the hell is going to say no to this tiny Tim character in a wheelchair? He could be quite embarrassing at times. I wasn't even certain how I felt about all this. Was I jealous and was I weirded out? Yes.

After all the Christmas cheer settled down that year, and I had made quite a handsome living at the Crab over the holidays, New Year's was upon us. Being the busiest restaurant day of the year besides Mother's Day I had to work. It was always a good time and lots of money. It could easily be a $200 night which in those days was like $400 by today's standards.

The place was bustling, we were all called in early to prepare for the guests. Balloons were hung in a huge fishing net above the main dining room's 20-foot-ceiling to be released from the balcony at midnight, party hats and noise makers were arriving by the box full, buckets being iced, with champagne cases stacked up behind the bar. The piano began to play, and I had a prime station in the main. The local sports athletes who normally wouldn't visit Charley's Crab brought their wives out, the wealthy business owners, nouveau riche or not, they all came out to celebrate the coming year with us and throw money at us.

There were three distinct table turns (seating's) and the people were informed of this ahead of time. So the diehard partiers were the last seating around nine or ten o'clock. This was the only night of the year the employees were allowed to imbibe, so after midnight, we were all stumbling around doing a half-assed job of cleaning and closing, our clothes disheveled and our wits as well.

"Come on, we're all going to Hurley's after, they are staying open late for us and putting out a buffet," one of my friends informed me. We made it for last call and needless to say it was a very early morning crawling home to Lake Orion just before sunrise.

Charlie and I didn't get to spend New Year's Eve together that year. He decided to take me out on a special date to the Ritz Carlton in Dearborn to see Tina Turner perform later in the week. God knows I loved me some Tina. I would run around singing "rolling, rolling, rolling, on a river" constantly.

The night of the show I got all decked out in a black leather skirt, a chenille blousy top, and my faux Chinchilla full-length coat. Off I went to Charlie's apartment and on to the Ritz from there. The weather was typical Michigan yuck, slushy and freezing.

Dearborn was quite a distance for us. Over twenty miles was the farthest we had ever driven together away from Farmington Hills. There was no freeway to get there directly, so we probably had to get to I-94, and backtrack up Michigan Avenue, or something like that.

The hotel was opulent. I should have felt out of my league, but that was exactly how my grandmother had brought me up. Believing that I deserved to be surrounded by some sort of regal atmosphere. There was a glass elevator in the middle of the hotel lobby going up several stories, and it was still spilling over with Christmas décor. People were milling around, some travelers, some people just having dinner there, and others making their way to the nightclub where Tina was performing. It was like dinner theatre with table seatings around a riser stage.

"What would you like to drink?" an attractive, blonde, young lady inquired when she approached our table.

"We will have a bottle of champagne, it is our New Year celebration," Charlie said turning to look at me.

She presented a wine list and Charlie ordered Mum's, (not Krystal or Dom) but Mum's. That was Charlie's speed, not too much not too little.

After several glasses of champagne, Tina Turner came out "guns blazing" so to speak. It was the first time I had seen her without Ike and she held her own just fine. I have loved that lady ever since I saw her in the Who's rock opera 'Tommy', as the Acid Queen. This was an exceptional treat for me.

She wore gold satin and heels that would send me screaming to a podiatrist. Flanked by her fantastic backup singers, she brought the house down.

When the evening came to a close and after a bottle of champagne and then some cocktails, we found our car and made our way back to Farmington Hills, in the rain the slush, and the snow. The long truck north on Telegraph road was pretty treacherous, and I was a terrible backseat driver.

On the way back, Charlie and I got into our first fight. Usually Charlie would simply withdraw into some protective turtle shell, but this time he was yelling right back at me. We had made it back to Grand River Avenue when as we were doing a Michigan turn around to the left, Charlie had apparently heard enough of my nagging and slammed on his hand brake.

A thunderous crash moved our car several feet, we were both dazed. There were no seatbelt laws then, so I was seated next to him in the front seat, and the crash put me on the floor.

Someone with a very huge pick-up truck had rear ended us. Just then our driver's side door swung open violently, with a blast of cold rain and air, and some big burley guy was yelling and punching Charlie.

"Stop he can't defend himself!" I screamed as I threw myself over Charlie to cover him.

In a split second and a rush of winter wind we were engulfed in punches. It was so dark and rainy that all I could see was a black jacket and wild hair flying.

One of the punches hit the side of my face, and the guy just kept pounding away and yelling. Just in time the passenger in his car came around and pulled the guy off Charlie. Someone must have witnessed all of this, and gone to a pay phone to call the police because the skirmish was still going on when they arrived.

We stayed in the car while the officers handled what was going on outside, and either they arrested the guy assaulting us or at least gave him a ticket because they took our information and sent us on our way. The ride back home was quiet, because the police suggested I drive us home and I was having all I could do trying to teach myself not to hit the pedals.

It would be several months before we would be called into the Farmington Hills courtroom to testify. Given the circumstances we were extremely intimidated and our nerves were ravaged. The courtroom was bright with fluorescent lighting as Charlie and I rolled into the courtroom that cold spring day. It was just like television. There was the judge sitting high on his throne of justice and the bailiff standing off to the side. At one of the two tables, I recognized one of the men from that night. It was all very contained and quiet, until I was called to the stand and identified the wrong man.

"The court calls Christine Olevnik to the stand," said the bailiff. "Is this the man who hit Mr. Charles Martin," asked the judge. "Yes sir that is the man I saw," I responded.

At that moment a friend of the defendant stood up and yelled across the courtroom,

"Your honor that is not the man who hit them, he is the man who rescued them." He proceeded to tell the judge there was a perpetrator who was working at a local gas station at that very moment, and they should go find him.

Yes, I identified the wrong man. It took so long for the case to come to trial, that my memory became foggy. Following that episode I now believe that perhaps 50% of the people behind bars may be innocent. I pointed out the guy who rescued us, not the perpetrator. Thank god one of his best friends jumped up and shouted, it was not him it was "so and so" and that was the end of that poor guy's persecution. The judge listened and sent for the correct person, and the poor soul who came to our rescue was released. That was a horrifying experience for everyone involved, and Charlie's relationship with me was never the same. We spent the remainder of that winter staying very low key. The event had been too much for us to endure.

Now it was a new year, a new spring, and the new season at Pine Knob was coming. It was a long winter and I was ready to open a new, and some old, chapters of my life.

CHAPTER 17

Set in Our Ways (Late 1977)

"You are never too old to set another goal or to dream a new dream." C.S. Lewis

So there we were living our weekends together Charlie and I, watching a great deal of television, and not much dreaming or goal setting. In a word, I had many other things going on. Joe Jackson released, "Is She Really Going Out With Him" and I was certain it was about Charlie and me.

Charlie had decided he needed some new digs, something he could own and build to suit his needs. He found his condominium in Northville. Yes, Northville. Where every man I ever loved was from including my ex-husband. Charlie was now living about a mile from where the ex and I had lived as newlyweds, with our newborn, in a barn, over the horse stables and dog kennels of an old hunter/jumper club. Talk about memories.

Most of the new suburban condominiums had taken over either lovely wooded areas and torn them all down, or farmer's fields that lay barren. These condos were built on the flat field variety of tall blowing grasses and abandoned shafts of wheat. They were very high end, not free-standing, but had a lovely façades of dark stained wood and brick with recessed front doors and easy access through the garage with a ramp.

During this transitional period, I didn't see Charlie very much, I was busy working and he had movers and other friends help him out with that laborious process. Instead I was busy working, taking care of the children, and going out at night after work to see some other bands that I loved.

One such band was 'The Rockets'. They were a mix of Mitch Ryder alums, Jimmy McCarty on lead guitar, Jimmy 'Bee' Bandanjek on drums, John Fraga bass player, Donnie Backus on keyboards, and the infamous Dave Gilbert (formerly of Ted Nugent and the Amboy Dukes) on lead vocals. They were playing at the 300 Bowl one night, a bowling alley and bar in Waterford, Michigan. The weather was cold and sleeting, but the bar was still packed with loyal fans. Not much for atmosphere, dark room, several tables, very unattractive plain black with black metal chairs. There was a rather prosaic, non-descript bar, on one side of the room, and a small dance floor which drew a crowd like free pancakes at I Hop.

We danced around the foot of the stage, which was nothing more than a short riser. Dave Gilbert's spit was hitting my head, I was so close. The locals were made up of rednecks, hardworking blue collar people, bikers in black leather, and "lake people" from Dave Gilbert's neighborhood of Union Lake.

That particular night I walked in, ordered a beer at the bar with my girlfriend Z who lived conveniently close and was my co-worker at the Crab. We sat at the bar quenching our after work thirst. Glancing over in the corner we saw someone slumped over on the floor. All I could see was a big shock of reddish blond curls.

"Who the heck is that, and is he all right?" I asked the bartender.

"Oh that's Mark 'the bird' Fiddrich, he's just passed out," was the response.

"Wow he looked a lot better pitching a baseball," I noted.

Just then the Rockets launched into 'Taking It Back' with David, ever the well primed with drugs and alcohol, brought the house down.

Just then Mark 'the bird' flew out of his corner and started gyrating. He was back.

My attention was on Jimmy McCarty. We had met at a club in Ann Arbor called the Fifth Dimension years before, when he was with Mitch Ryder. Tall, dark, and handsome, he had some evocative quality I could not resist. Even though deeply in love with Charlie, once in a while a girl has to get some real shoving love. Jimmy loved and shoved me that night, and several other "after the gig" nights that were to come.

When we were on the east side we would go to his house. One such night was after a Johnny Winter and the Rockets show. We had to be quiet as church mice because his little son Dylan was asleep upstairs. I have no idea what his marital status was, or if he had a girlfriend. It was not my business. I was with Charlie, and Jimmy knew that.

The following weekend after Charlie had moved in, I stayed over at his new place and helped him unpack all of those packed boxes I had been looking at for months. The furniture was all the same, nothing new for the new place of course, miser that he was. No new colors on the walls. They were simply stark white builder's grade. In the dining room table was the hand-me-down traditional maple set, and the old brown chenille couch pushed up against the long living room wall.

Charlie was an intense sort of person, just a high strung, live wire, and he had very particular ideas about how things should be done. He sat in the middle of the room in his chair like a king on the throne directing me.

"Put those over there....I want the pictures hung there....clear the table first," and so on. Soon several hours of this had passed and I was on my last nerve. Charlie and I never did any drugs together, he had a cocktail once in a great while, but never any other substances. I don't know how he tolerated my cigarette smoking. It must have been True blue love. There came a point however that day that I needed to go smoke some weed. Becoming too aggressive would not set well with Charlie, and as I said he was on my last nerve.

So out I snuck to the car, got my pipe, and ran out to the adjacent field, for just a little toke of smoke. As I stared across the old farmer's field of wheat I thought of the loaves of bread that never would be baked, the orgasms Charlie would never have, and the children he can never call his own. Tears filled my eyes as I wondered if I could spend the rest of my life with him.

"Where did you go?" he inquired.

"Just had to take a break and have a cigarette, I went way out in the field, and I didn't even burn it down," was my answer.

He didn't miss a beat and was right back to being the task master. The place was looking good. His Silver Bullet Band gold records hung on the wall, the furniture was in place and everything was open enough for him to maneuver around. I had embroidered the exact colorful lizard from a Door's album, about 12 x12 inches, and framed it for him. He gave that a place of honor. When all was said and done, I was walking by him with something in my hand and he pulled me right down into his lap and laid some very passionate kisses on me.

"Well that makes up for all the bossing around bit," I said with a smile. He knew he could always get to me.

"I am starting the construction of the elevator next week, why don't you and the gorillas come and spend the weekend, the guest bedroom is all set up, and they'll love it here," Charlie put out the invitation he never had before.

We had spent many fun times with my daughters, but never a sleep over at Charlie's house. He had come over to my condo and spent the night many times, bumping up the stairway, me carrying up the chair, he got around fairly well there. To be in Northville though, right by their grandmother and her family, would be great.

One time we took Charlie with the wheels to Cedar Pointe. I insisted Charlie go on all of the rides we did. I scooped him out of his chair and placed him into the Ferris wheel, and bumper cars. Even though I ended up scathing his manhood just a bit, he had more fun than he had experienced in a very long time.

Although I thought that a weekend at Charlie's would be interesting, and I would have to bring the dog along too, I couldn't leave old Tuffy behind. It would be the next step in our relationship. My girls were so excited about spending the night in Charlie's new house they were beside themselves, packing way too many clothes and toys.

"Just bring one toy and one game you both can play," I instructed.

"Does he have Atari?" the oldest one inquired, thinking he would have everything because he was a rich rock star.

"I don't think so, but you never know what he has in that basement, I haven't been down there yet."

We piled into the car and off we went to Northville. It was nearly an hour drive, and the natives were restless in the backseat of Speedy, testing each other's boundaries like kids do. Our Old English Sheepdog Tuffy, was sitting upright in the passenger seat making a really good shotgun partner.

"Okay enough of that you guys, please be on your best behavior over at Charlie's I want him to have us back again," I pleaded.

As we arrived dragging our backpacks, toys, tote bags, and overnight cases filled with Barbie dolls, the sheepdog bounded in and made herself right at home.

"We're here, ready or not here we come," loud enough to warn Charlie if he was in the bathroom ritual, which took nearly an hour minimum. There was no texting ahead, no cell phones, and if I had called from the road it would have been an imposition for him.

"Hi girls," Charlie greeted us with much exuberance.

"Charlie, do you have Atari?" they chimed out in unison.

"I have some stuff on the old Beta to play I think, it is in the basement set up, go on down and see." Laughing, giggling and being typical girls they ran downstairs. Charlie pulled me down to him in his usual tantalizing way.

"What time do they go to bed?" he wondered.

"Oh about ten o'clock on weekends," I said, knowing exactly what he was eluding to.

"Do you think you can hold out that long?" I responded with a smirk on my face.

"I don't think so," he said, as he ran his hand up under my shirt to

fondle me. Just then the girls came running up the stairs, the dog bar-
reling along behind them shouting,

"He has real drums Mom," the youngest chickadee sang.

"Well he is a drummer you know, wouldn't that make sense that
he has drums?"

"Ya, but I've never seen that many up close."

"Come on down and see what I devised," Charlie said. He still had
to bump down the stairs without an elevator and I had to bring down
his chair.

"Check this out," he transferred his butt from the chair to the
drum kit seat nearly falling over as I reached out to steady him. He was
so excited about the demonstration he didn't care if he tipped over.

My girls sat on some boxes yet to be discovered, and made an attentive audience. Charlie put an object in his mouth to demonstrate
that he could use his mouth to do the kick pedal on the bass drum, and
everything else was natural and fell into place for him.

"The only thing I have to do is work out the delay time and play
sort of in syncopation," Charlie explained though we had no idea what
he was talking about. My memories went back to sitting in Bob Seger's
basement with Pep's full set of drums taking up most of the space.
So long ago and yet the same wave of nostalgia drifting through my
memories. The children were thoroughly entertained by Charlie and
grew to adore him.

I made my way around the kitchen getting ready for dinner when
I noticed a small construction site on the far end. "What the heck is
this?" I queried.

"It is going to be a three floor elevator, they have the shaft built,
and some of the electrical in we just need the box."

"You kids stay away from here this is dangerous, there is just some
caution tape across this," I said.

We made a spaghetti dinner that night, something for everyone,
and Charlie and I toasted with a lovely red wine I had brought. We
were like a family. Tuffy lay at Charlie's feet after being fed, in between my feet and Charlie's chair. As promised, the girls stayed up

late playing in the guest room. They fell asleep around ten, and Charlie and I went to bed on the other side of the stairway. His independence was astonishing, I couldn't help but wonder how long he would be able to keep up the energy it took to be Charlie Allen Martin, in his old age. We made passionate love to each other that night. Once I asked him how his orgasms felt. He said it was like peaking and then no release. I suppose I pitied that aspect of our relationship because I had never been so satisfied by anyone without a penis. The irony of the whole thing was a great deal to endure.

In the middle of the night in the peaceful darkness I was suddenly awakened by a loud thud and then a harsh cry from the dog. Leaping out of bed I ran down to the kitchen and turned on the light. Peering into the hole in the floor I cried, "Oh my g "Oh my God!" as I looked into the basement to see poor Tuffy laying there in a heap not moving. I scrambled to the basement tripping over my nightgown on the down, nearly breaking my neck, I found the dog whimpering but unable to move.

"Oh Tuff "Tuffet are you okay?" I said in a low soothing voice as I ran my hands over her hind legs. She slowly got up and limped back upstairs and collapsed in the living room. I frantically barricaded the opening with some chairs laying on their sides, and stormed back up to bed.

"God dammit Charlie," was all I could say.

"What the hell happened?" he said, not fully awake, and wondering what was going on.

"Tuffy fell down into the basement!

"We can get her checked out in the morning," he said reassuringly, "go back to sleep."

The following morning the dog was getting around just fine. She looked rather bruised more than anything else, so after that incident and the weekend, I prudently reconsidered doing the "whole family thing" at Charlie's until the construction was complete.

By the next week, the winter blues were melting away and some signs of spring were forth coming after the long bleak Michigan winter. Charlie called me up one morning,

"Don't make any plans for Wednesday night, we are all going to see Bruce at the arena in Lansing."

Who the "all" was, seemed to be a big mystery. That being my night off it worked out well.

Off we went to the Breslin Arena in Lansing. The E Street Band had certainly grown in popularity since the time we saw them at Masonic Temple. The drive took two hours to Lansing, home of Michigan State University. We pulled right through the back gates and parked by the semi- trucks and tour buses. Arriving slightly late, Charlie and I were the last of our group to be escorted to a wooden riser platform, at the side of the stage left. Great views, and then I realized who we were standing with as the lights came down in the arena, everyone turning to greet Charlie.

There was Bob Seger with his girlfriend Jan, Drew Abbott with his girlfriend Crystal, and I think Chris Campbell and his wife Kris were there, my fellow Plymouthians. They were all very kind, but it had to be heartbreaking for Charlie knowing his relationship with his old bandmates had changed forever.

Naturally Bruce brought the house down, and Clarence in his flamboyant satin suit was outstanding. Just before the show was over we were asked to come back stage at the boss's request and we all funneled into a small backstage room with stark white walls, full of chairs, and not much else. Apparently this was a makeshift set-up because backstage crew were scurrying around bringing us a table set up with refreshments, beer, munchies. We all sat around rather silently looking at each other, the old Silver Bullet Band not knowing what to discuss with Charlie.

Just then Bruce's road manager, who I had been talking to earlier that night in the hallway popped his head in and asked Bob and Jan to come to Bruce's dressing room. We hung out for maybe an hour, then Bob came back saying Bruce wasn't feeling too hot and dispensed an armful of t-shirts to all of us. I wore that thing until it was thread bare. It had navy blue sleeves and the picture of Bruce leaning on Clarence Clemons' shoulder as he blew the sax. It was my favorite shirt ever. Guess that wasn't going to be the night I'd meet Bruce either. He sent his regrets to us all and we made our way back to our respective abodes.

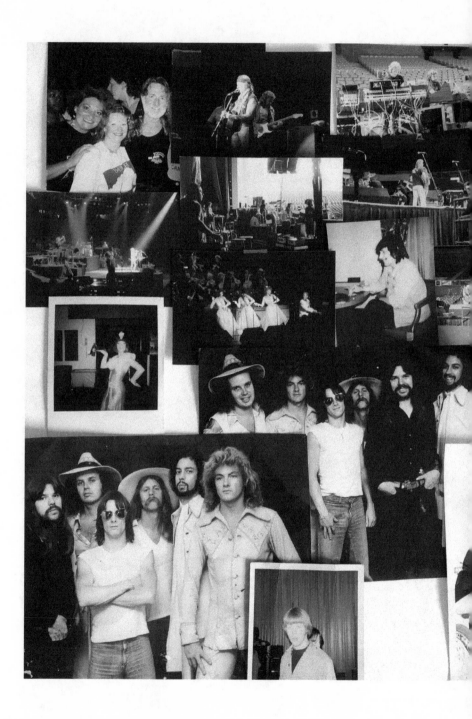

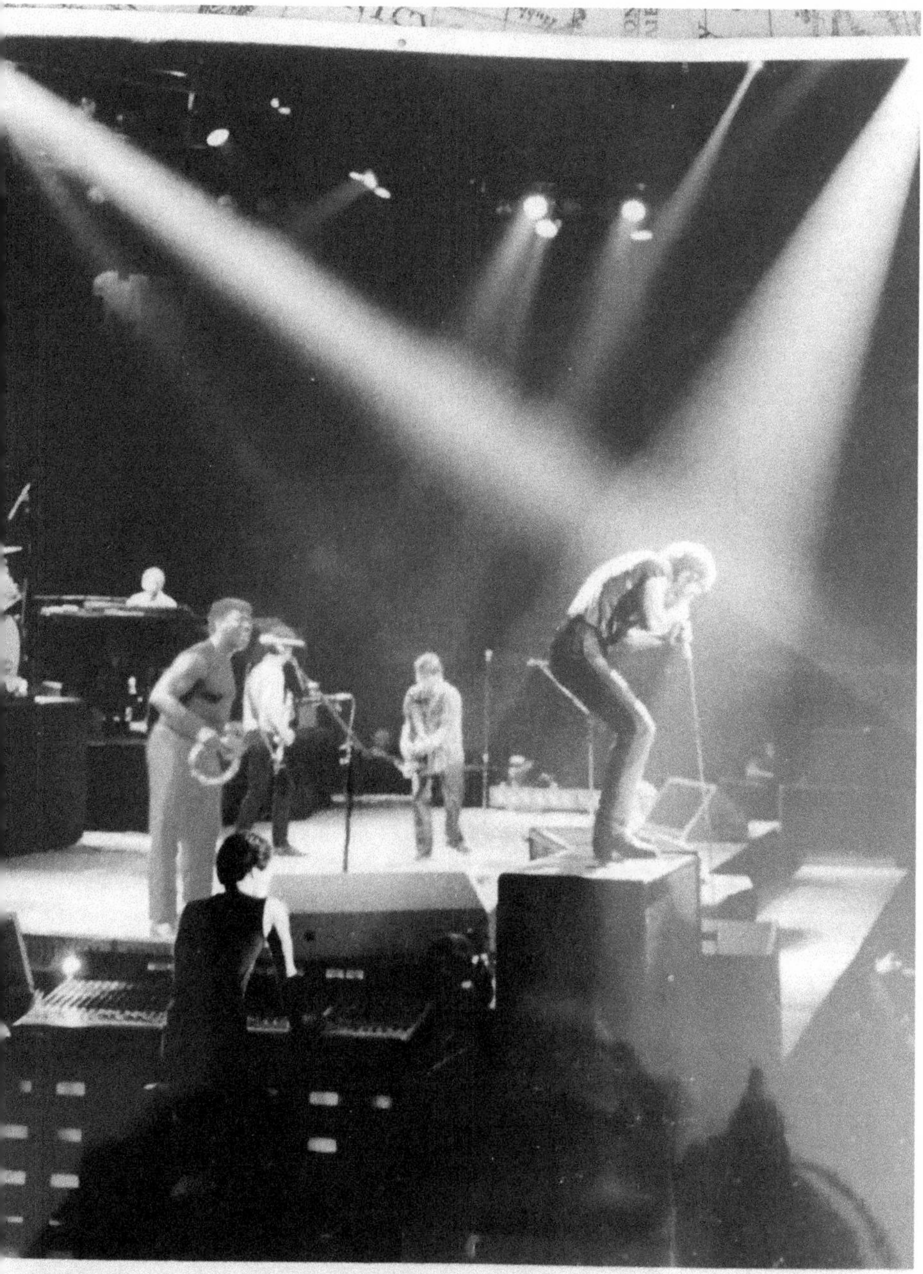

CHAPTER 18

All About Ring Around
the Rosie (1978)

*"I once had a rose named after me...but I was not pleased to
read the description in the catalogue: no good in a bed, but fine
up against a wall." Eleanor Roosevelt*

Eleanor Roosevelt is quite profound. I have great admiration for her.
She spoke her mind, and did it with grace and kindness. Although I
strived to be that type of woman, my alter ego sometimes took over.
For instance, I was more like Franklin Roosevelt in my affairs.

It was 1978, a new season at Pine Knob. The opening band was
America. I was only working at Charlie's Crab, not the crazy two job
pace of the previous year. I had to choose, and working both jobs was
nearly impossible. By that time, however, most of the bands had made
the Northfield Hilton their home sweet home. This made it easy for
me to secure backstage passes to most of the concerts. The girls in
the backstage trailer at Pine Knob who handed out the passes, knew
me on a first name basis. Jefferson Starship was definitely on my radar,
always Paul Kantner and Gracie Slick were at the top of my rock and
roll list. There was nothing more pure than Marty Balin's voice.

"If only you believed like I believed," lifted my spirits into thin air.

I danced all around the theatre, like a butterfly on the wind without a care in the world. Giving it my best west coast strut. Looking like a hippie at a love in.

Back to the old grind the next day, businessmen, early bird specials, local senior citizens to kiss up to, and always the families of the owners. I always got the Muer kids and Betty. They knew I doted on their children, and I was happy to spoil them with their daddy's money. Especially with large Sander's hot fudge sundaes, and all the colored mints they could stuff into their pockets. I believe it was sometime that winter we lost Chef Larry Pagliara to a sudden heart attack on the ski slopes in Colorado. The kitchen was much quieter.

Chuck "Rocky" Rochowicz had taken over the kitchen duties and he was excellent. He would get heated too, but in a sort of nicer way. Not in a throwing condiments at your head manner like Chef Larry used to do.

Summer was in full Michigan swing. Jimmy Carter was president, Menachem Begin and Anwar El-Sadat had kissed and made up, and I was having the time of my life. Two of my influences that year were Maya Angelou who had just written 'And Still I Rise,' to this day one of my favorite reads, and John Irving had penned 'The World According to Garp' which after reading the part where the girl is giving the guy a blow job, and they have a bit of a mishap, my practice of fellacio was forever changed. I could never go down on a guy again without thinking of Garp. On one particularly steamy July night Paul Anka and company came into the restaurant. We had been extremely busy, but things were winding down except for in the lounge where Bob Seeley was playing to his usual drunken crowd who stuffed the oversized giant snifter full of money while he obligingly played their requests.

I had been working in the Farragut dining room that night and Mr. Anka had requested a secluded table. When all the room had cleared out, I seated Paul Anka and his buddy at table 50, a cozy booth under the stairway to the mezzanine. The tables were covered with a decorative oil cloth and set neatly with rolled silverware. They ordered some drinks and proceeded to shove everything on the table toward the wall. Going up Approaching the service bar I said, "Kenny I have Paul Anka on my table, he is my mom's age and going a little bald, but still pretty good looking."

"Cool, he's playing I think four nights in a row at Pine Knob, it should be a really good money week for us," Kenny said.

Meanwhile back at the table, Paul and his buddy were laying out the longest lines of cocaine I had ever seen. Full length of the table, and hoovering the fine white powder up their noses as fast as they were laying it out.

"Hey sweetheart, ya want some?" Mr. Anka offered.

"Oh not right now I have a bunch of work to do, can't be partying on the job," I stammered out my excuse and ran off to bring them some appetizers and bread. He left me a more than generous tip that night and thank goodness because my car had just died on the way into work.

Speedy had been on her last legs and I sold her to one of the Crab cooks for $200 and bought myself an AMC Pacer. I called it my space car, and I loved everything about it. It rode low to the ground like a sports car, was easy to get in and out of, and plenty of space for my little family. Two tone gold with bucket seats. My very first, nearly brand new, used car.

My weekends were still spent with Charlie. I would take him on outings, to family picnics and even over to my ex-in-laws house one day. The house was probably a three-bedroom rambling ranch resting on 7 acres, with three or four more bedrooms built into the basement to accommodate their ten children. On the side of the house was a sloping hill down to a fire pit. We carried Charlie in his chair down the hill and had a birthday party for my daughter there. Horses romped in the adjacent paddock, and everyone was exuberant welcoming Charlie.

At work the following week Rodney Dangerfield came into the restaurant. He was playing at Meadowbrook theatre for several nights. He arrived in his usual boisterous manner, sporting a striped Hilton jacket, which he had borrowed from a bellman. He was being Rodney, cracking jokes behaving in a raucous and randy manner, with that fa-mous popeyed look of his. His eyes darting back and forth wildly. He asked for non-smoking. Rodney and his people were shown the Mezzanine. It was late at night and most of the diners had cleared out.

"How much to rent out this whole space?" he asked the hostess.

"Well we wouldn't charge you anything at this time of night," she responded.

"Good," he said pulling out a giant cigar and lighting it up. That was the first time non-smoking became a smoking section. He drank like a fish and had himself a grand time with all of his mates. He gathered all of the waitresses together and stood in the middle and had one of his buddies take a picture of all of us. What a free spirit character he was, sort of reminded me of my father. He was not set in his ways, he was living life to the fullest, and I expected to some extent I was envious of that.

CHAPTER 19

Living My Double Life (1978)

"Keep love in your heart. A life without love is like a sunless garden when the flowers are dead." Oscar Wilde

By early July, my heart was doing flip flops thinking about Stephen Stills and company in the form of CSN coming back to Pine Knob for an entire week. My arrangements at work were to take some vacation days. The girls were on a little vacation with their father, so I was footloose and fancy free. Knowing they would stay at the Somerset Inn, I made my way to the other side of Troy. It was early evening, the smoky hot sun of the July day just setting, as I turned into a parking lot hot enough to melt the rubber off your tires.

There were three tour buses parked on the outer perimeter of the asphalt lot. After many years of being together they were like the married couple who slept in separate rooms in separate beds, dreaming of a by gone era. Tensions among them could be cut with a knife. David Crosby was the most reclusive, still with Harper Dance's daughter Jan, very frail, tiny, mousy looking, she was so shy and retiring that even though we were seeing each other on various occasions backstage and around the hotel, she never said hello or acknowledged me when I would make an attempt at being friendly. Perhaps that was just her way, was my thought, or she was so drugged out she couldn't even relate to people anymore on any level.

Heavy into freebasing and who knows what else, David Crosby would spout out some opinionated political "stand of the day" whenever I was around a group. He was never around the rest of the entourage most of the time, but he definitely struck me as the activist type. Very much the rebel of the group. This was before the gun toting, thrown in prison David who made all the headlines in the eighties.

Then the peace maker, as I called him, Graham Nash, was the glue who held it all together, which I believe was exhausting for him. He had his radical moments too, very passionate about the environment. He was kind and had a more gregarious nature. He still spoke with that lovely British brogue. His wife, Susan, and newborn, Jackson, were along with him this time. I spent some time with Susan, a very nice lady, and even changed a diaper or two of Jackson's during our days by the Somerset pool.

Stephen was all about "the boys club" with the crew, sports, and everyone else, but when evening came along he wanted a woman to be there for him. That woman, that summer, at that time, was me. He had gotten a bit paunchy in his old age, but whenever I looked in those eyes any flaws went away, and trust me, he had several. A very large cocaine habit being one of them.

I walked into the English pub lounge seeking out a familiar face, and ran into Joel. He said Stephen was crashed out and sleeping one off, and to come around to the show tomorrow and see him, he would make certain I had a pass waiting for me. As I walked through the lobby and turned to leave, Graham passed through, "Hey, hello luv, what ya doin' here?" he said.

"Just came by to see Stephen, but I guess he is incapacitated at the moment," I said.

"Why don't you come and hang with us, we're having some drinks and dinner, and you can meet my business manager Mac."

"That sounds very nice, I do believe I will."

The dining room was set for fine dining with white linen table clothes, candlelight, which softened the large wooden beams and cream-colored stucco walls. By this time a large group of the crew, girlfriends, wives, and managers of CSN had gathered in the dimly lit dining area for a feast. We drank, conversed, and I was introduced to Mac (don't recall his last name), Graham's manager. We laughed, joked, and told stories long into the night.

Mac was very attractive and seductive. Through a series of quips, in a not so sagacious inspirational move, went back to his room with him. Needless to say, I had had way too many drinks, so my clarity of thought was shaken to its core, as we tumbled into bed together. His hair was long and light brown and his clear blue-green eyes stared into mine in a very meaningful way. He smelled good, and was smooth and gentle, and we made made love in a tangle of white sheets for several hours until we both fell sound asleep.

When I awoke a cloak of dread filled my soul and I was afraid that Stephen would find out about this little tryst and shun me. As I stumbled around in the dimly lit room gathering my clothes Mac awoke.

"Where are you going?" he mumbled with squinting eyes.

"I have to go...I shouldn't have done this, I came to see Stephen... please make this our secret...well you probably won't, but be kind about it, not braggadocios, okay?" I begged.

"I wouldn't say anything, you don't know me," he assured me.

I fumbled my way into the bathroom and got dressed, grabbed my purse and flew out the door. By this time I was sober as a judge, and arrived home to watch the sun come up over the condos. What kind of a bone head was I? Not only was I cheating on Charlie, but now I had cheated on Stephen.

Next night was the show, and I always tried to make a new dress and look my best. Madly clunking away on my sewing machine, I created a lovely silky jersey dress with a burgundy cropped jacket with shoulder pads, belted at the waist. Most of the time I would ravage my entire closet mixing up items before a mood would strike me. This ritual would go on until I knew a certain combination was right. I loved high fashion, scouring through the magazines for ideas, then create a more cost effective version.

That done I got into my space car and went north negotiating my secret back road into Pine Knob. There were no signs, one just had to know where to turn down the tree-lined gravel road. Arriving early enough to beat the rush I was parked up by the lodge and walking down when I saw the first limousine pull in the back gate. Someone rolled down the window and waved at me.

"Hello there...be right backstage!" I hollered out.

The crowds were beginning to fill the pavilion, so I wandered out to say "hi" to the guys at the mixing board. I also wanted to take a look at the giant screen that the Jacque Cousteau footage would be projected on. We truly are ruining this magnificent planet, god gave us. The acid rains, the destruction of the coral reefs, the red tide swarming in, and the deaths of all the ocean's indigenous natives we love. That sushi you love won't be around in twenty more years is my estimation if we don't clean up our act. People are so oblivious to it all. It is incredible how ignorant people can be. I digress. Okay, so I am a bit of a soap box queen myself, I have driven quite a few men away with my big mouth and left-wing convictions.

During the performance I wanted to be out front, due to the fact that tensions among the guys were too strained that night, I didn't want to be involved with anything but their performance. Even Graham was in a bad mood, and that rarely happened.

All negativity cleared away when the first notes of 'Helplessly Hoping' rose up to the crowds delight. They were simpatico. All was right with the world. My heart was soaring when Stephen sang 'Blackbird' which was one of my favorite Beatle's songs. Their performances were impeccable, the audience was encouraging and participatory, and the background film was astounding. The band would continue using that footage for many years taking their message to save the oceans to the masses.

Following the show, there wasn't much to do but party. The crew didn't have to load out, things would remain set up for days, and off we went back to the Somerset Inn..

We sat in the pub having our after show beverages when Stephen came sauntering in. He went over to a table of crew guys looking around and spotted me sitting at the bar. Making a bee line for me, he whispered his room number in my ear and out he went. Not wanting to appear too hasty, I finished my drink, made the rounds of saying good night to all the guys, and off I went to rendezvous with Stephen.

He was surprisingly affectionate and charming. He was much more comfortable with me the second go around, and I immediately reciprocated. We talked for a short time, he wondered where my kids were that night, and other small talk before he took my hand and led me to bed. We had mad sex. The method was the same as before, a prelude of kissing long deep and wet with interludes of oral sex transpositions, before the final chord was struck, to full blown intercourse. We were making some beautiful music together.

Exhausted we fell asleep in each other's arms. Upon waking the next morning Stephen was already up writing something, on the phone, talking to managers, "Hey what do you want for breakfast, I'm calling room service?" he asked me as I popped out from underneath the sheets.

"I'll have poached eggs and some bacon," I said. I had given up being a vegetarian not long before and I was back in full carnivorous swing.

Our food arrived as quickly as I have ever seen room service show up. The bellman tried not to acknowledge who Stephen was. Serving us quickly he glanced at me and looked away shyly, making a hasty exit. I hadn't even gotten a morning shower in yet. I wrapped myself up in the fluffy white robe the hotel provided and went over to the table to examine what was under the metal lids.

"What a gorgeous day. Look at the view you have?" I exclaimed pointing out the twenty foot window which ran floor to ceiling, allowing a view of the lush gardens and the pool.

"Uh huh," Stephen grunted and uncovered a club sandwich. "Is that what you eat for breakfast?"

"It's what I always eat on the road," was his answer, as he sipped his coffee pinky up.

"What's wrong with it?" he wondered out loud.

"Just not really breakfast type food, that's all," I responded in a matter of fact manner trying not to sound too critical.

When we had eaten I jumped into the shower and cleaned up my act. When I came out of the bathroom Stephen was dressed and seemed anxious about something, but in retrospect I am sure he had just had his first "bump" of the day without me. "Come on now get dressed we have to go somewhere," he requested in an anxious way while he rustled through some papers on the table.

Complying with his wishes I slid back into jeans and a shirt I had brought, and out the bedroom door to the elevator we went. We were walking along hand in hand, which I thought was just so romantic, but it was for another purpose. As we entered Nordstrom's Stephen's grip tightened, and he said, "Come on run."

As Stephen jerked me along, I broke out laughing getting a big chuckle out of him thinking he was this "big star" who would get mobbed if we didn't run through the store.

I heard the clerks behind the counters saying, "Do you know who that is?" to their fellow workers, then I knew he just didn't want to be bothered and least of all, have to introduce me. Believe me by that stage in his career a bevy of beauties were not "knocking down his door".

We slowed down once through the store and out into the busy mall. We ran past a restaurant where Linda B. had gone to work following the Chowder Society scandal. It was chic, French, and just her style. Passing several chain and novelty shops we raced into a shoe store.

"I need some new Nike's or Converse, or something comfortable," he said, dropping some brand names to the salesman.

After several attempts, as we sat amid twenty disheveled boxes of shoes, a choice was made. Happy with his find he once again took my hand and we sprinted back through Nordstrom's to the hotel.

"We have to get out to sound check," Stephen announced glancing at his watch, as we made our way back down the dimly lit downstairs hallway of the Somerset Inn.

"I have to get some fresh clothes and see about the kids. I'm pretty sure the girls wanted to come out to the show tonight, so I will see you out there," as I gathered what I had in the room. I planted affectionate kisses all over his face as he grinned that squinty-eyed Stephen grin.

My happiness welled up inside of me as I drove the ten miles home to my little condo in Lake Orion to await the return of my daughters. That week was absolutely magical for me. I enjoyed being with a man I admired and loved and lusted after, having the time of my life, included in the throng of crew and people that surrounded CSN as if I was truly a part of the gang. It was filling the void in my heart. Everyone greeted me like an old friend when I passed them in the hotel, backstage, or in the pub.

My mother drove up in her canary yellow Duster and unloaded the girls. I ran out to greet them.

"Thanks so much, Mom, would you like to come in for a minute? I want you to see the imported French wall paper I just put up last week." I was still trying to impress her. Even though she willingly gave me approval, I never knew whether she would turn around and cut me down in the same breathe. Not until many years later, when I graduated from college, would I achieve that recognition from her that I sought after, and yearned for.

We made our way up the stairs into the house, the girls dragging their overnight cases behind them. They dropped them at the top of the stairs.

"Hey those don't belong there. Take them to your room please," I said.

"Oh this looks nice. When did you find time to do it? I thought you were working all week?" my mother said.

"I told you I had friends in town this week, and I took some vacation time. The girls and I are going camping at the end of the week too, I'm not just hanging out partying the whole time," I said, still feeling compelled to explain my whereabouts to her.

I loved my living room. The French wall paper was a milk chocolate brown petite print with small white flowers and a matching floral
border. Borders on walls were all the rage and I wanted to be stylish.
I could only afford to paper two walls at $40 per roll, plus $48 for the
floral trim. That was marginally expensive in the 1970's. The windows
were covered with my rather thick, jute, macramé curtains, (more like
tapestries) interlaced with blue beads to match the floral pattern. The
curtains had taken me over sixty hours to create and I was proud of
my design. My couch had been found in an old barn by a friend who had
immediately thought I could do something with it, and I did. I stripped it
down to its scrolled wooden back, rounded arms, and claw feet and re-
covered it in tawny velvet with nail head and gimp trim. The rest of the
room was filled with hand me down antiques, a china hutch, a rocking
chair, an old dining room table and six chairs bequeathed to me.

"We are going out to the Crosby, Stills, Nash show tonight, so we
have to get ready," I said, shamelessly name-dropping.

"Well that was always one of your favorite groups, how did you
meet them?" she said with that motherly disapproving tone in her
voice which meant just what I thought it did she came just short of
calling me a slut.

"Oh last year working at Pine Knob, you know." I changed the
subject quickly, walking toward the girl's bedroom.

"Come on you guys. It's time to shower and get dressed for the
concert. I'm wearing jeans so you can wear your Jordache."

"Okay, I guess I'll be going then. Bye girls," my mother said.

"Bye grandma we love you," they yelled from their room.

"I love you Mom. Thanks again. Say hi to Dad and company for
me," I said as I walked her out to her car. My father had taught us to
always walk guests to their car.

My thoughts of Charlie tugged at my heart strings and I gave him a
call before we headed out for the night. I said I just couldn't get away
that week and I was taking the girls camping on the weekend. He was
not one to rough it. His idea of roughing it would have been staying at
the Holiday Inn instead of the Hilton.

"Okay then I love you...I am really busy shipping out shirts," Charlie offered up so I wouldn't feel guilty. I am certain he knew what I was really up to anyway. I had mentioned that I was going to see Stephen. Oddly enough there was no feeling of guilt in any way shape or form. We just lived in the moment.

Out at Pine Knob the people were gathering at the orange lacquered, backstage door verbally assaulting the poor security guy with, "Do you know who I am?"

"I don't care if you're the queen of England you have to have the right pass," he responded calmly.

I walked past most of them, saw Jackie from the Oakland Press, said hello, and squeezed through the throng with my daughters in tow. We made our way to the general refreshment and greeting room, I grabbed a Heineken and gave the girls each a Coke. One of the crew members came and placed us on the other side of the stage to watch the show amid stacks of Marshall Amplifier cases, and cables duct taped to the floor. The crew was scurrying around making last minute sound checks and taping the night's playlist on the microphone stands. Things weren't too fancy then, no teleprompters and so forth.

Moments later, Stephen, Graham, and David entered from stage right standing in the same configuration for their entire careers. The crowd rose to their feet with thunderous applause and the magic of the night began as a soft breeze filled the amphitheater. Stephen was changing guitars when he looked out into the darkness backstage to see me standing with the children between the cases and sound board. A big heartfelt grin filled his face and he wrinkled his nose. I was reminded that Stevie Nicks had said, "Players only love you when they are playing."

Graham sat at the piano playing 'Our House' while the others took a short towel off and refreshment break. Pitch perfect as always. What a talent he is, artist, photographer, and musician. The others joined him as he took a bow, and his place at center stage again.

That night and that week was the best one Stephen and I ever shared. Two years later things were not quite the same, and would never be the same again.

CHAPTER 20

Back to Provenance (1978)

"Try to be a rainbow in someone's cloud..." Maya Angelou

The week that followed was sad, but comforting for me. I knew that Stephen was really an elusive person, who had a different woman in every city, and would never be true to me. I settled back into life with Charlie and our long weekends living together. We were back to the old groove.

That summer was particularly hot. The sweat-filled working days in the restaurant were as busy as they had ever been. With acts like Barry Manilow, Neil Sedaka, and Neil Diamond, the older crowd were frequently filling up tables early in order to make the show at Pine Knob.

The first week in August, Jackson Browne came back to town for a three day stay. Of course I was going to see David Lindley to bid him a friendly "hello mate.". I walked into the Somerset Inn and welcomed the blast of breezy air conditioning as I approached the desk to have them connect me with David's room.

"Hi David, it's me Christine what are you doing?" "I was just doing some Tai Chai, want to join me for lunch?"

I agreed to meet and he gave me his room number. When I got to the door it had a sign hanging on it warning, "Beware of THE CLAW". This was David's concept alter ego who was always lurking around and startling people, or leaving goof ball notes around. Things do get tedious on the road and that was how he kept himself and everyone else amused. I loved his quirky personality, and his gentle kind way. So I went in and got clawed, then we went down to the restaurant and had lunch. The rush I would get from his music was so thrilling for me I could not resist. When he would sing 'Stay' I knew it was just for me.

This was the follow up year to the enormously successful 'Running On Empty' album tour and people were really into the singer songwriter. He is standing on the load out dock in 'back of the Pine Knob stage on that album, and I believe it was taken by my buddy Joel Bernstein. Jackson remains one of my favorite people to this day. Those three days went by so fast I felt as if I had blinked, and they were gone.

I only got to see one show due to my work schedule, but I got to know Russ Kunkel, and some of the other band members pretty well that year, such as his wonderful backup singers Rosemary Butler and Doug Haywood. Danny Kortchmar was there too, but this time he wasn't pulling the rip cord off my dress in the back, just sulking around as if he were better than everyone else. Sad to see David go that year, it had been a great three days of love making, small talk and friendship.

Later that month, was the Bob Seger and the Silver Bullet Band (silly bull shit band as Charlie called them) extravaganza. They played two nights, then had four days off, and played six more nights at the Knob. Bob had become the home town hero and the crowds adored him.

One of those dates, Charlie called me up to say, "Hey Seger called to invite me to the show and play keyboards, would you like to go?"

"Of course I would, oh man I have to find something to wear, I won't have time to make it," I said.

"All right then I'll pick you up at 7 o'clock, be ready, I'll just beep," he offered.

Jumping for joy all by myself in the living room, I danced around like a crazy woman, grabbed my purse and scrambled downstairs to the car. Winkelman's was where I went, that was the ritziest place I could think of on short notice. The store was fifteen minutes away in Rochester, and I got there in ten taking the back roads to Adams which had a higher speed limit.

When I arrived, I ran in combing through the racks feverishly until my hand touched on a slippery jersey fabric in an eggplant color. Soft, luxurious, and sexy. It had long sleeves with a cuff and three buttons in front along the lapel. The pants were wide-legged and flowing.

"This is perfect I'll take it," I exclaimed to the sales person. It came to $42, which was the most I had ever paid for anything besides a prom dress. That was sometimes my daily income.

No sooner had I finished preparing for the evening when Charlie was honking the horn. I ran downstairs, jumped into the front seat and kissed Charlie on the cheek. He was wearing a baby blue satin two-piece suit. Total throwback. I should have dressed him.

One would think for an important reunion night like this he would have splurged and gotten something new to wear. Not cheap skate Charlie. I thought he would at least go Alto Reed-style and wear white or black.

"Are you nervous?" I said.

"No why should I be? I'm just excited," Charlie said.

No matter what he said, I knew he was crazy nervous. He hadn't performed in nearly three years in front of an audience. He hadn't seen his old buddies in about that same time.

When we got to Pine Knob, we parked the car outside the gate, as if we didn't really belong there with the rest of the Silver Bullet Band. We went to the trailer and I secured our passes. They were the real laminated tour passes that we wore around our necks, not just the stick on type.

"Okay Rosie, here we go," Charlie signaled me to follow as he wheeled his way down the driveway ramp. Upon reaching the orange backstage door, I walked up the three cement stairs and without even knocking, two big burly bouncer fellows came out, scooped up Charlie in his chair and whisked him through the door.

A Detroit party was going on inside. Everyone dressed to the nines, Tom Weschler made everyone pose for pictures. Most of the people backstage came up and greeted Charlie with warmth and sincerity. It was a huge cocktail party, and I was greeted by Punch Andrews and his girlfriend Colleen with open arms and big kisses. People were stacked up wall to wall, disc jockeys such as Arthur Penthollow from WRIF, Oakland Press journalist Jackie, and other Detroit celebrities had come out the see the Silver Bullet Band.

"Get something to drink, I'll send Bill over to give you some direction," Punch instructed Charlie and me, pointing toward a couple of dressing rooms set up as bar and food tables. He was talking about Bill Blackwell the Silver Bullet road manager, and stage manager. Bill was a great guy, over six feet tall, slender, with gorgeous eyes and thick black hair. He frequently hung out at Charley's Crab.

The rooms were normally used as dressing rooms for the entertainers, but only one room on the stage right side was being used for Bob and company, all the others were on the stage left dressing room side. David Teagarden of Teagarden and Vanwinkle was playing drums at that time and he came up and greeted Charlie with great friendship, high regard and much respect. Then there was Robin Robbins on keyboards, Chris Campbell on bass, Alto Reed saxophone, Drew Abbott on lead guitar, and of course the wonderful backup singers, were some of the best in the business, Shaun Murphy and Laura Creamer.

Tom Weschler came over to Charlie and me, "Hey let me get some shots of you two," he suggested, and Charlie pulled me down into his lap, as he hammed it up completely putting on his fetching sexy look.

Then Bill came over and told Charlie when he would be playing. The audience more than exuberant, was already screaming "Seger, Seger, Seger!"

The group lined up and walked out onto the darkened stage with lights coming up slowly. Bob Seger appeared from the dressing room wearing solid black, with his hair flowing down his back, the longest I had ever seen it. Punch led him out onto the stage as he shouted his usual mantra, "Hey Detroit!"

The familiar sounds and songs lifted the spirits of everyone that night. None as much as Charlie, who was lifted right out of the chair that had stolen his career. Once again, he was in his element. He belted out such songs as 'Rock and Roll Never Forgets' and 'Let It Rock'. Bob played all the songs I loved, from the days of 'Heavy Music,' which reminded me of the first time he had played it for me on his mother's RCA Victrola in the living room in Ann Arbor. He also played 'Main Street', 'Fire Down Below', and 'Still The Same'. It was a night of reverie and revival. That night struck a deep resonant chord in my soul, and I was glad to see Charlie honored for his role making The Silver Bullet Band a success.

CHAPTER 21

Autumn Closing in (Late 78)

"Men always want to be a woman's first love...women like to be the man's last romance..." Oscar Wilde

Charlie had an old friend who lived in downtown Detroit in one of the oldest apartment buildings on Jefferson Avenue. He had owned a record shop on the east side, but was now making his own music and recording. His name was Tom Tassiff. Tom had that eastside look about him, a mix of Italian and eastern European features. He was dark and handsome with big brown penetrating eyes. Of course his hair was long, anyone halfway cool had long hair.

One morning I was mixing up some scrambled eggs for our breakfast and as the eggs hit the pan, Charlie said, "You make the best scrambled eggs I have ever had. They are so whipped up and fluffy," then out of nowhere, he added, "Would you like to sing backup on my buddy's record? He's putting it out ahead of ten other songs he has in the can."

"Well who's your buddy and what kind of songs?"

He told me it was Tom's album.

"I remember his cool apartment, Alden Towers, with the art deco style and the white marble and the dark wood."

"He has a friend with a recording studio in back of his house, and Tom has been recording there. He asked me to play keyboard and sing, and naturally I thought of you."

"When is this going to happen?"

"Oh tomorrow."

"How am I going to learn this music?" I said, in a snarky sort of defensive way. Trying to fiercely hide my pounding heart.

"We'll just ad lib...it will be fine," Charlie's famous last words hung in the air.

The next night as promised he picked me up in Lake Orion because it was on the way to the studio. There was no moon that night and we arrived in a remote area filled with trees and drove back toward one exterior spotlight over the gravel drive. Other cars were angled into haphazard positions along the back of the darkened house. Charlie and I exited the car and he made his way with some difficulty across the gravel on the skinny wheelchair tires. I held the screen door open as he knocked loudly.

A long haired, bearded guy, with a beer belly greeted us. Inside there was a sound-proofed glass-partitioned room with a free standing microphone on one end, a very sophisticated mixing board, and instruments everywhere. The entire space was well lit with spots where singers could plainly read their music.

"Hey Charlie and Christine good to see you...ready to sing?" Tom anxiously acknowledged our presence and frantically went back to listening to some of the tracks.

I was to sing an undertone during the chorus. He played it for me, stuck me in the booth and said, "Go ahead sing it," from his command post at the mixing board. The key was way too low for me, I could not project into my head register, or sing in falsetto, and I hated the song. It had absolutely no meaning for me.

"Christine, sing it like this," Charlie demonstrated.

"The key is too low, I cannot get that out," I said.

We tried changing the key, switching the lyrics, and the more we tried, the more screwed up the song got. There was my big chance to finally hear myself recorded and I was just stiff with nerves, and pissed off. I couldn't even get it done messing around with some other song. The disappointment could be felt on my skin. Wrong song, wrong key, wrong singer, goodnight.

Charlie's part turned out well. Tom was satisfied enough that he just stuck my part amplified into the background, I could barely be heard. After trying to get something down into the wee hours of the night, Tom cut us a demo and sent us on our way. It was my own little 45rpm record piece of crap. The beginning and end of my recording career in one night.

Charlie and I hunkered down that winter. I worked Monday through Friday at the Crab and took care of the girls. Every Friday I went to his house after work.

One night I was working in the pits, up two flights and around the brass-covered bar to the back of the restaurant. The hostess walked up to one of my empty tables, #84 a long spacious booth. She was followed by a couple of thirty something's dressed very nicely. The man was Matt Dillon good looking, in a classy suit and tie. The woman was tall and slender with long curly red hair, and a tight canary yellow satin dress, with five inch heels. She was having a difficult time walking in those shoes. Her legs wobbled as we poured her into the booth.

"Hi there, how are we doing tonight?" I said, taking note of how intoxicated the red head was. I glanced over looking at Matt Dillon with my, "and you think you are going to get lucky tonight?" expression on my face.

"What can I get you to drink?"

"Just a wine list please, we have been waiting in the lounge for this table for nearly two hours," he said.

"Honey, I have to use the ladies," the woman slurred.

"I'm afraid it is all the way back downstairs, let me walk you down. I don't think you can negotiate those stairs," I said.

"Okay honey let's do this thing," she said, as she struggled to stand back up on those heels.

We walked several feet, squeezing past tray stands that were set up with food-filled trays. For the most part, people were there for date night. The bar seats filled with guests overlooking the lounge, and Bob Seeley playing piano. I managed to maneuver the woman all the way down the stairs, into the restroom, and back up the two flights of stairs with very little stumbling or mishap. Then all of a sudden she made a sweeping gesture with her arm, and upended a tray with a metal bucket full of Manhattan-style Charley's chowder on it. I watched in slow motion as a bowl of the red, chunky, broth landed on a lady who had her back turned to us. She screamed, I don't know if it was hot, but I assume that it was. She leapt to her feet.

"You goddam drunk!" the man sitting across from her jumped up with a glass of wine in his hand. He took aim at my canary lady and threw the glass of wine. Suddenly she developed cat-like lightening reflexes. Laughing her head off, she ducked. The glass of wine covered a woman at the next table, and so it began.

"You can't do that to my wife!" the second man threatened.

The equivalent of an animal house food fight scene ensued across the entire dining room in a matter of seconds. Food was flying. I was running to the service bar to grab towels and napkins to clean everyone up when a slow motion Bloody Mary clocked me in the head. Just at that moment, my manager came running upstairs to witness me covered from head to toe in red tomato juice.

"What the hell is going on here people?" he shouted.

I began to explain. The canary lady had escaped all food and drink and was calmly sitting at her table. There was no one to point a finger at, and no point to any of it, so I gave up the explanation.

"Well it all started with a chowder accident," I said.

Furious at me and all that had happened, the manager comped every table and offered to pay for their dry cleaning. In retrospect it was all worth it to me. That was one of the highlights of my Charley's Crab career.

CHAPTER 22

Don't Let Your Limitations Block Your Epiphanies (1978-79)

"You must be the change you wish to see in the world..."
M. Gandhi

During that long bleak winter when Charlie and I were cloistered in his condo, he decided that our sex life needed a bit of a boost. He wanted to make it more exciting for me.

"I'm going to take you somewhere today that you have probably have never been," Charlie whispered in my ear one Saturday morning.

"Oh goody you know I love surprises," I said.

We got dressed, went out for breakfast at the Palace diner and started driving down 8 Mile Road from Northville. The farther we drove, the more the neighborhoods changed. We went from white suburbia to derelict Detroit, a sector that had been cast off. Hookers, druggies, and homeless people were the main residents of this side of 8 Mile.

"I'm sorry honey, but what the fuck are we doing here and where are you taking me?" my voice changing from syrup to vinegar in one sentence.

"You'll see." He turned onto a side street next to a tiny standalone shop call 'Good Vibrations'.

"Is this a porn store?"

"Yes, so I was thinking that we should get a dildo for you and me to play with....you know like a substitute, or something," Charlie explained.

"Charlie I'm happy with you, whatever led you to believe that I wasn't satisfied enough?"

"Come on, it will just be interesting."

Charlie assembled his wheelchair in the torn up, neglected street and I stepped out onto the curb and waited for him.

"You go first, I'm not strutting in there," I said.

The store was filled with things I had never seen before, or even in my wildest imagination. Posters of nude people in various sexual positions. Oils, tinctures, sexual aids. Charlie laughed non-stop as I picked things up and examined them with a quizzical look on my face.

There was a scruffy-looking guy in a dirty white t-shirt standing behind the counter. The shirt was full of holes and I decided the holes must be where he itches frequently, right over his nips. He looked us over and smirked.

"Here, take these over and ask him what they are for," Charlie said, handing me different sized balls connected with a string.

"Excuse me, what are these for?" I enquired.

"You shove them up your ass and as you are having an orgasm your partner pulls them out, very thrilling," he said in a greasy tone.

Charlie was laughing so hard he could not contain himself,

"Here this is what we want," he said as he rolled to a stop in front of at least twenty dildos of various lengths, widths, and even colors. Some were soft, some were bumpy, some had other textures, and some were so thick they looked as if they belonged to a horse or a cow.

"Do you think I should find one that reminds me of you?" I whispered.

"No that wouldn't get you very far up the orgasm chain, rock hard I was still pretty small, but no one ever complained," he offered up in all honesty grinning.

"Well what the hell, Charlie, I'm just happy with your hand and you know it."

"Here, I could strap this one on and we could maybe have something like the real deal," he showed me one that went around his waist.

"Here this one is perfect, not too long, not too thick, just right, geez, I sound like fucking Goldie Locks and the three bears."

"Let's get some stimulant lubrication stuff too," Charlie suggested.

Back out in the car, we sang along with the radio all the way home, eager to try out our new purchases. Rod Stewart was crooning "if you want my body, and you think I'm sexy..." and we belted out Queen, 'Crazy Little Thing Called Love' as we made our way down the filthy, streets of Detroit to the pristine vistas of Northville.

We were happy and there was champagne on ice waiting for us. Charlie went up the elevator first. He lit jasmine candles and placed red roses around the room. The satin sheets were on the bed and the light was just low enough to make me look good. No bumps, no zits, no freckles, no warts, no rolls, and no one else in the room with us. Perfect.

When I walked into the room wearing a light blue shear negligee, trimmed in white lace, a smile came over Charlie's face. Crawling across the bed to meet him, he undid the ribbon at the bodice with his teeth. His face found one breast and took it into his mouth. His hand found the other and he teased both of my nipples with extreme precision. He alternated passionate kisses, which only he could deliver, with the fondling of my breasts. My groin was throbbing and tingling. He presented the male member we had purchased, and inserted it gently at first, then with a thrusting motion as he simulated the back and forth motion of a fully functioning man. While this was transpiring my mind was wandering through fields of grass, blue skies, soft breezes and my clitoris swelled between my fingers.

"Just give me your hand, Charlie," I whispered in ecstasy.

He went down on me with a hunger I had never seen before, salivating all over me I began to come in short liquid bursts.

Charlie then gave me his hand. With a damn bursting rush of water that was unending, I saturated his bed with my orgasmic juices flowing over his hand from my vagina. Every fiber of my body felt relieved, saved, sanctified. My body pulsed and throbbed, as Charlie rolled over onto his back.

"What the hell was that? You let loose like a water balloon bursting on my head. That was fantastic, I've never seen any woman do that before." He was a bit shocked, and pure amazement oozed out of him.

"That was not pee either, that was coming straight from your vagina, and I've never seen anything like it."

I lay back in wonder. So that was what was really supposed to happen during sexual intercourse. It isn't the plucking of the cherry, the breaking of the hymen, the losing one's virginity, it is this. This is the God given ability to set forth a river in a woman that would sort out any inferior seed a man could expel. Why was no one speaking of this? I still to this day, even with a science degree, and inquiring of every gynecologist and urologist I have worked with, do not have my answers. I once had a roadie I was having sex with ask me,

"Do you think you're the only one who comes this way? Grant it you are much more than most come, but there are others," he set me straight.

This is what the persecution, rejection, molestation, raping, belittling, degradation, disfigurement, brutality, objectifying, the heinous treatment of burning women at the stake, beating them into submission, slavery, suppression, repression has all been about. Keeping women from achieving their optimum sexual potential in life. Both men and women are guilty of these atrocities. Let this new found release be the requiem of the female soul. It became mine.

During the remainder of the winter, and early spring I started to get restless, longing to see a musical performance. Charlie arranged to see his buddies Lowell George and Little Feat playing at the Royal Oak Music Theatre.

We drove together from Charlie's house to the venue, which was a theatre filled with the old burgundy velvet, wood-handled chairs designed for the small butts of a bygone population. We went directly to the back stage door where we were warmly greeted by the band's road manager, who gave Charlie a hug and a "how ya doin' man?"

The music was lively, with the thumping bass of 'Fat Man In the Bathtub' filling the small auditorium, and I was mesmerized by the style of the drummer Richie Hayward. Not wanting Charlie to feel bad, I held my tongue, but he could probably read my face. These were crafty musicians. Lowell George was a down home sort of fellow in his overalls and white t-shirt. Billy Payne was on keyboards displaying phenomenal talent, and Paul Barrere, Sam Clayton, and Kenny Gradney filled out the remaining members, along with the Tower of Power horn section blowing our minds. Great music the likes of which I had never heard before. A lively mix of blue grass, mixed with rock, mixed with Louisiana southern style.

When they played 'Dixie Chicken' the entire crowd got up on their feet and started singing and clapping along, including Charlie and me backstage. They were promoting their album 'Waiting For Columbus', and played nearly every song on that record. During the break Charlie introduced me to the band.

Richie Haywood was wiry or should I say wired? Bandana tied around his neck, sweat dripping down his face, he gave me a hug and said howdy, then Billy came off stage right, and into the wing where Charlie introduced us. Billy chatted cordially with us for a bit, then excused himself to wipe away the sweat. I would cross paths with those two again in the future, but that was how we met. Lowell said "hi" and the rest of the band was preoccupied doing their own thing with their own people in the dressing rooms under the stage in the basement of the old theatre.

We stayed for the encore, and then the frantic load out began. After changing his clothes, Richie came up to say good-bye,

"Hey you guys want to smoke a joint?" he offered.

"No man I don't smoke, she might want to," Charlie said, and he wheeled away to talk to Lowell who had just stepped out of the light into the back stage darkness.

Richie and I stood there looking at each other so I said,

"Thanks Richie I would love to," and we stepped further into the night air and had a smoke. We made small talk about where the tour would take them, where he was from, where I was from, what my relationship was with Charlie, and so forth. I think I gave Richie my phone number that night, he got it somehow, because several years later, he called it.

Sometime near the end of that year in the early winter months, I met Mark Volman and Howard Kaylan of the 'Mothers of Invention' from Frank Zappa's band. I have always been a big Zappa fan ever since. I first saw his poster in the head shop in Ann Arbor, the one of him sitting on the toilet.

One night Flo and Eddie (a.k.a. Mark and Howard) were playing at the Royal Oak Music Theatre. After unsuccessfully trying to get out of work early, I headed for Royal Oak anyway. When I frantically ran into the theatre, they said the guys had left already. Not to be discouraged I knew the seedy little motel where they were staying, the Sir Sagamore on Woodward Avenue. It looked just like the knight from King Arthur's round table on my Camelot album.

It was a cold, dark, windy night, and probably midnight when I knocked on their door and introduced myself,

"Hello I'm Rosie, I am really disappointed that I missed your show would you like to smoke some weed with me?"

Howard, who had answered the door in his underwear and t-shirt, turned to Mark and said, "It's Rosie, would you like to smoke some weed with her?" Then Mark responded with,

"Sure come on in Rosie, I'm Mark and this is Howard." That was the beginning of a lovely friendship.

The room was dimly lit, they were in t-shirts and boxers, and it really was a crap shoot who I was going to be with at that point. Mark put forth the invitation to stay with him. We were quietly respectful of the roommate during our sex that night and I made my way home afterward. We were friends from then on, anytime they played Detroit, or nearby.

One time on a hot August night they played the Plymouth club on

Ford Road called Center Stage. I brought my friend Doris "Clitoris" with me. Their show was original, funny, upbeat, and I was crazy about them. Backstage after their performance we presented Mark with a birthday cake and Doris and I sang happy birthday in two part harmony. Mark and Howard said,

"Dang that was really good...you two should be an act." We plowed through the cake ravenously, and went to party at the Plymouth Hilton. The lounge name was King's Row or something like that with the logo being the King of hearts card. Mark was my king of hearts. We celebrated his birthday in royal fashion, and then went to his room and made mad passion love into the wee hours. Soon after that they sang backup on Bruce Springsteen's 'Hungry Heart' on The River album.

That night was so magical for us, I believe that was the night Mark asked if I would like to come to California and stay with him. Not having any clue what their life styles were at the time until I read Howard's book 'Shell Shocked.' The entire Mother's of Invention scene was to bring home a woman to be part of their family, live with them, as if she were a muse of some sort.

On another closely related mission of mine that winter, my groupie friend P.J. (her name was Patricia Jacques) and I hooked up with Frank and his body guard. Prior to Zappa's performance at Masonic Temple, one very frosty winter night in November, I went to the backstage door through a darkened alleyway. A single light over the door was all I had to navigate by. P.J. had called me up that day and invited me to the show, knowing Wednesday was my night off. She and I had met at a Ted Nugent show. I was seeing Cliff Davies, and she was doing whatever it was she did.

I walked up to the rather large black man, a typical hulk of a body guard type, who had a singular beam of light shining over his skull capped head.

"Hello my name is Christine Fowler and I am meeting Patricia Jacque here tonight, go find her for me please," I said shivering and jumping up and down to maintain body heat.

"Okay wait here," he said as he looked me up and down, then

disappeared inside slamming the heavy steel door shut in my face.

Several minutes went by, and when he returned his demeanor was quite different.

"Come on in, sorry about that, but we have to check everyone you know," he escorted me through some long abandoned hallways, and up some stairs.

The old wooden floor creaked under my feet as I followed the smell of cigarette smoke to an open doorway on the left. Sticking my head in, there was Frank Zappa himself lying on an old army cot puffing away.

"Hello Frank, I'm Christine, my friend P.J. told me to meet her here."

He sat up and laughed, "I thought you were the Fowler's sister, Tom and Bruce Fowler are in my band."

"Well I suppose I could be related in some remote way."

"Stay around for the show, okay? P.J. is out there somewhere just go that way and you'll find her," he said as he continued to mentally prepare for the concert.

P.J. seemed to know everybody. I did not know anything about her. She was always very secretive and that may not even be her name. Things were always more interesting when she was around.

The band came on playing the famous riff 'I Am The Slime' one of my personal favorites. The body guard sat on the stage right out in front as if he were an integral part of the program. Women threw their panties and Zappa egged them on.

Following the show P.J. and I were invited to come back to the Renaissance hotel to have pure unadulterated sex and sleep. Frank did not drink or do any drugs whatsoever. The body guard, P.J. and Frank and I got into the limousine parked in the alley as thirty or so screaming fans lined up for a glimpse.

We had sex and slept, and when I awoke at about 4am, I dressed, tiptoed quietly out of the room and hailed a cab. The next night at work, one of my bartenders said, "Did I see you getting into Frank Zappa's limo last night?"

"Yes you did."

CHAPTER 23

Fear of Commitment
(1978-79)

"The difference between involvement and commitment is like ham and egg. The chicken is involved; the pig is committed..."
Martina Navratilova

Sometime in the early spring Charlie decided we should get married. We were driving somewhere and once again, he had not told me the destination. I cracked the window to feel the warm sunshine and spring breeze on my face. Like a dog, eager for fresh air. We were heading for Bloomfield when Charlie turned to me and said,

"You know if we ever want to get married you have to get divorced."

The statement itself blindsided me. We had never discussed the possibility or even an engagement before. Yet another man proposing to me in a left handed, back door sort of way. Ugh. Where is the romance? Once again, just an expectation that I should fall into.

"So where are we going?"

"We have an appointment with T. Patrick Freydell, the Silver Bullet Band attorney," he responded matter-of-factly.

I had heard of this big wig attorney. He was skilled in a contractual agreements and had always been Punch Andrews and Bob Seger's go-to guy.

Arriving at the yellow brick, high-rise building in one of the most affluent areas of Michigan, we valet parked in the garage and entered the building. I followed along in a puppy dog way behind Charlie.

At the receptionist's desk, he paused to say, "Charlie Allen Martin to see Mr. Freydell," in a pompous sort of manner.

"Oh Charlie don't be silly, I know who you are," the poised older lady in a gray business suit with a tapered skirt laughed at his theatrics.

Entering the office we were invited to sit opposite the desk. The receptionist softly closed the heavy walnut door behind herself smiling.The room was classic with bookshelves along one wall and a grand wooden desk positioned in front of them. The large floor to ceiling window provided a panoramic view.

Just then a man with dark, coifed, black hair wearing thick rimmed glasses and a business suit bounded into the room. He shook Charlie's hand and told him it was great to see him. Charlie introduced me as his girlfriend, Christine Olevnik.

"How do you do Mr. Freydell very nice to meet you." .

"Well, let's get to it, answer all the questions and then I will draw up the documents and ask for a court date."

The process took about half an hour and we were done. In retrospect, I should have taken a nice trip to Mexico since all the attorney did for me was change my name legally back to my maiden name. My ex-husband was not contesting. We had already agreed that I should have the children, and our property had been split up years before. Charlie said he would pay the legal fees when we were married.

There it was again, "when we get married." I didn't like the ring of it. The conversation that ensued on our drive home did not enhance the relationship.

"Charlie we have to consider the girls," I said.

"I love the gorillas," he reassured me.

"Yes but every time they frustrate you in some way, just being kids, you do that frozen shutdown emotional thing you do, which can't be good for you or for the girls. They sense your emotional self-protective nature when you don't get your way," I said.

"I love you, but I want something more permanent. I don't want you running off and doing whatever it is you do with everyone you do it with," he said, finally being honest.

"I seriously do not know if that is going to work. Where are we going to live? Are we all going to fit in your two bedroom townhouse? What about my job? I can't commute from Northville. My girls are in a fine school right now, I don't want to rip them out of there again."

My older daughter had already changed schools three times and she was only in elementary school. They would be closer to family members in Northville, but the concept was too far-fetched for me to grasp just then.

All of the issues were coming to a head during this ride back to the condo. I was able to be the chicken, but I was not ready to be the pig. In the end, I had to pay for the attorney's fee of nearly $800, I got the divorce, and my name was Fowler. That does not sound like much money now, but in 1979, for a mere waitress, it might as well have been a million dollars.

That was the end of the Charlie Allen Martin affair after nearly three years. I still loved him and I fell into a funk. We remained friends for a long time following our paramour years together. Shortly after our time together, he married a lovely woman named Susie.

Many other things were happening simultaneously in my life. Charley's Crab and the Northfield Hilton had become the quintessential go to spot for the whole Detroit area with all of the "stars" coming and going.

CHAPTER 24

Devastation (1979)

"Hell is empty and all the devils are here..." William Shakespeare
My world was upside down.

For weeks I walked through my life trying to decide what to do next, trying to answer my daughter's questions,
"Won't we ever see Charlie again?"
Vacillating between cheerfulness during work to sobbing mournfully the rest of the time, I made it to the following weekend. My friends could not console me, I had no dreams left, and my emotions were splayed open and raw, like a gutted fish.

The events that followed gave me a wakeup call. There was a deep foreboding, hanging over the moonlit sky that night, and a serious funk looming in my soul.

There was a dive bar called Heaven on Dixie Highway, in a white trash area near my home and Pine Knob. Johnny Paycheck had released his hit single, 'Take This Job and Shove It' a couple of years earlier and was trying to ride the coat tails of that hit playing the bar circuit.

My mother had collected the children earlier that evening and I was alone with my miserable thoughts. I threw on a pair of jeans, a blousy white shirt, tied a bandana scarf to my purse, and attached large hoop earrings to my head and off I went to drown my sorrows.

Heaven was packed that night. I had been there once before checking out the local 'Doors' cover band Pendragon, when it was a rock and roll bar. Now strictly country, the décor had not changed one bit, just the musical selections. The same old linoleum-tiled floor, the same old round cheap tables, with initials carved in the wooden table tops. Pictures were drawn in marker to leave a legacy of the partiers that had come before. The same old metal chairs with red vinyl seats.

I sat alone at a table watching Johnny Paycheck's warm up band play try to get the place primed. Pain leaked out of every pore, self-loathing was the theme of the night as a cacophony of unfamiliar music surrounded me.

"What could I get you honey?" a gum chewing waitress asked me.

"How about a vodka and tonic with a lime please, and just keep 'em comin' sweetie," that was heavy stuff for me. I was out for trouble when I drank Vodka, Rum, Gin or Tequila.

The band played 'Whisky Bent and Hell Bound,' as I tied my red bandana to my wrist and went out on the dance floor. I didn't give a shit if I was dancing by myself, but a couple of young men jumped up and made a sandwich out of me. I welcomed the attention and the flirtation. Let the good times roll.

By the time that Johnny Paycheck got on stage the room was spinning. I was making my way to the back door for some fresh air when someone grabbed my arm from behind.

"Hey there sugar, where ya goin' let's smoke a doob," a long-haired young man suggested. He was part of the crew working Johnny Paycheck's tour, and we climbed into the cab of a truck which held equipment.

"Have a pull of this too," he said, handing me a flask. We were extremely stoned by this time, but I didn't care and I drank it. I was turning to leave the cab and go back inside when he said, "Where ya headed so fast honey? Won't you do me a little favor and suck on this." He exposed himself. Full of self-loathing, desperation and devastation I complied. I hated myself at that moment and what my life had become, and so I just kept on. One of his buddies climbed into the cab in the first one's place and I sucked him off. Then another and another. I could hear voices outside saying, "Hey what's going on in there?"

"Some girl is giving out blow jobs."

By the time Johnny Paycheck got into the truck I had reached my limit. I may or may not have gone down on him too, but everything was starting to blur. That was enough self- deprecation for one night. I found my purse on the floor of the truck, stumbled across the gravel of the darkened parking lot, found my car, and locked myself inside. The night was cold, and a biting breeze cleared the stench that covered me. Seeking out my Altoids, I popped two in my mouth and sat there slumped down for at least an hour until my head cleared. I drifted off to sleep, and when I awoke the lot was emptying out. I spotted the roadies carrying out speakers by the single light over the back door.

I began sobbing about what I had done, what they had done, what the night had turned out to be. Making my way home skirting the edge of Pontiac toward Lake Orion, wallowing in self-pity, I continued to cry over losing Charlie and what to do now. I needed to reflect, go deep inside, and figure things out. When I finally reached the comfort of my own home, I dragged myself and my little red bandana up to bed.

Charlie insisted we remain friends, but he wanted something more permanent in his life. Some crazy part of me could not quite commit to one man yet. At least not to a man in a wheelchair who could not digest a constant diet of children being around.

CHAPTER 25

City of Angels and Fresh Start in Frisco: 1979

"The whole of life is about another chance and while we are alive until the very end, there is always another chance..."
Jeanette Winterson

That spring, as the season began at Pine Knob, a fresh new sagacity was washing over me. I decided to choose men more wisely and curtail my partying a small bit. I wanted to spend more time with my children and make more money.

Most of the regular bands opened Pine Knob that year, but the J.Geils Band stood out. They played for three days in a row. They were established as a Detroit band, even though they were from Boston. Personally, I had never had the opportunity to see them, but I loved their romping stomping sound. The harmonica was one of the lead instruments in their band instead of a searing guitar or strong vocalist. I loved all of their music.

The Allman Brothers came in next. The bands were staying at the Northfield Hilton. On one occasion I would see Gregory Allman walk into Hurley's when they did stay there. He was quite tall and his long blonde hair was down around his shoulders. I went up to him and said something stupid like,

"Hey how are Cher and Alijah Blue?" His response was "har-rumph...." as he turned around and walked out.

The rest of his group were partying hardy, so hardy that one of the crew thought he was invincible and walked out on the open cement cross beams one story up, that were only meant to be architectural. In a very drunken state, he fell to the hallway, hit his head and was DOA at the local hospital. In classic "Allman Brothers are jinxed" fashion, this tragedy was added to the long list.

That particular year, 1979, Stephen Stills was on a solo tour. I had hooked up with him in my home town of Plymouth when he played at the Center Stage theatre out on Ford Road in Canton, Michigan that spring. He had his close band buddy with him for that season, Mike "Fins" Finnigan on keyboards, George "Chocolate" Perry on bass, and probably Joe Vitale on drums. I teased him that night because for some unknown reason he looked at his damn watch every two minutes. I asked him after the show if he was playing 'Beat the Clock' which a popular television show at the time. He laughed it off and said he didn't want to run over and pay the fine.

Later in June, Stephen played Pine Knob as a solo. Once again he and his band stayed at the Somerset Inn. I don't even recall if I made it to the concert or not, but I certainly remember what happened the night when I showed up at Stephen's usual suite and knocked on the door.

"Hi there...did you enjoy the show, you didn't come back after-ward?" Stephen greeted me.

"Oh yes luv it was great, doing a lot of your 'Thoroughfare Gap' stuff huh?" I guessed since that was his release of the year.

"It appears that your old injured knee is bothering you," I noticed he was limping around.

"Ya but it's okay, just turned it wrong tonight" was Stephen's response.

"It's holding up fairly well in that jockey shot on the album cover," I quipped assuring him that I owned it and had played the grooves off of it.

As I entered the room and the seating area I was aware that someone else was in there with us. Stephen introduced me to his backup singer. If we were in animation you would have seen two large green headed monsters looming up with teeth bared spitting fire at each other. As it was we cordially greeted one another, then Stephen in a surprise move turned to her and asked her to leave. She was blindsided, shocked, surprised, and all together put out by that request. She argued with him for a moment over at the door, and then conceded. I still wonder to this day if she stayed on tour after that insult, because I am certain he was shagging her.

We sat for a while making small talk, and I noticed his acoustic (I think it was a Martin) guitar leaning up against a chair. I picked up the guitar to strum some chords thinking I would show him my chops when he started to laugh, presumably at me.

"That isn't open E tuning," he chuckled. "It is difficult to explain." He took the guitar and began demonstrating. "It's like this....and that. This is what Jimi Hendrix did," he showed me.

"Sure," was my unintelligible answer. In that moment I decided I would lay it all on the line, I stood up and declared, "I love you Stephen. I'm in love with you."

Silence followed. It was as if he had not heard me, but then that Stephen grin came over his face. He took me by the hand as he had so many times before, and led me up the spiral staircase to bed. Not wanting to push the subject any further if he was not going to reciprocate, I gingerly followed.

We were together one other time after one of his shows. He was staying at the Troy Hilton this time and after making me comfortable watching television in his suite he excused himself saying he had to go talk to some of the guys and would be right back. I went into the bathroom to wash up and noticed about four emptied white paper squares lying around. Obviously he was out of cocaine and on the hunt. When he returned hours later he woke me up on the couch and suggested we go to bed.

"Come on let's get some sleep," he pointed to the large bed in the corner.

I don't know if it was the fact that he woke me up out of a fantastic dream or what, but as we were making love I could not stop having multiple orgasms. One large wave of ecstasy after another overwhelmed me as he turned the passion up to warp speed. Finally he had climaxed, and rolled off of me, both of us gasping for air. Falling asleep together in the bed I had turned into a cold lake. Stephen jumped up.

"I can't sleep in this!" and off he went through a door into another room. I was too exhausted to follow him and I fell asleep in the huge wet spot. The next morning I woke up and went to look for him in the other room. He looked like a little boy curled up sound asleep in a twin bed. I kissed his cheek and he woke up. After having breakfast together I said good-bye to him. That was the last time we made love. The bass player George "Chocolate" Perry and I would maintain a friendship that later found us in some awkward situations being around Stephen.

During the following week at work I tried to get my mind off of Stephen, and some of the events that ensued helped me do just that. There was a regular who would come into the Crab in a rather pronounced way. His enterage of several beautiful women, and his superfly apparel always commanded attention.

Everyone said he owned a modeling agency in Troy, but I think it was more like an escort service. He was a dark-skinned black man, built like a linebacker, sharply dressed in very expensive Armani threads, a beautiful woman on each arm. He lavished each one with gifts, and a carte blanche dining experience. Not only was this notable, but what he was driving up to the little valet booth was almost more impressive. An Excalibur. The vehicle topped even the Rolls Royce owned by Robyn Robbins of the Silver Bullet Band. Whenever we wait staff saw this particular gentleman enter the dining room we would all run out and drool over the car.

I was their server that night on table twenty, when one of the managers came running briskly up to the table, and bending over whispered something in the gentleman's ear. He leaped up and ran out of the restaurant as if it were on fire.

One of the valet boys had decided to take the Excalibur for a joy ride and had wrapped it around one of the large light poles illuminating the Hilton parking lot. Tragedy struck on so many levels it was absurd. The valet company lost their commission, the boy lost his job, and Muer nearly lost his shirt paying for the cost incurred. That was a nice little distraction for a while, we talked about that one for weeks, and we also lost the man's patronage.

One night at work as I plodded along through my nightly tasks and smiled graciously to the customers, I turned to my friend Norma and said,

"I seriously need a vacation, somewhere I have never been before, or somewhere I have been, but with a different outcome, what do you think?"

"That sounds pretty good to me, what are you thinking of doing?" She assembled glasses on her tray at the service bar.

"Well I thought I would go visit Zsa Zsa," our fellow waitress who had decided to up and move to Los Angeles.

"That sounds great. I wish I could do that," she said, snapping her fingers.

I took money out of my savings account and headed for the local travel agent's office. In the travel office I looked at the romantic getaway posters filling the walls. It all looked very exotic except for the six desks lined up in a neat little row with a chair beside each one.

"Hi there may I help you?" a short haired, middle-aged man wearing a pin striped suit greeted me.

If I worked in one of those agencies I would wear nothing but Hawaiian flowered shirts all day long, was what I was thinking. I suppose he wanted to look like he was all business as he was going to take more money than I had ever forked over for a trip.

"Sure I need a round trip to Los Angeles, California, please," I glanced around the room and took a seat.

"Lodging, renting a car, want to go to Disneyland?"

"No just visiting a friend, and she will pick me up." He printed out my ticket, and gave me directions. Since I had flown only one other time before when I was 16 years old, I needed instruction in a big way.

After much anxious anticipation, the departure date came. I boarded the LA flight in Detroit, and readied myself for the four or five hours in the sky.

When the plane touched down, I was filled with excitement and prospects for the unknown. The airport was the busiest one I had ever seen, jets soaring in from everywhere.

Darlene greeted me outside the LAX baggage claim area in her yellow Corvette Stingray convertible, and off we went to get our wild on. She lived in Westwood at that time, and I noticed we were going in a different direction.

"We are staying the night out at my boyfriend's house, his name is Bob, and he lives in Malibu," she informed me. "And his wife's name is Barbie," I said laughing at my own stupid joke.

"You know Malibu Barbie, not any reference to you at all," although we used to call her Zsa Zsa, she looked like a Barbie doll without the long legs. Darlene had the tiniest waistline I have ever seen.

As we drove along the Pacific coast highway, the rocky cliff rose out of the sea to the east, making the twists and turns with the sun sinking into the azure ocean, slowly like a big orange ball. I was a kid in a candy store.

"Look at the ocean....there's Alice's restaurant out on that pier... oh man this is so cool," I was like a Jack Russell terrier looking out the window taking it all in.

"Here we are," Darlene said. There was a large oasis of grassy land tract that preceded a guardhouse.

"Hello Ms. Rea nice to see you again," the security guard greeted her with a smile.

"Bob owns three houses in here right now, he is a contractor, we are staying at the ultra-modern one tonight and I'll show you the others tomorrow," Darlene informed me as she pointed out the neighbors' homes to me.

"Cher has this big Egyptian house down there. The huge white one, then Linda Ronstadt lives there and she pointed to a Swiss Chalet looking place, and Larry Hagman and his wife Maj live right across the street there." Darlene gestured up and down the small road that traversed the area.

As Darlene clicked open the garage door, I saw a Bentley and a BMW in the pristine garage. Not one tool, not one drop of oil, spotless.

We went inside and made ourselves at home. Bob was working late, and I could meet him tomorrow. She showed me to one of the guest bedrooms, sliding glass doors in a Japanese-style, trimmed in mahogany and green glass, which opened to the room, en suite, and a balcony. It didn't appear to be lived in. I flopped onto the forest green bedspread, exhausted. As casually as falling into a field of grass.

Down in the kitchen we foraged for snacks, and then went to our respective rooms and fell asleep. Awakening from a deep slumber to voices in the hallway I heard Darlene say,

"She's asleep. You'll meet her tomorrow."

"Maybe she wants to join us," a male voice offered up in a slightly inebriated state.

"No I don't think she's into that," the voices trailed off down the hall to the bedroom.

Way too tired to care what they were up to, I dozed off again. Dreams filled my sleep with wondrous adventures.

The following morning my room was filled with California sunshine. I went downstairs. Darlene was still in bed and Bob had gone to work. The doorbell rang and I decided to answer it.

Opening the door I saw a woman in a black robe with this crazy white hair in all sorts of disarray, and big black glasses on her face, "Hi, I'm your neighbor, would you happen to have a cup of sugar?"

"Well come on in, I have just been through all of the cupboards looking for coffee, but I haven't checked these jars yet." I lifted the apothecary type lids of the canister set and fulfilled her request. Thanking me, she was out the door as quickly as she came in.

Man, I thought to myself, these California people were of a different breed. Looking around I got a sense of how palatial the house was. Sunken living room with fireplace, high end furnishings and large picture windows opening to the backyard entrance where orange and lemon trees provided succulent offerings.

"Hey sleepy head, I'm the one with jet lag, so you must have had a rough and tumble night?" I said when Darlene showed up. We enjoyed a small breakfast of coffee and oranges picked from the backyard, and then she gave me a tour of the homes in the neighborhood before we went running on the beach. Bob had built an enormous Victorian-style home on the northern side of the modern home, and the southern side was a Mexican adobe-type home with white stucco and red tile roof.

We stopped into the hacienda because it was vacant. The attention to detail was remarkable. Hand-painted tiles trimmed out the centrally located kitchen, tiled floors, and heavy wooden beams made it feel as if we had walked into Barcelona, or maybe Zorro's house. I could not imagine what these homes were selling for.

After the tour ended, we cut through the ocean front homes on a sand lot. As we ran along the beach Zsa Zsa pointed out the houses that she knew to be occupied by celebs, and the thick sand in my Nike shoes gave me a challenging run. Looking eastward and skyward, up over the various mansions, I saw a shining dome glowing in the morning light.

"Hey Darlene who lives up there?"

"That is the Jean Paul Getty mansion. He was some really wealthy guy," she said. Of course he was the wealthiest man in America during the mid-century. Then pointing to the north of the mansion, Darlene continued my education.

"That is Pepperdine University," Darlene raised her arm to the other end of our site line. The beach was glorious, and the color of the water was brilliant blue just the way I remembered it.

When Bob returned from work that evening he scooped us up in the Bentley. Making small talk and introductions I was jostled to and fro in the back seat, as we made our way along Highway 1, the ocean road. We spent that evening with Bob at a five star coastal restaurant wining and dining.

He was much older than Darlene, much more mature, and much

wealthier. His blond hairline was receding, and he sported a deep brown tan. Bob was in good shape for his age. He was probably only about forty years old, but that was ancient to me. The restaurant was opulent. I remember long white sheers blowing in the wind. Our table was candle lit with a fresh gardenia perfuming the space.

"So Christine, where are you from?" Bob asked.

"Oh Detroit and I grew up in a small farming town called Plymouth."

"Hum, never heard of it, well you girls order whatever you want. I have some friends I need to talk to." Off he went.

"Does he always treat you like that? He didn't seem very interested in us?" I said.

"He has a lot of real estate friends at the bar he needs to talk to," Darlene made excuses for him, and then we laughed and ordered some of the most expensive things we could find on the menu.

A small jazz combo played in the dimly lit lounge off in one corner, while Bob was drinking Martinis with his cronies at the bar. Bob watched me walk to the restroom, and as I was returning to the table he grabbed my wrist and pulled me over.

"This is Dennis, one of my friends, would you like to hook up with him tonight?" Bob said.

"No offense, buddy, but you're not my type." I jerked my arm back and walked away, which raised an uproar among the men.

When I got back to the table I told Darlene what had happened. She gave me a little chortle, basically ignoring what I had said. To each his or her own I suppose.

"He doesn't mean any harm, they're just getting smashed up there, here have some more Chardonnay." We feasted on our lavish array of food and had our own little party, reminiscing.

Feeling rather inebriated after our last bite of cheesecake, we poured ourselves into the Bentley and back to Bob's we went. Stumbling up the stairs to my little room, I flopped onto the bed, listening vaguely to the snickering in the hallway as Darlene and Bob banged the hallway walls giggling like school children on the way back to his master boudoir.

CHAPTER 26

77 Sunset Strip (Summer 1979)

"You have brains in your head, and feet in your shoes. You can steer in any direction you choose..." Dr. Seuss

We made our way back to Darlene's humble apartment the next morning, hung over as hell.

I thought Westwood was a pretty cool place. I could walk to the downtown area, lots of little shops, and a Peaches record store. Across from Darlene's studio apartment at Sepulveda and Wilshire Boulevards was a cemetery with all white headstones in neat rows.

"What the heck is over there?" I asked her as she sipped her morning coffee.

"Those are the Vietnam war soldiers in the VFW cemetery," she responded.

The sheer number was shocking to me. Those were only the soldiers from this area. There must have been hundreds lined up covering a couple of acres.

"I knew several guys from Plymouth who died in Nam, but until you see something like this you don't really have a sense of how many guys died over there, and in some really horrible ways too," as if there is any good way to die in a war.

As we had our morning coffee I was perusing the local newspaper circular when I came across an ad. It was for a local bar on the strip.

"Hey I'm friends with the band that is playing here tonight? Would you like to go?"

"I don't think so. I have work this week, and the weekend at Bob's was enough for me," was Darlene's answer.

"Okay I think I am going to rent a car for a couple of days just to hang out at some places. I saw a car rental place over in Westwood there. Is there some guest parking I could use?" trying desperately to think ahead through my fog. The parking garage below the apartments was jam packed every time we had pulled into it.

"Sure and you can always park on the street, that sounds like a good idea. Here is a spare key to the house so you can get in whenever you want, don't rely on me being here much, okay?" Darlene offered.

"Of course that's fine, I am pretty self-sufficient, don't worry about me," I reassured my hostess.

That evening I made my way early while it was still daylight to the Starwood nightclub on the strip. Back then you could pull into any corner gas station and get directions for local landmarks, and actually get accurate answers.

My friends the Rockets from Detroit were opening for Spencer Davis Group and another band I don't even recall, but what really struck me were the murals painted on the outside of the building. It was a cinderblock painted gold exterior with the Sales brothers Tony and Hunt depicted on these murals. I knew Soupy had two sons in a band, but I didn't know they were so famous out in L.A.

It was a steamy hot night and the strip went from a calm slight flow of traffic to rush hour status by sundown. It was my first time having sushi and I stood in line with some very trendy L.A. hipster people. Their attire was disco chic to Madonnaesque, colorful garb, glitz and glamour. The vibe was very different, though. Maybe it was the salt air, but people in general were different than Detroiters. Wanting desperately to fit in, I had my black vinyl pants on, some sort of striped shirt and vest combo, with a scarf tied around my thick brown hair.

The club was dimly lit with black walls. It had a cavernous feeling, smelling of stale beer and cigarettes. In the corner there was a raised stage with huge spotlights trained on it. I got myself a drink and looked around for a familiar face. Near the restroom doors I saw Johnny B. Badanjek.

"Hey B. it's me Christine...from Detroit," I exclaimed and threw my arms around his neck.

"Oh ya, what are you doin' here?" he grinned. Johnny B. was about as laid back as any man could be without falling asleep. Mr. Super casual, the B. man.

"Where's Jimmy?"

"He is warming up back stage, go say 'Hi'."

I made my way through the crowd who were moving to the extraordinarily loud music en masse. Upstairs were several little rooms and I simply followed that familiar Gibson guitar sound to one of the rooms and poked my head in.

"Hey Jimmy! I was out here in L.A. and thought I would check you guys out," I said.

"Oh wow," he came over and gave me a hug. then said he had to prepare and I should go find a spot to watch the set.

The Rockets came on stage after sufficient anxiety had built up in the crowd. They brought the house down. Songs like, 'Turn Up The Radio' and Fleetwood Mac's song 'Oh Well' had people dancing, cheering, and swooning.

British rocker Spencer Davis with 'Gimme Some Lovin' and 'I'm A Man' fit the bill just right providing great synergy with the Rockets. I cannot recall if Steve Winwood was there that particular night, but he most likely was.

Good ole Spencer made himself a prominent figure after his set, when he crashed into our little Rockets dressing room announcing that he had arrived and passed out in the middle of the floor. Everyone jumped to his assistance and gathered him up. He acted as if nothing had happened and started carrying on conversations with everybody in the room including me. The tiny space was filled with Hollywood radio personalities, newspaper people, throngs of groupies, and people providing the drugs.

"So, we are doing this coastal tour this week, but we are ending up at this huge festival called 'Day On The Green' up in Oakland, why don't you come?" suggested Jimmy during the course of the night's festivities.

"Oh man that sounds great, I'm staying with this chick who doesn't really like the rock and roll scene or partying much, but I'll ask."

"Well try to make it, we'll be back in L.A. after that, and my son is coming into town for a while. I can see you then if not in Oakland," Jim offered. I had not known Jimmy McCarty as a family man before, and began looking at him in a different light.

CHAPTER 27

California Coasting
(July 4ᵗʰ 1979)

"Never mistake motion for action..." **Ernest Hemingway**

After much cajoling, I convinced Darlene that we should spend the following weekend in Oakland, California. We were personally invited backstage, and one of her favorite bands, 'Journey' was the headliner. She was still apathetic about the entire adventure and didn't want to drive that far.

"Fine, I'll drive your car, and you can just chill out, and sleep or whatever. I have driven this coastline before with my husband when we came through here," I said, trying to sound confident.

We climbed over the doors of her bright yellow Corvette Stingray convertible and slid into the black bucket seats. The engine revved up with the power of a bazillion horses, and off we went.

Sunshine, ocean breezes, early morning lack of traffic what could be better than that? I will tell you what could be better, a speedometer that worked.

"Hey, how fast do you think we are going Darlene?" I noticed I had no concept in that car.

"I just keep up with the semis. They are usually watching their speed," Darlene said as I opened her up on an empty clear stretch of road.

"Oh my god I have never driven anything like this. My old boyfriend Dave from Northville had one, but he never let me drive it. This is really crazy," I exclaimed with the glee of a child at Christmas.

Cruising right along, going slightly faster than most of the trucks, I began to tell Darlene about the Rockets band members so she would know them once we met up with the guys. Just then the red bubble of death appeared in my rearview mirror.

"Son of a bitch we are getting pulled over!" I yelled at Darlene.

"Shit, just be cool. California cops don't mess around. Don't tell him about the speedometer or he will give us a ticket for that too," she said.

"License and registration," he said, peering over his mirror sunglasses. Great just like cool hand Luke.

"Do you know how fast you were going?"

"Uh, no not really," I admitted.

"Well I clocked you at 83 mph young lady, you need to slow it down," he said .

He promptly came back and said, "You can pay this right here or you can mail it in."

"I will mail it in. I don't have much money on me," my voice was audibly shaking.

"All right then. Here you are. Slow this thing down," his dad voice was in high gear.

We crept the rest of the way into San Francisco. A stop for coffee helped us shake off the early morning blues as we crossed the Oakland Bridge full of seagulls swooping and cawing. Somehow we found our way to the stadium. It was still early by rock and roll standards, maybe 10 or 11 am, as we parked the car by the back stage gate. We made our way, strutting our stuff, and looking like we owned the place. I was sporting a white flouncy gauze shirt, jeans, with a long scarf, and a flippity, floppity hat. We walked up to the backstage gate.

The sentry was a very large bouncer-type guy. I explained that we were with the Rockets from Detroit. He looked over his list, and I was actually on it. He looked skeptically at me as we marched proudly through the layers of security guards. There was no inspection of bags, metal detectors, or armed security back then.

The back stage area looked like a wagon train of white trailers . In front of each trailer lay a Persian rug of various patterns. The trailers were marked in order of appearance on the stage with Journey's trailer being the closest. In the center, were round patio tables with Cinzano umbrellas shading the diners. Kraft services (and this was the first time I had seen Kraft services...love them) was set up like a big cantina on one end, and opposite that was a basketball court and a volleyball court complete with AstroTurf.

Suddenly I felt right at home, when a group of clowns dressed in mostly Aguste and whiteface were running around. If I didn't mention it before I will now, my father was a tramp, clown that is, with the Shriners.

The theme for the day ala Bill Graham productions was "bring in the clowns". The moment was magical, and surreal for me. We found the Rockets' trailer. Once inside I went about greeting everyone, and introducing them to Darlene. My popularity suddenly grew to epic proportions when they saw her. They had to pick all of their jaws up off the floor, and naturally David the lead singer tried to scoop her up first.

Jimmy came over to me and gave me a big kiss, "Good to see ya darlin' glad you could make it, go out and help yourselves to anything you want, they even have breakfast out still if you haven't eaten," he offered.

"We are opening the show so we have to get on stage right now and sound check, set up, all that stuff," he said.

We made our way outside. As a warm breeze tossed my hat to one side, I spotted Journey and some members of Thin Lizzy a relatively new band from Dublin who had a hit called, 'The Boys Are Back in Town.' Charlie Martin would always sing his own version, "the boys are black and brown." Thin Lizzy had formed in the year of my high school graduation, 1969.

"I think I should pace myself today and drink white wine spritzers, what are you having?" I asked Darlene as we stood in front of the open bar next to Kraft services.

"That sounds good. I'll do that too," Darlene answered, scanning the tables with a scrutinizing eye.

"Let's go check out the stage," I said as I sucked down my first drink of the day.

As we walked to the other end, I glanced up, and there in front of me was a beanpole of a man, not very tall, dressed all in black with sunglasses on and a beret on his head. I recognized him right away, Peter Wolf, the front man for the J. Geils Band.

"Hello there, I'm glad to see Detroit is being represented today," I said to him.

"Ya me too," he looked over the top of his glasses, as we walked by.

"Who was that?" Darlene said.

I told her.

"I cannot wait to see them," I added. "This is going to be a great day."

My womanly intuition was kicking in.

When we reached the steps up to the darkened stage, black curtains flanked the back and sides in order for the lighting to be affective. They furled in the wind as if attached to some pirate ship, sans skull and cross bones.

Looking out over the sea of people that were gathering, some of the stands were filling up, and perhaps half of the stadium ground was being staked out by concert goers. The Rockets blasted 'Turn Up The Radio' and the crowd went crazy.

Following their set, we wandered back to the trailer for the usual, *how do you think the set went?*

"I could hear you just fine, but it does suck to be the first act, everyone checking your sound to improve the quality of theirs," I empathized.

David had some drugs lined up so he started partying. Jimmy and Johnny B. had some old friends to visit, and the other band members went their own way, which left Darlene and me to fend for ourselves the rest of the day. For the most part we drank, ate, wandered around, sang songs with bands warming up in their trailers, and picked out which people were legitimate radio and promotion people, and which ones were the drug dealers.

Promo guys were easy. They were all dressed as clowns. At some point during the afternoon Jimmy called me over to one of the clowns.

"Bill Graham this is Rosie from Detroit," Jimmy McCarty had just introduced me to one of the biggest guys in the industry. We exchanged small talk, I told him I was a singer too, and he said to send him a demo. He excused himself wishing me a good time, and off he went. Many years later, he would appear in the movie 'Apocalypse Now' landing on the helicopter pad to entertain the troops. We would also meet again backstage at a Pine Knob Santana concert.

Now looking around, it appeared the Kraft services kitchen had opened and lunch was being served. The aroma of fresh shrimp and barbeque wafted through the air, and we decided to sit down and eat with everyone else. We got in line and there in a white three-piece suit with an ascot around his neck,was Eddie Money whispering sweet nothings in Darlene's ear. He was clearly enamored, spurred on by alcohol I'm certain, and he would not leave her alone. Darlene, on the other hand, wanted nothing to do with any of these people. She was tolerant at best. Back then Eddie was very handsome with shoulder length brown hair, flashing eyes and a baby-face. He beamed from ear to ear when he was around Zsa Zsa. I had died and gone to rock and roll heaven. Heaven was filled with rock stars and clowns. This could not have been a better day.

After lunch, I went over to the basketball court to shoot some hoops. I had been on the junior high girls' team, but we were only allowed to play half court, and so my true skills were never quite developed. If I made one of those shots my day would have been perfect. However, after close to 100 attempts, I attracted the attention of Phil Lynott of Thin Lizzy. He came up and asked if he could have a go at it.

"Sure, go ahead. I don't want to play horse though, because you will kill me."

"Well, you know we don't play this sport in my country," he said.

"Never the less, you are a very tall guy, and I am a short chick, da...." I said.

He took shot after shot, and he wasn't doing any better than I was. The boys were back in town, but clearly not the basketball team.

"Here let me try again," I suggested.

We kept missing the basket. After a while, we were laughing so hard we were almost rolling on the turf. Our grandmothers could have done better. I laughed until tears were running down my face. Then we both shrugged and walked away.

I didn't go out to see the UFO set and just caught the tail end of Nazareth. They were a heavy metal rock band from Scotland and had many big UK connections, with 'Hair of the Dog' being one of their big hits.

Meanwhile, the Rockets were really partying heavily, Dave Gilbert had hooked up with several pie-eyed groupies and was walking around backstage. Jimmy and B mostly stuck to the trailer or trading guitar licks with some of the legends who were present. Many of San Francisco musicians who were not performing that day showed up back stage. Besides Eddie Money, someone said Paul Kantner and some of the Starship members were there, and perhaps some of Carlos Santana's group.

The afternoon turned into evening with the sun setting slowly in the west with a giant orange and pink glow. There is nothing like a California sunset. Being slightly full of wine spritzers, with one emotional eruption after another, I was fading fast.

Journey came on last and blew the crowd away. I noticed the throng of concert goers had grown immense.

"Come on, let's go up on stage and watch the show," said Jimmy coming out of the trailer and putting his long lanky arms around Darlene and me. We tagged along, and the rush of it all finally hit me. Here I am in a place I thought I would only dream of, with a man I adore, listening to perfect music.

That night we trundled off to the Rockets' motel across the bridge, in a "mom and pop" strip of white-painted compartments strung together with an office at the end and a neon sign blinking on and off with some letters burned out. "The Oass" not Oasis. Jimmy and I shacked up in one room, Johnny B said Darlene could have one of the beds in his room, and being the absolute gentleman he was (since they had not made a connection that day) Bee proclaimed,

"And I will leave you alone, promise."

The following morning Darlene and I climbed into the canary-colored Corvette and headed down the road. This time she drove.

"I am meeting up with Jimmy later today. Guess where he's taking me?" I said to Darlene.

"Well as if I could ever guess, where?"

"The Colonies."

"No. Malibu?"

"Who the hell does he know there?"

"I don't know some old producer guy who is famous for creating the Charlie's Angels pilot or something."

"That should be fun, I have got to get into work. They are going to think I have quit or something,"

"I guess he is bringing his son, Dylan, who is four. The only catch is I have to pretend I am just a friend, no sneaking away or obvious signs of affection in front of the kid. Very strict rule," I added.

"Well, have a good time. How can you not, Malibu by the ocean doesn't get any better," Darlene smiled her beautiful smile and dropped me off at the apartment door.

When Jimmy picked me up in his burgundy Chevy Malibu rental car, Dylan was next to him in the front seat. He opened the back door for me.

"Hi Dylan, I'm your Dad's friend Chris."

"Hi."

"Are you excited about today?"

"Ya."

Man of many words, like his father. I chattered on in the backseat leaning over the two bucket seats in the front of their rental car. There were no seatbelts then, so we were jostled about as we wound around Highway I on our way to Malibu. Johnny B was along for the ride, and sat quietly sunken in the seat with his head near the window. Just as the waves were crashing against the shoreline, 'My Sharona' by the Knack came blasting over the air waves, and we sang along. Even Dylan chimed in.

We drove past local surfers. The ocean waves looked like they were topped with whipped cream. The austere cliffs rose up on the opposite side of the highway.

Passing Alice's Restaurant, and the pier, we finally reached the colonies and were greeted by the uniformed security gatekeeper, acting as sentry to the carefully guarded community.

We turned opposite Darlene's boyfriend's house, past Cher's white ode to Egypt, and other houses all of which had diverse, unique styles. We came upon a rather non-descript Cape Cod that could have been anywhere in the Midwest or New England.

"Here we are, Ivan's house," Jim skidded the car across the gravel drive.

The stairway to the upstairs apartment was lined with black bowls with blue crystal lobelia spilling out of them. The tiny blue flowers blowing in the ocean breeze soon became my favorite flower to plant at my own home each year. The sound of the surf was amplified when we entered through a glass sliding door to greet our host.

Jimmy introduced us to the old man wearing glasses. Ivan was taller than me, but not by much, paunchy, with salt and pepper hair and a balding dome.

Johnny B. was next to greet our host as if they were long lost friends. Then he proceeded to make himself at home.

"This guy knows everybody in the world," Jimmy hugged Ivan's shoulders with one long arm.

"And now he knows me," I said, which got a chuckle out of the old coot.

CALIFORNIA COASTING (JULY 4TH 1979)

"How about some cocktails, make yourselves at home, there's some food in the fridge, just help yourself to whatever you find. I have a bit of work to finish up and then I'll join you," Mr. Ivan Goff said as he returned to his study.

I made myself a vodka and tonic with fresh lime while Dylan and Jimmy ran out to the beach. In the bathroom across from the toilet were pictures of JFK and Ivan, Winston Churchill and Ivan, movie stars and Ivan adorning every inch of one wall. Strange place for such pictures, I thought, take your shit while contemplating all of these world-renowned people.

I joined the beach crowd romping in the Pacific. Johnny was playing some great tunes on the RCA Victor turntable in one corner of the patio (?). Once again, I was having a blessed day.

The couple next door came over and introduced themselves, their names escape me, but they were teenagers and invited me over to see their parents' house.

I mentioned that there was a lot of architectural diversity in the neighborhood. "People just kind of do whatever floats their boat, don't they?"

On the right side of this house, there was an Olympic size pool and contemporary, modern, expensive furniture inside. I was just checking the pool temperature when the young man said, "Hey I have some great monkey paw herb, want to try it?"

"Why not, I enjoy the herb now and then," I said.

We got so annihilated I was almost hallucinating. Along with the rum and cokes, I was feeling alright.

"I better be getting back, my boyfriend is going to wonder where I am," I said as I made my way to the beach door several hours later.

Our host had finished his work. He danced around the living room and grabbed me to dance with him. I joined in happily. Dylan was playing outside. Jimmy turned around in a swivel chair, took my hand, and pulled me down into his lap, laying a big old French kiss on my mouth.

"I thought we were not going to display affection," I said, with a smirk.

"We aren't. That was just a reminder of what you're missing today," he said as he got up to forage for food in the kitchen.

"Well, if he's not going to enjoy such a lovely young thing, then I will," offered Ivan who began twirling me around to some old Motown song.

We danced, drank, and sang the whole afternoon away. Before I knew it the sun was setting on our little celebration of life, and it was time to get Dylan home, and me as well.

"Nice to meet you, Ivan," I said as I walked barefoot to the car carrying my sandals, still wearing a bathing suit covered with a t-shirt.

"Nice to meet you, come back any time, I am always here," he said.

I slept all the way back to Westwood. Jimmy dropped me off at Darlene's and said,

"See ya in Detroit." That was the end of my L.A. adventure.

CHAPTER 26

Meanwhile Back in Detroit (1980)

"Action may not always bring happiness; but there is no happiness without action...." Benjamin Disraeli

Fast forward to the 1980's. John Lennon was assassinated. I cried through my birthday, which was the same week. The following year, Hinckley attempted the assassination of Ronald Reagan, the video game PAC MAN was released, and everyone in the world was watching the royal wedding. Women were finally being recognized as credible enough to hold an appointment to the Supreme Court, and I was trying to hold my little family together and still make a living at the restaurant. In between baking cupcakes for the school bake sale, I was still chasing musicians around town.

In my world there was always something else going on. Something quite separate from all the other facets. I was trying to recapture my youth, while playing the responsible adult parent. Always defining myself by whatever band I happened to be with at the time, in a vain attempt to recapture my lost youth.

The early Pine Knob season was exciting as always, spring had sprung, I was young, and life was full of possibilities. John Denver was the opening act that year and of course they stayed at the Northfield Hilton. That was the year I met Bernie Wyckoff, John's road manager. He was tall handsome and gentle, and didn't look at all like a Bernie. He was a good lover and patient with me, always available to me, and kind, whenever they were in town. Very sweet man.

One late evening in May, a group of eight or so John Denver people came into Charley's. Most of the dinner crowd had cleared out by then, just a few stragglers, women who the men were attempting to lure into bed and playing hard to get, businessmen on the road from EDS, and Kmart Corporation, or people just too drunk to know it is time to decamp.

John's group sat at the Wanderer table right at the front of the main dining room. I was their server that night, and John was pounding tequila shots and ordering up oysters, clams and shrimp like he was Neptune himself commanding the ocean.

"Let's have some Dom Perignon," John instructed me, "bring about four bottles to start," he instructed me, which delighted everyone at the table. Even back then Dom was about $90 per bottle, the most expensive champagne we carried.

He was a much bigger partier than I expected him to be. As I walked past him, he grabbed my wrist and pulled me down onto his lap. Giggling like a school girl, I played along.

"So have you ever had an oyster on the half shell?" he said.

"Sure I have, it's prerequisite for working here," I flirted back, moving my face two inches from his.

"Okay then, but you haven't had an oyster my way." He squirted lemons generously over the frozen plate of iced oysters, then gave each a dab of cocktail sauce and horseradish. Preparing a shot of tequila and some crackers next to the plate.

"Okay follow me, do what I do," he said, lifting the mouthful of mollusk up to his mouth and slowly slipping it in.

"Now take it into your mouth," he said hanging on my every move, "now chew a couple of times mixing the flavors."

"Ah!" he exclaimed shooting the tequila. "Now you."

"I never drink on the job."

"You have to have the whole experience," he insisted.

"All right then," I said, and I reluctantly slugged back the Jose Cuervo.

"Now take a bite of oyster cracker," as I lifted the cracker to my mouth he grabbed the back of my head and kissed me long and hard.

We had the attention of all the late night diners by then, and the room lit up with applause. I stood up and took a bow, while the whole table laughed uproariously. Having learned the name of the table, which was named after a ship, not the Dion song, they started singing the Dion song.

"'Oh, well I'm the kind of guy who'll never settle down. I'm never in one place, I roam from town to town," they all sang. What a fun night that was, and of course I ended up with Bernie, who picked up the tab, and tipped me very generously, while the rest of them crawled back to their hotel rooms arm in arm singing. John always made certain I had concert tickets and passes waiting for me whenever they played Detroit.

Tom Petty and company had played at the beginning of June. There was a different tone around the band that year, so I sent TP a handwritten letter via his record company saying how much I loved him, and the music, and I hope he didn't lose his feeling or style for what had brought him success thus far. I wanted him to remain true to his original style and not make any drastic departure from what made everyone fall in love with his music.

My friends Jackson Browne and David Lindley were there for the 4th of July celebration. We all enjoyed watching the fireworks from backstage, which were being set off on top of the ski slope. They were absolutely glorious and made the patriot in me soar with pride.

Dan Aykroyd and John Belushi aka Jake and Elwood, had formed the Blues Brothers Band. Riding on the coattails of their successful movie they did a string of concerts that year.

Now I had no idea how crazed their fans could be until they stayed at the Northfield Hilton next to the Crab. Working the two nights they played Pine Knob I made fantastic money. I witnessed screaming girls, women hanging over the balconies to flash the band, convertible cars, limousines. It was just like an Academy Award night with the red carpet leading to the front door of the hotel. Screaming fans were flying around the circle drive yelling and blasting Blues Brothers songs on the radios. It looked like something out of Caligula, one big drunken hotel party.

During that same year another life changing event happened. I met Carlos Santana and company, and the man my daughters called "Messy Head". His name was Chris Becker, and we became close friends with benefits. He was not a handsome man by most standards. His thick, black, wiry hair stuck straight up most of the time, and his pop eyes were a particularly noticeable feature. There was barely anything on his body resembling a muscle. He was tall and lanky, but in some obscure way I found him attractive.

Nothing ever developed out of our relationship, he had a girlfriend back in San Francisco living on a house boat, but we were good friends for many years. He had been my connection to many celebrities.

Each year when Santana came to Detroit a wonderful couple, let's call them Mike and Peggy, because I can't remember their real names, would have us all over for a backyard barbeque at their house on Upper Straits Lake. The house was large enough to accommodate everyone, two stories with a walkout, and we were welcomed to partake in volleyball, swimming, boating, food, friends and good times, underneath the weeping willows that surrounded the yard. "Killer" was their road manager. He had wild curly hair and John Lennon glasses. Each time he would make his famous lemon herb salmon wrapped in foil for all thirty or more of us. Corn on the cob would be roasting and the aromas of all this lifted through the air.

Mike organized the volleyball and boat tours, while Peggy, the attentive hostess, made certain our drinks didn't run out. You could smell that party for miles around, not to mention the cannabis. It was a family affair, and something my children thoroughly enjoyed every year. One time, I glanced over at my 11-year-old daughter on a chaise lounge next to Carlos himself carrying on a lengthy conversation.

"What were you and Carlos talking about for so long? I asked Chrisanna later. "He was asking me about school, and if I liked his music, and would I come out to the shows. He was really nice mom, is he married?"

My girls were constant matchmakers for me. They just wanted me to leave all of my options open. Those were some hot summer nights.

Kenny Loggins played with my old friend Rick Roberts and Firefall that year. I got to catch the show but never connected with Rick again. Later that night at the Northfield Hilton as I walked through the hallway, Kenny and his wife snuck out for late night snacks at Denny's. I passed them hiding in one of the doorway cubicles with their carryout Styrofoam boxes like thieves, and I greeted them.

Next on the roster that year was the Rockets followed by four nights of the J. Geils Band. Sometime during that week with the Beach Boys in the hotel, Santana, and some other band from California someone coined the phrase, "this is like the Hotel California", making a reference to the Eagles song.One night Diana Ross walked into the restaurant. She was playing for four days at Pine Knob, and came in slightly ahead of schedule. All the wait staff were upstairs leaning over the brass bar railing overlooking the downstairs lounge when she came in. She wore a white jumpsuit and a large brimmed white hat over all of that gorgeously wild hair. We called her name and she slowly lifted her head and waved to us. There are a select few women that have really made a lasting impression on me, but she certainly is one of them.

Another star struck moment for me was waiting on Gina Lollobrigida. She arrived with an entourage of ten one night wearing a long red satin evening gown. I was her server. She could not have been nicer, and is one of the only people I have ever asked for an autograph. A true iconic bombshell of the 1950's and 60's. As little girls, my next door neighbor and I would giggle over her costumes, which wrapped around her breasts exposing everything but the nipples, in magazines like *Life* or *Look*.

Bob Seger and the Silver Bullet Band played three nights that season with Catfish Hodge, one of the famous Hodge brothers. All legends in the Detroit area. I was welcomed slightly less than before by Punch and company since my break up with Charlie, but he still gave my kids and me some tickets to take in a show or two.

REO Speedwagon came into town a few weeks later and that's when I became friendly with Neal Doughty. One of their crew had given me a pass for the show. Neal and I locked eyes immediately over the food table back stage, consummating our passion that night after the Pine Knob show.

He was shy, yet appealing. In a way he reminded me of Michael J. Pollard of 'Bonnie and Clyde' fame,but when I mentioned that to him once he was seriously insulted. He didn't believe that I thought Michael J. Pollard was very sexy. Neal and I would get together several times, in several different cities. Kevin Cronin struck me as quite a character. Aside from Bonnie Raitt, I don't believe I have ever met a faster talker. Give him some white lines and he could chatter on for days.

One bleak and rather chilling December, Neal asked me to come out to the show in Ann Arbor at the University of Michigan stadium. That was big time. They were promoting their new album 'High Infidelity'. Driving through snow and lousy weather for forty miles, I showed up at the hotel around four in the afternoon, and went to the front desk. Back then everyone on the road used crazy names like Mickey Mouse and Donald Duck. Having a lapse in memory that day I forgot Neal's fake name, so I had the clerk ring his room. He came down to fetch me and we snuggled all the way back to the room and played hide the sausage for about an hour before the gig. There is really nothing significant I can remember about our love making except for the feeling that he couldn't really let go with me and be himself, as if there was someone at home he was saving the true emotional lust for. It made me feel excluded and not really even thought of as a friend.

The show was great, one of the best I had seen, but the guitar player Gary Richrath happened to be in a fight with Kevin, because he was fucked up on whatever drug of the day, heroin or something else. Backstage Kevin was laying into him. Gary was struggling to walk a straight line.

"Look at you man...what have you been doing? You can hardly stand up."

"I am getting it together man...I will be ok," Gary reassured him staggering toward the stage stairs.

"Come on Christine this is band shit, let's go find you a spot," Neal evaded the entire scene and took me by the hand.

Thankfully he did get it together and the show went on without a hitch. They made their peace after the show at a huge party in one of the Chrysler stadium suites. There was a live local band, the place was decorated for the holiday, and all of the Detroit radio celebrities were there. There must have been a hundred people there after the show, quite the gathering. Having one too many drinks that night, Neal and I left early and made our way back to the hotel for some more mad and passionless love making. We smoked a joint that I had found at the party, and got completely stoned out of our minds. That was the last time I was with him.

New to the music scene were the Cars. Their runaway successful album propelled them to the top of the charts, and I was crazy excited to see them. They played Pine Knob with a group called Martha and the Motels, who would become my friends, and invite me to come backstage to their concerts whenever they were in town. I was in Ann Arbor the next time I ran into the Motels in a bar called "Chances Art" on Liberty Street. As it turned out the women of rock and roll were for the most part, nicer to me than the men. Debbie Harry, Pat Benatar, Heart, and Martha were all very cordial, welcoming, young women. There was no lovely lesbian sex, they were just stand up kind women.

CHAPTER 27

Moving with the Groovin' and Smoozin' (1980)

I believe when life gives you lemons you should make lemon-ade, and try to find someone who life has given vodka and have a party".....Ron White

The restaurant changed atmosphere and personnel with each mana-gerial move. During this time it was a rather masculine lady named Paulette, whose obedient husband and son also worked there.

One day I strolled into the restaurant early to open the place wearing black and whites, my bow tie hanging down, the smell of fish chowder hung in the air. Kenny the bartender stood by the ornate ce-ment birdbath filling it with superior bottles of wine.

"Hey, you better look out. Paulette is on the war path and she is looking for you," he said.

"What the heck did I do?" Dread filled me. As I entered the kitch-en I found Paulette ranting and raving at the cooks on the line.

"Meet me on table 85 in ten minutes," she shouted at me like the drill sergeant she was.

I made my way to the very back to booth number 85. Still contem-plating my demise, I nervously tapped my fingers on the table. Paulette came storming around the copper bar and along the narrow passage toward me, sliding in across from me.

"Now you are probably wondering what we are going to talk about?"

"Well yes, I don't have a clue."

"It's my opinion that you are wearing too much make up."

Now I had not changed the colors or method of my application of makeup since I started there four years earlier. Eye shadow, eyeliner, mascara, no powder, no fake lashes, no painted in eyebrows. "Wow, really, I thought it was something serious."

"It is serious you look like a slut, okay, change it."

"Well, all right then," I said. I was in shock.

Some managers greeted the musicians I hung out with more hospitably than others. On that particular night following the "you are a slut" conversation, Paulette told me to bring over whoever I wanted, she felt like having a party.

The last dinner stragglers had left the lounge and the door with the mermaid painted on it was shut and locked. The lights were dimmed in the dining room. Bob Seeley had played the last note, and I called my friends to come on over to the Hilton.

Paulette the restaurant manager opened the walk-in freezer, supplying pounds of shrimp, crab, lobsters, and salads. We found some cheesecakes and chocolate Decadence desserts, and brought them out. We loaded the push carts with food and wine, dinner plates, and opened the service bar. There was Joe Walsh, Waddy Watchel, Russ Kunkel and my acquaintance from the Crosby, Stills and Nash band, Chocolate. All in all about ten others from two or three bands staying in the hotel at one time, all at the beggars banquet fit for a king.

Paulette sat at the head of the table, and welcomed all the musicians. It was a good night. It certainly earned me some brownie points in the music world, and little by little my reputation grew. It is a much smaller world than anyone would ever guess. Everyone is fair game as far as George "Chocolate" Perry thought, and so, despite being Stephen Stills' girl, we ended up together that night and became good friends for some years.

Summer was coming to an end. Johnny Mathis and Henry Mancini were performing at Meadowbrook and I had the pleasure of being Johnny's server each night following the shows. He had always been one of my favorite singers. He would come in alone, order his favorite gazpacho, and quietly go back to the hotel as if he were a nonentity.

In those days, gay men unless they were named Liberace, kept their sexuality under wraps, although it was blatantly obvious. Henry Mancini and about twelve other men would dine together at the Captain's table, completely unabashed. I am so glad times have changed and not many are afraid of coming out the way they used to be.

When Sha Na Na came to town that August it was hot steamy and sexually driven. Jocko and I rekindled our passion for each other over cocktails at a nearby club down Crooks Road, and then went back to the hotel for a fling.

Some of my favorite people and bands were finishing out the Pine Knob season that year. Bob Seger and the Silver Bullet Band had several nights, REO Speedwagon, the Cars with their opening band the Motels with my buddy Martha.

At the end of the August the Toledo Speedway Jam was about to happen. A willing accomplice, I dragged my friend "Z" along to catch some sizzling asphalt music. Normally this was the home for Arca stock car racing, but not that day.

The band from Boston, The J. Geils Band was going to be the headliner. I had not seen them since our meeting in Oakland, California. It was an opportunity to get my motor city breakdown on.

My connection that day was Howard Leese of Heart. Howard and I had met when the band played Pine Knob for the first time. We also had an encounter in downtown Detroit the previous winter at a party with the Kinks at the top of the Pontchartrain Hotel. Ray Davies was taller than I thought he would be.

Ann and Nancy, the Wilson sisters, had been together for some time, Howard had transitioned from session player to lead guitar. He had a great stage look, lanky physique, blondish-brown hair that fell in cascading ringlets to his shoulders, and a fairly fashionable dresser. He was quiet and reserved, but somehow we became a couple for the remainder of that summer.

Z and I dressed up in our best groupie garb, hats, scarves, jewelry, full on make-up, and ready for anything attitudes. Jumping in my AMC Pacer space car we headed south on I-75 toward Ohio. Already a sultry, summer, the asphalt was so hot you could fry an egg on it. I lit up a True blue cigarette and Z lit up a joint, looking at each other saying, "Never too early never too late," and we were on our way. Arriving in Toledo at the speedway, we found our way across a large expanse of parking lot to the back gate.

"Who are we meeting here again?" Z asked.

"Well it is Howard Leese from the Heart band you know they do that song, 'Straight On' for you," and I sang a few bars for her in my ala Ann Wilson rock girl voice. It was from the 'Bebe La Strange' album which they were promoting.

"Oh ya that is so hot this summer, I have heard it everywhere," as we reached the guardian of the gate with his clipboard.

"Good morning ladies, what can I do for you?" he queried.

"My name should be on the list Rosie, or Christine, with the Heart group plus one," I informed him in my most charming demeanor.

"Here you are," and he handed over two stick on passes to access everywhere for the day. We peeled off the backs and stuck them in strategic places.

"Oh my god, Z, these are all access, I can't believe it, we can have a blast, but you have to listen to me, and follow my lead, so we don't get kicked out of here, got me?" I educated her to the difference and variety of acceptance in certain areas. My friend had a way of being star struck and showing her exuberance to the point of embarrassment at times. Thinking back, if I was a true friend I wouldn't have thought that way.

Outside of the venue people were flocking to the gates carrying coolers full of beer, only to find out they were not allowed in. For only $15 one could witness some great music, but you had to purchase the venue's beer. Good old Belkin Productions. Masses of people began guzzling beers at 10am in the morning and offering up their beer to us rather than waste it in a hot car all day. We gratefully declined and went on our merry way.

Roadies were scurrying madly about the place, Kraft services was setting up food and coolers full of a variety of beverages, and tables to sit around with red and white checked tablecloths.

The familiar strains of "Two Tickets To Paradise" got the crowd rolling and the party had started. After a heart pumping set, Eddie came running off the stage, dripping with sweat, tie undone, and in his New York accent shouted, "Get me a fucking towel!" One of the crew complied, and as he mopped his saturated face, he ran back up the stairs to the stage. Everyone went crazy. As the busses pulled in through the back gate and circled around, I recognized the Heart bus and ran over to greet Howard.

The sisters were as fiery as the day was hot, and ignored my greeting as they stepped down from their carriage. Howard was a little bit friendlier, putting his arm around me and laying a big old kiss on my cheek.

"We had a long weary road trip last night, don't mind them, and then they were fighting with everyone," he offered in compensation.

"I understand that's cool," I said.

I introduced him to Z.

"How long have you been here?"

"We just got here in time to see the first act, not too long, we had to work last night, so this is super early in the morning for us," I gave him one of my wide-eyed looks.

"Well make yourself at home. We have to get dressed and warm up and I will see you later. We're at the Holiday Inn so come on over after the show, okay?" He dashed after the rest of the group holding his wardrobe.

We strolled around the venue, checking out people, slugging some brews, and generally trying to stay cool. The aroma of cannabis wafted through the air and Z and I looked at each other and smiled, "Good idea," she said, and we found a semi secluded place to light up.

Having a serious raging munchie attack we were given Kraft food services tickets by one of the road crew. One would think we had never seen food before. Pure gluttony prevailed.

The final bus pulled in through the gates and out strolled the Geils band entourage. As I walked toward Peter he gave me that same gunslinger, stopped dead in his tracks pose, he gave me in Oakland.

"Hey, Pete, how's it going?" I said as he smiled at me. Then Jim Donnelly their road manager stepped off the bus exclaiming, "Could it be any fucking hotter....hey what are you doing here?" when he saw me standing there.

"We thought we would come down here for the day, a day tripper from Detroit to say howdy, and give you a big old Detroit welcome to Toledo." I gave him a smartass curtsy, finger under my chin.

"Cool, let me get the guys settled in and we can talk," he said as he walked away.

Jim came back to have a drink with me several minutes later, and said they were heading up to Castle Farms in Charlevoix. Would I like to come up?

"Of course I would love to, the kids are with their father for the rest of the weekend, where can I stay?"

"We are going up for the show and driving straight back to the airport."

"Ok, then I will just drive up there during the day tomorrow because I can't spring for a hotel or anything."

"You could stay with one of us."

"That's fine, I will be much more fresh with a good night's sleep after all this," I said and bid him farewell after he had shared a couple of spoonfuls with me under the tablecloth.

Following the show late afternoon, Z and I headed for the hotel where Heart was staying to say good-bye to Howard before hitting the road to Detroit. Upon entering the lobby, Ann Wilson was clipping through the lobby at a quickened pace.

"Hello Ann, great show today, really hot wasn't it," I said.

"Ya, hi there, thanks," and on she went toward the bar.

"Stay here, Z, I have to talk to Howard for a bit." I gave her $5 to get a couple of drinks while she waited.

Making my way to his room I knocked gingerly on the door. I could hear the television in the background. Howard flung open the door,

"I didn't think you were coming."

"I am a woman of my word," as I finished undressing his half dressed body.

We attacked each other ravenously since his erection was way ahead of where I was. Our love making was never fabulous, but passionate none the less, and I did think he was a good kisser, which to me was everything. It's always in his kiss. That tryst lasted about an hour, and the elevator took me away from him in a split second. The Heart band was on the road again.

When I got home that night I decided that I should sew something to wear up north. I had some black taffeta, and faux silk in purple and chartreuse. Just like the fairy godmother in Cinderella I magically whipped together a wraparound dress in black, and a cropped purple jacket with green lining like it was a dream. My rock and roll dream was encapsulating and haunting. I wanted to be around the music, I wanted to make the music, and I wanted to be an influence and muse for the musicians, and make them happy whether it was my witty repartee or the great sex we would have.

The drive up to Charlevoix took about four plus hours, so there was plenty of time for me to fantasize about Peter Wolf, Seth Justman, and company. Some weed for the road helped pass the time as I recalled how romantic the castle is. I pictured my men in tights like Robin Hood, and suits of amour jousting for their maiden's hand while steins of beer crashed together in merriment.

Pulling up to the familiar gates, I drove right in without being stopped. Sound check was going down and it was "nothin' but a party, nothin' but a house party". The faithful followers of the band showed up and we all hugged it out and greeted each other.

Dusk was soon upon us. We enjoyed a beautiful buffet of food and drink while they warmed up. In the meantime they did whatever it is they needed to do to prepare for the stage. Some drugs, some singing, some arguing.

We all took our spots for the show as a most exuberant crowd cheered. The chorus of the first song, and the soft summer breeze lifted the words "I just can't wait," out over their heads and the tree-tops. Closing with 'First I Look at the Purse' the band brought down the house.

Some heavy duty partying followed the show backstage with Jim making certain everyone was "taken care of" in the way of drugs and drinks, including the radio personalities and the affluent up north people who had paid their way into the inner sanctum of Geilshood.

Danny, always the gentleman, dressed in silk suit and tie with a nice hat, came up to chat with a group of us, while Pete ran in and out of the room, and Seth stood quietly to the side listening to people fill his ear with their idle chatter.

Soon it was time to head back to the Detroit airport hotel. My car was to follow the bus, and several others were behind me in our caravan. The diesel stench of carbon monoxide filled my lungs for the long journey back to Detroit, and I wondered if they were trying to kill me.

When we arrived at the hotel, dawn was breaking over the eastern tarmac and the sunlight streamed across the glass façade of the hotel. Dragging our asses behind us we made our way to our rooms and I crashed in Jim's extra bed.

Several hours later, I awoke to Jim on the phone arranging for a special delivery to the hotel,

"Yeah man we are all here, come on over," he said to whoever was on the other end.

"The only thing I need right now is room service and a shower," I said.

"Go ahead. Order up whatever you want," he said to me, his hand over the receiver.

Much improved, smelling fresher, and changed into comfortable summer clothing from my overnight bag, I vigorously ate the Quiche

Lorraine and grapes off my room service tray, while Jim went to meet his connection.

He came back grinning from ear to ear half an hour later. "Come on," he said. "We're going to Danny's room."

Danny Klein, the bass player, was wearing suspenders. He was barefoot, bald and looking more disheveled than he had at the party the previous night.

"Hey do you know Christine?" Jim inquired.

"Yeah I've seen her around, we talked at Cobo and last night."

Hours were spent talking about Detroit and Boston, this and that musician, and doing line after line in between. Pretty soon, Danny gave Jim the high sign to leave us alone, and sent him out of his room in order to have someone on one time with me.

It started out slowly, but then I was driven like a mad woman to please him, and we continued for several hours. When Jim returned, he and Danny went outside the door to talk. Curiosity killed the cat, and it broke the heart of this cat when I overheard them say,

"I want to take her back to Boston." "No Danny, you don't want that one, that's Rosie. You don't want that one, trust me."

My heart sank. I never felt the same about Danny again. Later in September of that year they would play five nights straight at Pine Knob. They stayed at the Northfield Hilton, I brought them Charley's Crab left over bread in black plastic bags, and I was invited to be on hand for the famous photo shoot that consisted of the multi-colored paint fight that splashed over their white painter's pants reigning in the Centerfold era. By this time my attentions and admiration were turning to Peter Wolf.

CHAPTER 28

Change Would Do Me Good
(1981)

"I went to a restaurant that serves 'breakfast any time'. So I ordered French toast during the Renaissance..." Steven Wright

Our restaurant was changing for the better. Mr. Muer and his wife Betty had taken an extensive European tour that year, and as a result the Chef Larry era came to an end. Our uniform little black vest changed into tuxedo jackets. We still wore the signature Muer bowtie. We hired a pastry chef, and made fresh daily roulades and flans that would tempt a nun to indulge. Our main dishes went from heavy Italian influence to French influenced fare. Pot a feu, salmon en pappiote, loupe de mere, and of course our famous bouillabaisse were ever popular. Even the wine list became more sophisticated. Along with all of this new cuisine came new, larger, heavier plates. White porcelain plates 15-inches wide would hold an entire Dover sole almandine, carefully filleted tableside by yours truly. My back was killing me. Good thing I was having plenty of sex to offset the pain.

That winter as a little birthday gift my friend who worked for Bill Graham productions and Carlos Santana called me up. It was mid-November and the Rolling Stones were coming to the Pontiac Silverdome in my neighborhood.

"Hey Chris aka messy head, what's going on, you never call me this time of year," I exclaimed in joyful surprise.

"How would you like to be a guest of the Rolling Stones November 30th and December 1st?" knowing full well what the answer would be.

"What do you mean?"

"They are playing with Iggy Pop and Carlos Santana, and I have an all area, parking pass, press pass, and just about anything you want to do, pass for you."

"Oh my god, I can't believe it! I have not seen them live since the winter of 1964 at Cobo Hall, this is phenomenal," I said.

My big teenage crush was on Brian Jones, a founding member of the Rolling Stones, who died the year I graduated from high school. My first guitar was a Gretsch, just like his. My mother found it justified to give it away to Plymouth State Home for the mentally ill when I was away in Florida one time.

"I don't know where anyone is staying yet, but at least we will be at your place."

"That is the nicest birthday present anyone could give me this year, and, man, right about now I need a boost. My kids are good, but just when something happens to put me ahead, something else shitty happens, or I suppose that's just called life. I need a pick me up and you are just what the doctor ordered, thank you."

According to the tabloids, Mick Jagger did not want to do the tour at all but deferred to Keith and Ron Wood's coaxing and they set about having the biggest money making tour ever. Over 50 million dollars rolled in. They set records for years to come. Their album *Tattoo You* was being promoted and of course I had bought it, and memorized every word, and pretended it was all about my rose tattoo.

The only Rolling Stones connection I had was Chooch McGee. He had told me about being Keith Richards's guitar roadie when we hung out on and off one summer. I thought that was all bull shit until I saw Chooch at the shows working as a guitar tuner. Then there was Nicky Hopkins.

Nicky was such a dear man, I adored him. He had the arched back, gentle saunter of an unassuming man with fingers that were made to play a piano.

We met when he toured with a band called 'Night' who had a very stylish female lead singer. Their one hit was a song called 'Hot Summer Nights' and that was how I would categorically sum up my fling with Nicky. We made mad passionate love for two nights. He was quite open with me about living happily with his wife in Encino, California. I told him about my elderly aunt who lived out there at one time. I remember he smiled politely.

Soon the week of the Stones arrival happened. Ian McLagan, Ron Wood, and maybe Bill Wyman showed up at Charley's Crab one night to listen to Bob Seeley play his romping, stomping, brand of boogie woogie beats, and secretly I was certain they were there to meet me. Everyone working that night ran up to me to let me know they were in the house. The real connection as I learned later, was a bartender who had promised to score some heroin for Keith.

The frigid gnawing winds of November in Michigan can be wicked, but the heat coming off of the first show was spectacular. I arrived early so I could track down Chris, who was there to work for Carlos. Entering the heavy backstage steel door, my hand's bare skin adhered to it for a moment, no one was there to security check me in. I was standing in the middle of a wide cement driveway where the trucks could enter easily. On one side was the backstage area, and on the other side, near the elevators, was a ping pong table.

"Just make yourself at home, goodies are back in that room, or you can wander around wherever you want to," Chris said.

Of course, I had made an outfit to wear for the evening: flared, pin-striped pants in navy blue, and a shrunken wool, maroon-colored cropped jacket, with leather piping, and one ginormous brown leather button holding it together, finished off with knee high boots. Looking good, if I do say so myself.

Some of the crew knew me and greeted me warmly, but the majority were strangers. Making my way out front, I was stopped cold by the stage set. It was the most creative set I had ever seen, made up of enormous, brightly-colored panels designed by a Japanese artist named Kazuhide Yamazaki, with the legends of Americana rock and roll leaping off the panels, guitars, cars, records flashing. The tour became more of a festival than a show. Mick even rode up in a cherry picker and balloons were released for the celebration. No one had ever done anything like it before. Even seeing the Beatles twice was not as exciting as this spectacle. To put things in perspective for you, the L.A. show had a little known singer named Prince who was apparently booed off the stage, if you can imagine that.

So Prince and Iggy Pop both the opening bands for the Stones during that tour, had relatively the same experience, only there were vegetables involved being hurled at poor Iggy. The show that night began slowly in full light in the stadium and on stage, when Iggy made his way out in front of his band. He was just two songs into his set when the screaming, booing, and rotten tomato lobbing began.

I was perched two rows up in the vacant seats behind the stage with a good vantage point witnessing the onslaught. In my naiveté, I did not realize this is a normal occurrence for an Iggy show. I kept yelling back at the crowd to "knock it off".

A major gap in performances occurred between Iggy Pop and Santana. The extravagant stage set up took place for what seemed like an eternity. Walking back to the loading docks and backstage rooms I got a bite to eat. The food tables were spread with snacks, baked chicken, mostaccioli, roasted herb potatoes, and some salads, welcoming various shifts of people to partake.

When I finished eating, I noticed the driveway contained three black limousines parked on the slope down to the dome. I assumed the Stones had arrived. My heart was beating right out of my chest.

Looking over at the ping pong table I saw Bill Wyman and someone else playing with the enthusiasm of Chinese tournament players. I watched for about thirty minutes, just to kill the time.

Chris came to fetch me.

"Okay, come on, Carlos is about to start, and I have a great spot for you," he said, guiding me up the stairs to the stage.

The mixing board which was set up stage right, had some seats around it. He put me right next to the sound technician.

"This is unbelievable," I said.

"It sure is," he agreed.

The familiar "Oye Como VA" got the crowd going, the house lights went down, and the unmistakable sound of Carlos Santana's guitar met my ears and touched my soul.

Halfway through the set I felt a presence behind me, something telling me to turn around. I turned around, and there in the dark, with his knees nearly touching my back, was Mick Jagger. He was all bundled up in a winter coat and beige rain hat.

I think I said hello, I certainly smiled, but I cannot remember. I was beating time on my legs and singing along, so I'm sure my love of the music was apparent. When the set ended, I turned around to talk to Mick, but he had gone. There went a missed opportunity.

Exiting the stage, the large garage door had now closed and everyone had to use a small side door. Barely making my way through the dark, there was Mick standing by the door talking to someone. As I passed by, I smiled and he said,

"Here you go," as he opened the door for me in a gentlemanly fashion"Thank you very much," was all I could manage, and he continued his conversation.

He was looking rather peaked, but much more handsome than any pictures I had seen. Mick was not photogenic. Only Annie Leibowitz or Mick Rock could do him justice. When I went through the door, Keith Richards had finally emerged from his inner sanctum, his level of highness had reached an acceptable peak, and he was ready to rock. If there is any such thing as the living dead, he was the poster child. He had a purplish-white skin covering the boney structure of his face and lines as deep as the Grand Canyon outlining his features. He was almost frightening.

Just then someone from the Santana group grabbed me by the arm and said,

"Come on with me we have to get you situated."

"Sure, situated where?"

"Just sit up there for a minute, then when they hit the stage, you can go out there." He pointed to stage right, just the other side of the keyboard player, behind one of the Japanese stage screens.

From my lofty perch, I witnessed Mick going into a makeshift dressing room built on stage out of cable boxes and amplifier cases. I watched him undress. He was "jumpin' jack flash". Then a familiar face was carrying guitars around and setting them up. It was Chooch McGee, my old buddy from the previous summer. He had ended up living in Wyandotte that season on someone's boat and getting work as crew on a tug. I attempted to yell and get his attention, but he was way too busy. Then Bill Graham dressed in jeans and a gray hoodie, grabbed the microphone and announced the Rolling Stones.

In the words of Patti Smith, I was "eclipsing my own dreams with reality." As soon as Mick jumped out in a canary yellow jacket and white knickers, out came the third song 'Let's Spend The Night Together' and of course the crowd went into a frenzy. By that time, I was up behind a blue and red screen, singing along to every word ten feet above the crowd, dreaming I was part of the band. I was the only one allowed up there besides the band, not even Iggy or any of Santana's crew were up where I was perched. Next was 'Shattered' followed by twenty other hits. Everyone got their money's worth that night. The show rounded out with 'Satisfaction' and it seemed as soon as they were off the stage, they were loaded into their black limousines and they were gone.

That was one of the highlights of my life, one of the top five concerts I ever attended. I was treated like a queen. Of course, the queen got laid. Just not by Mick.

CHAPTER 29

Out Ahead of the Pack
(1981-82)

"To live is the rarest thing in the world. Most people exist, that is all..." Oscar Wilde

Earlier that spring before the season really started rolling, Chris called from San Francisco. There was a music merchandiser's convention in Chicago at the McCormick Place, and he was wondering if I would be interested in working the booth with him. Silly question. So the following week I took some vacation days and drove to Chicago. We stayed in the lap of luxury at the Hyatt Regency.

"So do you do this show every year?" I wondered out loud.

"Sure when I can get away, it helps pay the bills when things are slow."

"I don't think I ever asked you where you live."

"My girlfriend Nancy and I live on a house boat in the San Francisco bay area," he kept talking while he gathered items in a backpack for the McCormick Place.

"You never even mentioned a girlfriend."

"I didn't know how you felt about that, you have stated on several occasions that we are just friends. I love to party with you," as his voice got softer and he hugged me around the neck pulling me into his chest.

"Ya ditto," I grinned.

Every musician who was going out on tour that summer had a vested interest in this event. All the major guitar companies had big rock stars demonstrating their products. Fender, Gibson, Les Paul, everything from tuning forks to tambourines.

When we arrived early that morning, I strolled through the booths and watched as the dealers set up the displays. We had some sort of an amplifier in our booth, and on the other side was John Sebastian playing an acoustic guitar and singing away.

"Hello there, John, my name is Chris. I'm here with the amps just the other side. I loved your band the Lovin' Spoonful, big fan," I boldly complimented him.

"Well thanks very much. Where are you from?"

"Oh Detroit, I'm here with some friends for a couple of days."

"Well then, I will see you around, stop back over when you can," he said.

We chatted again about the transition from folk music to pop and rock genres, and later that fall at the Royal Oak Music Theatre he gave me a backstage pass, and the entire balcony to myself, while he opened for a fresh new stand-up comedian named Robin Williams.

Out in the corridor, Eddie Van Halen was demonstrating how he could wail on his Stratocaster. Paul Simon was in another small amphi-theater playing an acoustic guitar and singing along.

That afternoon we met up with a couple of the guys from 'Journey' for lunch. Chris introduced me to Neal Schon and a couple of the other guys, and we shared some deli food and sandwiches, while I en-tertained everyone with some lame quips like, "You can tune a piano, but you can't tuna fish."

Back at the convention center, I walked around noticing that it was pretty much a boys club. No women-owned businesses, or booths. It gave me the idea of making guitar straps, or t-shirts like Charlie tried to do, something to sooth my entrepreneurial spirit. Alas, I never got that going due to a lack of capital funding.

That night we decided to go to Ron's of Japan for dinner. Chris said it was like a Benihana.

"What is Benihana?" I asked.

"Never mind, you'll love it," he said, as he opened the restaurant door for me.

Delicious aromas of steaming vegetables and savory shrimp, took me back to my childhood, and UT Gardens where my grandparents used to take me for dinner.

The host took us to a large half-moon table. He placed menus and chop sticks around the cook top.

"There will be other people seated with us," explained Chris seeing the perplexed look on my face.

Just then the entire band 'Loverboy' was ushered over to our table.

"We will be your new best friends tonight," one of them said.

We ended up having the time of our lives, telling jokes, practicing the flipping of the shrimp into pockets, drinking Saki, and just talking about their tour and the road mishaps they had experienced.

Later that night Chris and I strolled slowly back to the hotel along the deserted streets of Chicago. It was there we happened upon the last bastion of American retail: Woolworth's, still parked on a corner it had inhabited for more than forty years. We got someone to take a picture of us with the camera I had remembered to bring for once.

Early the following morning, I had to high tail it back to Detroit. I picked the girls up at my mother's, and ran home to prepare for work, and the opening of the Pine Knob season.

There was a new sort of acceptance for "Rosie" among the prominent players of Pine Knob. The bands 'Foghat' and 'Whitesnake' had given me backstage passes to their Pine Knob and Cobo Hall appearances. Suddenly, I found myself welcome at more than one venue.

When the Doobie Brothers began the season early in 1981 they had an opener that seemed a bit odd. It was Carl Wilson of the Beach Boys. His departure from the group had taken place just a few days prior, so they had to get a substitute for one of the original Wilsons.

Carl was very kind to me. He and Gina had come into the Crab for dinner the night before and I had served them. He invited me to the show. During sound check the next day, I hung out with Gina, his "soon to be wife" and the daughter of Dean Martin.

We were in one of the dressing rooms off stage. She was a beautiful woman. She wore no make-up, but she had dainty features, sparkling eyes, and dressed plainly in blue jeans and a white shirt. She was busily crocheting something while I prattled on about my children, being a working mother and how great it had been to work in the ski lodge restaurant for an Italian family.

The Doobie Brothers band members were just there doing their jobs, not interested in making any Detroit friends, but the road crew was fantastic as always. All the gang from the Charlevoix motel were still with them, and we could party down, party high, party every which way. We had so much fun until the first night of six shows. The concert ended right at curfew, 11pm according to the city ordinance. There was no load out, so we headed back to the Hilton. No sooner had I walked into Hurley's to greet everyone when one of my friends from the Crab came running in screaming,

"Chris your car is on fire!"

We all ran out, to see what was happening, and there was my AMC Pacer going up in flames. People were scrambling everywhere trying to move their cars out of the way. When the Troy fire department roared up and began to fight a losing battle, the flames rose 30 feet in the air. Parts were sparking, explosions erupting, and everyone was out on their balcony or out the main floor sliding doors watching in awe. I began to cry. The whole Doobie crew was trying to comfort me. My car was soon a black carcass.

"How will I get home? I have to get to my children, I have a babysitter," I said, sobbing woefully.

The roadie ring leader, a congenial black guy named Tyrone, was my buddy, and he reached into his pocket and handed me a set of keys, offering up their rental.

"Here, take one of our rental cars, we are here all week, and we have another one."

So the Doobie's helped me out of a tight spot that night. I threw my arms around his neck and gave him a big kiss, wrapped things up with the fire department, and made my way home to my daughters. The insurance money was sufficient enough to get me into yet another used car, but there would never be another space car.

By September, the end of summer was upon us. The night chill required a sweater, revealing clothing covered up a little more than usual.

'Journey' rolled through town, and the 'Kinks', neither of whom I got to see due to my work schedule.

Then a firecracker of a girl showed up at the Hilton with her band. It was Pat Benatar. She was small, but mighty, so I dubbed her Mighty Mouse to her crew, who suggested that I not call her that to her face. It was really meant as a compliment. Pat was very kind and hospitable to me. At any rate, that night at the show, and they only had one night, she was furious with Neil Giraldo, her guitar player. He had been partying a little too hardy and broken his arm the night before. He was sporting a plaster cast and was all bandaged up.

"What the hell are we going to do? How the hell can you play?" Pat was screaming as they entered the reception room full of food and beverages with him trailing after her.

"We'll be fine. I can still play. Come on, I'll show you," he said, and as quickly as they came in, they headed for the stage and his demonstration. It was easy to see where "love is a battlefield" came from.

The show went on and Neil played with his bandaged arm and without any flaws. It was also apparent that he was an extraordinary guitar player, which is why Rick Derringer "rock and roll hoochy-cooed" him right out of his band.

Pat was the best female front person I had ever witnessed. The power in her came from another place. I guess the tour worked because she and Neil were married in 1982, and unlike so many crumbled cookie relationships, they are still together to this day.

CHAPTER 30

What Can We Do About 1982?

"We accept the love we think we deserve..." Stephen Chbosky

My daughters were growing up so quickly, and of course I had working mother's remorse most of the time. They were 12 and 9 years old, and becoming prepubescent. What the hell kind of an example was I going to set? All I could be was myself, after all, and try to show them kindness to others, generosity, and Atari. They were overjoyed at the joysticks and played endless games on the television screen. The following year, Disney would open Epcot center and we would take a driving vacation there with friends.

In the rest of the world, USA Today newspaper had its first publication and would now be a standard under every hotel door in America. Public enemy number one in France, Carlos the Jackal, was terrorizing the citizens. The shit in the Middle East was at a boil when Israeli forces invaded Lebanon, and Israel returned the Sinai to Egypt. For us ecology-minded people, the International Whaling Commission ended "commercial" whaling. Also, the largest robbery in history to this day took place when an armored car in New York was highjacked for $9,800,000. Maybe he should have paid off the Jackal, and given Lebanon a little country somewhere.

Meanwhile back at the Crab, the Beach Boys were opening Pine Knob as tradition would have it, but they did not bring in a great restaurant crowd. My friends from the music merchandise convention 'Loverboy' came in next for a couple of days. I am retty certain I attended that show one night. Then hometown star Smokey Robinson showed us some good preshow business.

Early in June, Eric Clapton from my old favorite band 'Cream' was bringing his solo act to the Knob for two nights. I had to work both nights, but I was determined to meet him and have him sign a record that I had found in the racks of the drugstore where I used to work. It was a 'Best of the Cream' album with an Iron Butterfly 'In-A-Gadda-Da-Vida' label on it, which played the Cream. Late night after the show, Eric came into our bar, had an orange juice, no ice, and headed out the door. After punching out, I chased Mr. Clapton through the mermaid door and stopped him in the hallway of the Hilton on its bright red carpet, "Eric...Eric...would you mind?" I handed him the album. He began to sign the outer cover.

"I'm sorry no, I want you to sign the label please" and as I exposed the vinyl and showed him the label, he sort of huffed. "That's unusual," he said and gruffly brushed me off.

When I met up with one of his crew in the bar area, I asked why he was so grumpy. Eric had seated himself on the other side of the dance floor to listen to the local band play, and had ordered up another orange juice.

"He quit heroin and alcohol to do this tour," he said. "That would make anyone grumpy." I ordered myself a Gran Marnier and Amaretto coffee drink and hit the dance floor.

Eric stayed in our hotel for a week after his shows at Pine Knob. From there, he was flying up to Canada to do some fishing. The pristine lushness of the Canadian north should have soothed his soul, but he remained grumpy.

That week my friend John Denver and his road manager Bernie were in and out for one day. They still provided me with some comp tickets, which I gave to family members. The month of June would not close out without me falling in love with a member of the band Asia.

Back in my "Cheri" days, she had introduced me to the band King Crimson. Little did I know that the newly formed super group from the UK were members of my other favorite groups, 'Yes', 'Emerson, Lake and Palmer', and 'King Crimson'. They had been the most progressive, innovative, and unique sounds of the seventies.

The day was overcast and so was my mood. There was not much on the horizon for summer fun, and so my routine run to Hurley's after work was mandatory. None of my friends could be persuaded to join me that evening, so I sat alone chatting with the bartender until a tall very handsome gentleman with a British accent inquired about beer varieties. Everyone who knows me is aware that even if you were reciting a nursery rhythm in a British accent, you will have me eating out of your hand. So there I was gushing all over him, introducing myself, asking his name.

"John. It's a pleasure," he said. "Are you here with someone?"

"We are playing at Pine Knob tomorrow," he said.

"What band are you with?"

"Asia, ever heard of us?"

"I think they just started playing one of your songs on the radio, is it the 'Heat of the Moment'?" I sang

He chuckled, and we went on talking for a while until he invited me up to his room.

My favorite combination: British, blond, tall, and a good kisser. There you have it. We tumbled into room 237, barely in the door before taking each other's clothes off. He was well endowed and he let me have my way with him. We tried most of the positions I knew. Very Kama sutra.

It was during those three lovely days with John Wetton, formerly of King Crimson, currently of Asia, that I realized men from across the pond were not circumcised. I had slept with Gary Brooker (of Procol Harum) by then, and it was starting to occur to me in the form of a generalization. Which also raised many other questions about penises. Did they have a more difficult time having orgasms, did they have premature ejaculations problems, and if one retracted the foreskin prior to a head job would there be more sensation? Unfortunately, none of my burning questions were ever answered, but then again, the only other Brit I had a fling with was Elton John's guitar player, Davey Johnstone, coming right up the following week.

The weekend was approaching. Saturday morning I had my crying session, which was a depressive ritual I had for years. I felt better after a good crying jag, and carried on. I would like to say oh the whippoor-wills were singing in the old oak tree outside, but that would be hog wash, it was just another steamy summer workday. My biggest fear was that I would succumb to depression like my mother had. I started taking herbal supplements of St John's Wart and that seemed to help me over the sinking albatross around my neck.

My mother had picked the girls up early because I was opening the Crab and had to leave around 3:30 to get there on time. Sauntering through the heavy wooden doors swinging my black apron filled with my wine passport, multiple pens, a wine opener, and lipstick, I noticed someone sitting at table 31. I punched the time clock, shouted hello to everyone in the kitchen, and grabbed a tray full of silverware and brown linen napkins. I placed the heavy tray boldly on the Wanderer table and pulled out a chair to sit down. It was then that I glanced over at the table in the dimly lit, otherwise empty dining room and said hello to Jimmy Buffet.

"Hey, how are ya doin'?" I smiled and greeted him as I rolled my first set of silverware in a tight cigar shape, while impersonating Groucho Marx and lifting my eyebrows up and down.

"Pretty good, they were nice enough to feed me before the crowd came in," he said, complementing our hostess, Cheryl.

"That's so cool, but celebs really don't get bothered too much here. People will say hi to you, but keep on walking. This is sort of a snooty place, and Troy is a snooty city, not as bad as Birmingham or Grosse Pointe, but still you know what I mean. Anyway famous people come in here all the time," I said.

"Really good food, and I'm a fish snob," Jimmy said.

"Hey, you have a sailboat don't you?"

"Yes it's a pretty big schooner."

"Well I was talking to Dan Fogelberg last fall and he said he was borrowing your sailboat to take a Mediterranean cruise."

"Oh ya, yes he did. He took his whole family and a crew, and had a great time. So are you coming out to the shows this weekend?" Jimmy said.

"I'm afraid I have to work."

"Too bad. The crowds, they call themselves parrot heads, are a real fun bunch. Anyway, Bonnie and I arranged to have one of the meeting rooms in the Hilton to have a party tonight, why don't you stop by?"

"That sounds like a good time, Bonnie Raitt?"

"Ya she's the opener tonight."

"Oh crap, I love her. I sang *"Let's give them something to talk about,"* as I cleared his plate, which he had all but licked clean.

He laughed, got up and left it at that, walking back through the silent, empty lounge into the Hilton.

The restaurant was super busy that night. EDS people, Kmart people, local television people came in I waited on Bernie Smilovitz, his wife and another couple at table 4. Our cash readouts for the night topped $7000, which was a huge amount of money for the 1980's. Business was booming, and life was good again. I was going to Jimmy Buffet's party.

Luckily I had a change of clothes with me, just jeans and a blouse with some boots, but better than smelling like fish chowder. I brought some friends with me, and went into the designated party room. They had a fully stocked bar, and the road crew supplied all the blow. I hooked up with one of the crew and we made several pilgrimages to the ladies' room stalls. I think we horrified some of the other women in there.

Back in the party room, Bonnie arrived and someone introduced me to her. We talked about Jackson Browne, CSN, and some other mutual friends. I have never met anyone who could talk like that woman could talk. Maybe it was the cocaine, but man she had a motor mouth. We had a ball, we laughed we played music, we drank a ton, and when the night was coming to an end we went our merry ways to get it on behind closed doors.

It was already July and Santana came into town the night before they were to play at the Knob this year for a four day run. I had not received a call from Chris or anyone else, but after the first show the wonderful couple who had the house on Upper Straits Lake were in the bar hanging out with Carlos and company, and invited us all again to partake in a picnic. It had become an annual ritual, but it wouldn't be the same without my friend old "messy head." Chrisanna and Damian had dubbed Christopher that one morning when he woke up and looked like he had just stuck his finger in a live electrical box.

"Hey Killer where is Chris this year?" I asked one of the crew members.

"He was having some family trouble with his girlfriend Nancy and they may lose their houseboat in San Francisco. He couldn't come out on the road this time," he said.

Unaware of this relationship, or anything about his personal life really, my heart was slightly broken that day. That was the end of our relationship, I never saw nor heard from Chris again.

Peter, Paul, and Mary played a sleepy set the following night, then George Benson and his silky guitar licks played the Knob, and the restaurant crowd was fairly good for him.

As I mentioned previously, Elton John was playing Pine Knob. He was one of the most renowned acts to ever play this little outdoor amphitheater. Only the Jackson's or Madonna could have topped his draw during that era.

Of course they were staying at the Hilton, and I had observed Elton literally running through the lobby in his wild stage costumes before and after the shows. The band 'Quarterflash' led by a female vocalist, was their opener for three nights and I got to know those band members. The 'Quarterflash' group invited me to the show.

Backstage was available until the Elton people arrived and everyone was "invited" to go out and take their seats in the general public. My seat could not have been any better. I settled into a front row seat right behind Elton's white baby grand piano. Great view of the 88's. The sound was not lost at all, even though it was miked up and amplified for the audience. Elton came out looking like the painting 'Blue Boy' by Thomas Gainsborough right up to the wide brimmed hat with a giant plume of feathers cascading off of it. God, I loved the flamboyance. It was one of the best performances I had seen to date. 'Someone Saved My Life Tonight' was my Cheri Chronicle anthem.

Later, back at the Hilton, I was standing with a group of people in the lobby when Elton flew out of his limousine still in blue boy garb, and ran at break neck speed right past us. I wondered why he was a bit paunchy if he was always running like that. Meanwhile at the party in one of the suites, I met the very tall and lanky Davey Johnstone. Of course his blond hair and British accent was the first attraction, but then getting to know him better, he was friendly, unassuming, and natural with me, which I appreciated. We had a very provocative fling that night on his substantial member, which, of course, was uncircumcised.

Now it was near that time that my friend Mervi, a petite, natural blond, from Finland began working at Charley's Crab. She was certain that she deserved the best material things that life had to offer. This, of course, did not coincide with my transcendental, unearthly beliefs at all, nonetheless, we became friends.

She was into country music, which of course the rocker chick in me could not comprehend, but all that aside, Willie Nelson was in town. We arrived in Hurley's that night to find these rowdy guys in cowboy hats ordering up large quantities of tequila like they were extracted by a time machine straight out of Mickey Gilley's and deposited there.

"Hey ladies how are y'all doin' tonight?" one of them inquired. This was Poody. Light-colored, long hair flopping out of his hat as he tipped it to us, from atop his six foot plus frame.

"This here is Dusty," Poody said as he grabbed a smaller fellow around the neck in a big old hug. They all had nicknames like that.

"You girls look like you could use a shot of tequila," he said as they selected one from their lineup of about ten shot glasses on the bar filled with amber-colored liquid. The aroma was overwhelming mixed with lemons and limes to accompany the shots.

My girlfriend and I accepted their invitation, salted our hands and grabbed a lemon for the ritual. It wasn't quite the same as sitting on John Denver's lap with an oyster chaser, but it was pretty damn good.

"So, where's the party tonight?" Dusty smiled and put his arm around me.

"One of the waitresses next door is having a house party tonight," I said.

Mervi grabbed my arm and dragged me across the bar.

"You are not thinking of Marie's are you," she said in a firm loud whisper.

"Well sure, she invited us and said we could bring a friend," I offered as an excuse.

"You know she only wants a few people there, not the whole Willie Nelson crew."

"I know but what a hoot to crash that party (of snobs)," is what I was thinking and half said.

Now Marie was favored by everyone at the Crab from managers to guests. She was very popular and her sister worked with us too. She was petite with curly black hair, dark eyes and a dry wit that could cut like a knife if she chose. Still, I remember when my shoulder was dislocated at work, she was the one I ran to in the kitchen to pull it back into place. Tough lady.

"We have a party. Let's go," I said as we all piled into my little white Datsun. It was not designed for three burly guys and Mervi, but somehow we jammed in there, and off we went.

When we arrived we were less than welcomed by Marie, who reticently let us into her home. It was a lovely sprawling midcentury ranch with plush furnishings. Once the guys started bragging about who they were, and offered everyone at the party tickets for the next night, we were finally embraced by the group.

We partied long and hard into the night, dancing and carrying on in the family room, still doing tequila shots until we found Dusty passed out on the living room couch. It was about then that Marie decided she had been a gracious enough hostess and sent us packing.

By the time we reached the hotel we were all ready for bed, so Mervi and Poody paired off, and Dusty and I paired off, and away we went for smoke, sex, and sleep in that order.

Now I had witnessed Kris Kristofferson not looking much like the Rhodes Scholar he was, passed out drunk on the stage at Pine Knob with poor Rita Coolidge having to carry their act the rest of the night. I had met Waylon Jennings when he sat at table 31, big, grumbling and gruff, therefore I really didn't know what to expect from Willie Nelson. Luckily, he was not either one of those. He was sweet, gentle and kind to Mervi and me through the many times we saw him over the years. He always welcomed us back stage and took care of us for tickets. A very standup guy.

It was already August and the summer was speeding by with rapid velocity. James Taylor was coming into town, and I read somewhere that he claimed to not be able to remember parts of his life. I was one of those things. Early one evening, before the dinner rush he came in and sat at table 12 in my station with two other men, in front of the grand fireplace in the main dining room. Granted, I looked very different there than in the Pine Knob disco with my little orange polyester dress. He didn't remember me from the other time we had met at the bar in Somerset Inn, or backstage at his shows. He didn't recognize me. I think I was just a "type" to him. He was not really flirtatious, but beguiling in some smooth way, and man, those eyes of his were intriguing. They weren't drinking, just some wine and tea, very simple dining, but when he left with a warm good-bye and thank you, he left something else behind. There tucked underneath a saucer was his room key at the Hilton.

Something came over me. I was put out that he didn't remember me, or if he did find me remotely attractive why did he wait six years from the first time we met to show interest in me. Slightly pissed off,

I marched over to the desk in the Hilton lobby and dangled the key in the manager's face saying,

"Mr. Taylor left his key behind, would you see that he gets it?"

He looked at me dumbfounded, as if to say, there was probably another intention for that key. Reluctantly, he accepted it, and off I went back to the restaurant.

That night I got a late night call from Westwood California. It was George "Chocolate" Perry asking me if I would like to go out on the road with him for a few days, when they came into town next week. I made arrangements with babysitters, assured my youngest daughter I would be back for her birthday. Then I made certain the kids were alright with that, and their father would be around if they needed anything. It was to be my first time on the road with a famous band. How glamorous.

Time was creeping by like the melting Salvador Dali clock. Not even meeting Debbie Harry and seeing 'Blondie' perform the following week kept my excitement at bay. Even my old buddies the 'Rockets' were playing the Knob, and that didn't stop me from being anxious. I even missed David Byrne and 'Talking Heads' who had my new favorite song coming out, 'Burning Down the House' and my other favorite song 'Psycho Killer' because it had a French word in it.

The night of August 15th, George called to say he had arrived and they were at Somerset. There was a great deal of selfish motivation on many fronts when I think back on the dynamics of the relationships in the CSN group. I was still in love with Stephen, but he was still stubborn and aloof, George I believe really loved me in some way and thought that making love constantly was the way to my heart. I just wanted to be near Stephen. It was pretty twisted. We could not be on Stephen's bus. Graham had some extra people along already, and David and Jan invited us to travel with them.

I knew Jan because everyone talked about her mother, Harper Dance, who worked I believe, at Criteria Recording Studio in Miami. They were heavy into freebasing back then and looked very torn up for it. Jan was a mousy, skinny, quiet little thing, and David was bloated, heavy and full of large reddened sores all over his body. Still he was as opinionated as ever, which is what I loved about him, so David's bus it would be.

The kids came with me to the first show, and I hung out at a couple of sound checks during the next few days. One day instead of checking the sound we all banded together in the great raccoon rescue. A baby coon had gotten himself trapped up in the rafters and was screeching through the sound preparation. We got blankets and nets, we decided who would be the best climber in the road crew and sent him scaling the metal girders along the wall. Twenty or so of us stood below in fearful concern for the roadie and the raccoon. When it was bagged, we all cheered, but then it was getting too late to sound check. Graham was a bit perturbed with us and sulked off.

The next day, the children were taken to their Grandmother's and George came over to my house to spend the day while I packed for the tour. Rarely did I take any of these musicians or roadies home to see my house or meet my children.

That was my private place, my private space. There was David Lindley, George, and Linda Ronstadt's guitar player, not Waddy, but one of her guitar players on tour who had been granted the privilege. He was just lonely and wanted to have a normal day. So we went out to lunch, went to see one of the Star Wars movies, went to my house for a while, where he attempted to make my crappy old guitar sound sensational. No sex, just companionship, then back to the show that night. He didn't force himself on me, just a really nice friendly guy. Both he and David Lindley had tried playing my piece of crap acoustic guitar, and they couldn't even make the damn thing sound good, so then I didn't feel so bad. However I digress, Chocolate was still sitting on my antique velvet couch waiting for me.

After the CSN show that night we all boarded our respective buses and off we went down I-75 heading for Ohio. It was midnight. George took me to his sleeping birth, like on a train I thought, and we rocked that bus all the way to Toledo, I don't know how that driver kept the thing on the road through the motion of the ocean.

At one point I said to Chocolate,

"What is that smell? That smells like a chemistry experiment gone wrong."

"That's those two freebasing back there," he nodded toward the main suite in the rear.

"Oh Lord what if we get busted?" I said.

"That's not going to happen, don't worry," Chocolate said with great confidence.

Somehow I was not convinced.

When we went up to the front where some of the crew were playing cards, we all listed slightly when the bus made a turn into a rest stop. One of the guys pushed down the window shouting at another tour bus going in the opposite direction.

"Hey it's the Doobie Brothers bus....where are you guys heading?" he yelled.

"Pine Knob, how about you?"

"West Virginia!"

It had never occurred to me that I should ask Chocolate where the hell we were headed, I didn't care if it was the moon. I just wanted to go. As Stephen's bus pulled up next to us, we headed into the convenience store. We were poking around getting drinks and snacks when Stephen started yelling, "Oh my God look what I found!" It was a brown shirt that read, 'Give me Chocolate or Give me Death'.

He was so excited he had the guy go to the back and bring out all the boxes of shirts he had, and bought every last one of them. He handed them out to everyone in the entourage except for me, and insisted they all wear them for the crew shirts on the next show. It doesn't take a genius to figure out who that gesture was intended for. The intention I believe was to exclude me, and it worked. I went through the five stages of grief one at a time while my heart was breaking. Denial, anger, I stopped short of depression and went back to anger, but by the time the tour was ended I was in acceptance.

Back on the bus in our love nest that George hardly fit into, the poor man kept hitting his head, we cuddled up again. That was exactly the metaphor for the moment, I thought, this man is beating his head against a wall trying to make me feel something I don't.

We got to the Hilton in West Virginia around 9am. The buses circled in a dance of the diesel dragons. We all stumbled into the glamorous hotel that stretched up a dozen floors to a domed skylight. We found our respective rooms.

There was no avoiding the need for sleep, so George wrapped me in one of the white Hilton robes, put me in the shower, and then to bed, alone. I heard the door softly close behind my friend, and out went my lights.

When I awoke, the television was on and light blasted through the full-length windows. There were several trays of room service goodies waiting for me, but no George. Then I heard the turn of the key clunk, and George said, "Here I got something that will pick you up with your coffee," and he laid out several white lines.

"So we don't have to smell the Crosby bus anymore, we are going on Graham's bus tonight," Chocolate said to calm my fears of getting busted. As if getting busted for my hashish and marijuana would not be so bad.

Sound check, back on the bus, have dinner, then the show. It all went so quickly, that I didn't even have time to take it all in. The music, of course, was phenomenal. Their harmonies were well-blended like a sweet recipe of home cooking. I loved their stage set, and the whales soaring through the backdrop when they did their tribute to Jacques Cousteau.

Back on Graham's bus we were welcomed and so was my hashish. That was the drug of choice for the night at the rear sector of the tour bus.

"Thanks Christine that is really good stuff, you always have good hash," Graham said.

"Well thank you, it's my one indulgence, I think my guys get it from Canada."

The conversation about the environment, religion, politics, and etcetera went into the wee hours of the night until Nash called an end to our get together and ordered us all to bed like unwilling children. We obliged and soon we were in the next city.

After about four days of this lifestyle, I was finished. Not much of a road warrior, I must admit. George took me to the airport and stuck me on a plane for Detroit. Glad to see my daughters, and glad to be home again.

Somewhere in that mix of summer flings with Chocolate, he called me from California. He was going out on the road with Joe Walsh this time and wanted me to go with him for several venues through Ohio and Indiana. The only one I could afford to miss work for was the Blossom show right after playing Meadowbrook Music Theatre. I managed to get a ride to the campus of Oakland University that afternoon to meet up with the band for sound check. The dirt roads were still vacant at this time of day, and I walked right up to the box office, had them call back stage, and George came out to meet me.

"Hi baby," he put his arm around me and laid a big old kiss on my forehead.

"Hello there, good to see you again, so soon in one summer, very unusual," I said with a hint of sarcasm.

"I know, but you will love this show we have been rehearsing in LA, and Rosemary Butler is singing with us too," he offered as an excuse.

"Oh my god I love her, what a voice, I know her from Jackson's band," I said.

"So are you ready for the road again? You have a really small bag there," Chocolate pointed out.

"I know, I can only go to Blossom with you, then I have to be back for work, I'm sorry it has to be short."

"Oh man, that's a bummer, I was hoping to take you around Columbus and see some other sites, not just hang in the hotel."

"Well let's just enjoy the time we have."

"It won't be like the CSN tour. We're all on the same bus here, but Joe is a hoot, you met him a couple of times," he said.

We made our way through the empty seats of the amphitheater, which sloped steeply toward the stage, surrounded by green grass lawns and mature forests. The setting is pristine, and the acoustics are wonderful too.

Backstage we entered a room with food laid out, and beverages for the crew who busied themselves unloading crates and amps from the truck. None of the crew faces were familiar, which is at this point in time was a good thing.

Joe arrived carrying a guitar case, and George stopped him. Turning in midstride as he was going toward one of the dressing rooms.

"Hey man," that old familiar Joe voice.

"This is Christine, remember you met her once in the Book Cadillac Hotel in Detroit."

"Well the first time we met was playing ping pong at Punch Andrew's Christmas party in 1976, and you were with the Eagles guys then," I corrected and reminded both at the same time.

"Oh ya, I remember you," Joe smiled slightly, road weary.

"She's going with us tonight to Blossom for tomorrow's show, and I tried to convince her to stay on longer, but she has to work," George said, sort of asking Joe's blessing for the occasion.

"Sure man, that's cool and all," he said as he turned back toward the dressing room to unload his gear.

"Well go hang out where ever you like. We have to set up and rehearse, then we can have some food before the show, okay baby," he kissed me and excused himself.

Rosemary walked through backstage just as the microphones began humming. She stayed to herself, and several minutes later I could hear her doing some runs to warm up her voice. That beautiful voice.

The horn section set up next. Those guys were a riot. They had these masks and pig faces that they wore to liven up the audience. People began filling the seats and before I knew it, Joe was singing "life's been good to me so far..."

Joe was hands down one of the premier guitarists of our time. He had a string of solo albums in the following years that never peaked like his days with the Eagles.

That man could make us laugh though. He was always spoofing and goofing. He kept us thoroughly entertained after the show as we said our good-byes to the people who had come out to see Joe from the Detroit area. Joe was from Ohio and so many of his old acquaintances came out for the Blossom show. The venue was nearly identical to Meadowbrook or Pine Knob in charm and atmosphere, surrounded by woods and open country.

After a loving and affectionate two nights filled with great music, good times, laughter, and my friend Chocolate, I flew back to Detroit. I often wonder now how he is, where he is, how his life went post Rosie.

Later in August of that year, a bunch of us from work were having a going away party in one of the suites in the outlying rooms surrounding the pool area of the hotel. The party was for our very handsome, and beloved manager, Jim, who was with us for too brief a time.

The party was interrupted when a couple of very drunk guys from John Cougar Mellencamp's band tried to crash the door. When we sent them away and wouldn't let them in "no matter who they were" they retaliated by pulling the fire alarm out in the hallway.

We didn't really hear much commotion until the fire engines pulled up outside the sliding door wall, sirens blasting and red lights firing. One poor fireman, still in his striped pajamas under his hat, coat, and boots was pulling the hose from the pumper truck to start extinguishing the fire.

The guest of honor, our manager, ran outside. "There's some mistake we didn't call and there is no fire here!"

The police had been notified and they started a hotel-wide search for the culprits. Some arrests were made, and the next day we heard on the news that the concert was delayed while members of the troupe were bailed out of jail. John Mellencamp never stayed at the Northfield Hilton again.

CHAPTER 31

Time for a Detroit Breakdown

"I was trying to daydream but my mind kept wandering..."
Steven Wright

The phone rang several weeks later and it was one of my fellow group-ies who hung around with Stephen Bladd of the J. Geils Band. She had some rather exciting news to share with me.

"Christine, the guys are going to be in town for over a week to do a live show at Pine Knob, and they are recording! Did you know about it?" Maryanne asked.

"No honey, I have been pretty busy with work and kids this week. Where are they staying?"

"Of course at your hotel, the Northfield Hilton, and they are plan-ning some nice surprises for all their Detroit friends too, I just can't wait."

The J.Geils Band was riding the wave of success that 'Freeze Frame' and 'Centerfold' had brought them. I kept thinking,

"How the hell did they get a hold of those pictures of me from the WABX deejays?"

I was the X centerfold for sure at least one of them, with Steve M sharing his photographic trophies. It is a small world, and the music world in Detroit was smaller than most.

Every night that week I had to work, and every night I would fill a black garbage bag with our left over Charley's Crab bread and run it out to the band limo as it pulled up out front. They all loved my bread. The bread was special. Each morning, long rolls of pizza dough were spread out on baking sheets drizzled with seasoned olive oil, then a blessing of sea salt, poppy seeds, and oregano was lovingly tossed over the bread, and baked to perfection in a convection oven.

After work I headed over to hang out with whoever was around, and everyone was around, roadies, groupies, friends of the band, local radio personalities. My fellow groupie friend PJ, who was with me from the Frank Zappa days, and had hung out with me at the Ted Nugent recording studio A2, was in the hotel that night in Seth Justman's room. He was either so painfully shy or just not interested in us that he never made a move as we cuddled up on either side of him on the bed in the darkened hotel room. In hindsight, he was probably waiting for us to have our way with him. I think PJ probably did after I left the room.

Who knows where Danny was. I didn't see him around at all except in the limousine when I had given them the bread. He was pretty cranked from the show and maybe just fell out in his room. That was how the entire week went until the Friday night when I was finally off work and able to go out to the concert. It was 'Showtime' and my daughters were more than excited to be going to see the guys live. Everyone knew I was bringing my children and it was to be a "family affair" type of night, low key on the language, drugs, and other behavior.

My little family was all dressed up in our best outfits, the girls with their Farrah Fawcett hair and Jordache jeans: 'Happy Days' meets 'Charlie's Angels." They were thrilled and full of questions.

As we walked down the wide Pine Knob driveway toward the loading dock on that sultry summer afternoon the smell of chicken barbequing overwhelmed us. It was early afternoon, very early by rock and roll standards.

"Wow Mom, that smells really good," Chrisanna commented.

"This is their last night here so we are having a big barbeque and party before the show," I said.

There were two huge white canopy tents set up with tables for dining and the food. To my daughter's delight, on one end of the table were two video games, just like the arcades set up under the big top.

"Can we play Mom?" the girls giggled, unable to control their excitement. It was Pac Man and Donkey Kong for free, no quarters involved.

"Of course you can, but it's not just for you guys, so share if someone else wants to play," I said.

Now I understood why the manager had asked me what my kids liked to do. I should have said ride ponies, they probably would have gotten ponies. It was wonderful of them to think of the children, it meant a great deal to me.

The barbeque was fantastic, the chardonnay and beer flowed freely, several salads and scrumptious desserts were catered for the event. All of the people that were close to the band had been invited. It wasn't a press party full of strangers, or a drug snorting sexposé, just special.

As the concert hour approached, Pete Wolf showed up and made his way through the picnic toward me.

"How was everything? Are you all having a good time?" he smiled, and a genuine look came over his face.

"This is beyond belief what a great blow out for the last night, well done," I said.

"Okay go see the manager. He has your tickets. I hope you like your seats and enjoy the show," he turned and walked off to his dressing room.

The orange sea of seats were filling fast. Back then it was nothing fancy, no big screens, no cones of acoustic projections, just plain, seats and lawn.

We made our way to about the 7th or 8th row center, which was eye level to the stage. The adoration of Detroit people for this band was apparent as soon as they hit the stage with 'Just Can't Stop Me' followed by 'Just Can't Wait' our faces were blown off.

They were Jewish, they were from Boston, but they were loved. Perhaps it was a throwback to the Purple Gang in Detroit, the Jewish mobsters, but they were adored.

After the show we were brought back stage before anyone else, and their manager found me and said that Peter had something special set up for us. We were escorted to the stage left side where there were no other people.

"This is where Peter wants you to wait," instructed their road manager.

"Okay girls, this is something special that I have never had before. I think we are welcome to anything here," I explained to my children.

In front of us was a black, fabric-draped room, with a slanted table filled with food for kids. There were gummy bears, Kit Kats, fruits, etcetera, all designed for children. A huge display of food and beverages.

"Wow, you guys look at all this. It's for you. Isn't that cool?" I said.

"Yeah Mom, this whole day has been crazy cool, it is for us, isn't it?" my oldest said.

"Pretty sure it is for us," as Peter Wolf entered the room, his road manager announcing his arrival.

"Hi Pete! This is incredible, thank you," I managed to get out of my mouth,

"This is my oldest daughter, Chrisanna, and my youngest, Damian. Girls, this is Peter Wolf."

"Damian, huh?" Pete offered his hand and they both shook it.

"You're welcom, what do you think?" he asked.

At that moment my youngest said, "You have silver shoes!"

They were actually gold. Peter just gave her a slight smile.

"Honey those are gold shoes. Tell Peter how much you loved the show."

They both started chattering at once about their favorite songs and Donkey Kong. As hastily as Peter had entered the room, he made his exit. Shy? Perhaps he had to go get his party groove on, who knows, but there we were standing in the room full of food.

I told them to take whatever they wanted, it was late, and we had to get going. There was much protesting.

As I passed through the throngs of people back stage, I said my goodnights to everyone, and made my way to the backstage door, down the stairs, and up the long driveway with my children, one on each hand.

Autumn was upon us. The moon hanging over the chair lifts was larger than usual. The loadout was happening, and I left the party people to their own device.

A night or two later, working upstairs in the section of the Crab with the wooden booths. There sat six lovely, stylish, punked out beautiful girls at table 80.

They did not look local at all. They had that west coast meets Cyndi Lauper-style about them.

"Hello ladies how are we doin' tonight? Can I get you something to drink?"

The blonde said, "I would like an Absolute martini, straight up."

"I am so sorry you girls look so young I am going to have to see some ID okay?"

"We left them back in the hotel," said the black-haired beauty.

"I'm so sorry can you go and get them?"

They hesitated looking around at each other, but eventually got up and went to retrieve their proof. One of them stayed.

"You're not drinking?"

"No I'm taking some antibiotics I'll just have a coke please."

Several minutes passed and they returned, submitted their orders, and continued with their dining experience. They were all just 21 years old, so I wasn't too far off base. When I went up to the service bar my bartender asked me,

"Do you know who they are?"

"No not really."

"Those are the 'Go Go's' and that is Belinda Carlisle you just carded."

The other end of the season highlight was when after all those years, following the Grande Ballroom appearance, I actually met Ian Anderson at a Hilton party. I was invited, knocked on the door, and in a whoosh of flaming long red hair, he opened the door to greet me.

"Hello luv, welcome, come on in," as he staggered out drink in hand, and that was it. My bungle in the jungle moment.

CHAPTER 32

Crazy Changing Climate (1983)

"If you want to conquer fear, don't sit home and think about it.
Go out and get busy..." Dale Carnegie

At some point in time, Chuck Muer decided that we all needed a Dale Carnegie course. He believed that it would solve whatever dilemma we were facing, whether it be in communication, in memorization, in speech, and so forth, but furthermore would help make the Crab a better restaurant.

No course was going to solve my biggest barrier to life and that was my fear of love. Whenever I met anyone that I was attracted to, I clammed up tighter than a shell. It rendered me speechless, shaking, and unable to stand without faltering. So everyone that I had been sexually involved with up to that point, I hadn't been overly infatuated with: not my husband, not Charlie, not even Stephen. Mick Jagger and Bruce Springsteen to mention two men had left me dumbfounded.

It was 1983 already and due to David Crosby's arrest in Texas, CSN was not touring that year. Big changes were happening though across the board. The way people's lives would be affected by Microsoft introducing Word, Motorola having the first mobile phone, and seatbelts becoming mandatory in automobiles worldwide. On the home front, we were at a staggering 12 million people unemployed, which left little interest for the IRA siege in Northern Ireland, or the bombing of the US embassy in Beirut.

One morning I was awakened by a slosh, which was more like a wave, of my waterbed tossing me back and forth so violently I fell out of bed onto the floor. Come to find out there was an earthquake in central New York City, and one in Cleveland that reached all the way to the great lakes. Yes, indeed, things were changing.

Pine Knob opened with the Beach Boys as per usual for a two day run. This time for the first time they stayed at the Northfield Hilton. Dennis Wilson walked up to the hostess stand and asked for a table in jeans, a t-shirt, and no shoes on his feet. We politely asked him to go put on shoes, which he did, and he was seated in my station at table 51 in the Farragut dining room. Damn those torpedoes.

Wheeling my little three-tiered cart full of food down the ramp I served the table next to him and turned around to see him barefoot again and lounging across the table with his feet up. He was accompanied by Mike Love's daughter whom he had just had a child with. If I recall, that would make her his cousin, and she was all of about 15 years old or so. Talk about robbing the cradle. She ate quickly and left him there in a tequila stupor. Fortunately, their concert wasn't until the next night. We bantered about for a little while, and then he staggered out.

It was reported the following day, the band had gone to Arrowhead golf course nearby, and Dennis had taken off down the middle of I-75 on a golf cart waving a bottle of tequila. Luckily they wrangled him in time for the show, and no one was injured.

Now Dennis had been one of my teenage crushes before Paul McCartney happened to me. That floppy blond hair, the surfer mystique, the great physique, and his swagger. That night after work a few of us went to Hurley's for an after work drink. There at one of the upper tables surrounded by red velvet chairs filled with young girls, was Dennis Wilson. I was walking by to say hello to some other friends who were seated nearby. Suddenly he grabbed my hand, pulled me down into his lap, cradled my head gently in his hand, and laid one of the best French kisses on me that I have ever had. He was simply irresistible. Now I understood the allure, and it was worth the wait from 14 years old to 33 years old. I promptly stood up smiling from ear to ear and proceeded to my friend's table.

That was the last time I saw Dennis Wilson. He drowned that following winter while fishing for memories he had tossed into the sea. Diving for pictures he had thrown overboard, he had been overwhelmed and drowned right next to his schooner. At least I got a kiss good-bye. As swiftly as the ocean washes away footprints in the sand, Denny was gone.

Sweet winds were blowing across the valet parking area when I went to work a few days later. Some woman must have had some very aromatic perfume on that smelled like passion flower. The BMW's and Cadillacs were getting backed up which meant a good money night for once.

It was a strange year for music all together. Disco was still raging on with Donna Summer still hot on the charts, Ashford and Simpson, Barry Manilow, but even the old standbys were only at Pine Knob one or two nights, no big headliners.

Meanwhile a hot new band from California was playing their first gigs. They were called the Red Hot Chili Peppers, and they had not made it to Detroit yet. The Clash and the Cure were hot, but not playing Pine Knob. So when a call came in from one of my friends to go back stage at Cobo Hall to hang out with the Clash, of course I said hell yeah.

It was Mary, or PJ, or someone, who decided we needed our Casbah rocked. We had tickets and after show passes, so of course we were right there for the encore and made our way through the bright house lights that had come up after a great Clash show. They played all my favorite tunes, 'London Calling' and 'Should I Stay or Should I Go' and of course, 'Rock Z Casbah'. This was a real boon for them because they had played places like the Motor City Roller Rink before.

Joe Strummer came out first in a soaking wet white tank top with a towel around his neck.

"Hello ladies, what's shaking tonight?"

"Oh hey there Joe, loved the show, are we partying tonight at the Ren Cen?" my friend inquired.

"Sure, come on up. We will think of something," he added while he scrubbed at his wet hair with the towel.

Then Mick Jones came out with some east side girls hanging on him. You could always tell west side girls from east side. They were as distinctive as NY vs. LA. Thinking I would say something clever, and he would have to come over to me. I spouted out something like,

"Hey I'm a friend of Elton John's, do you know him, he's British?" Mick turned away and gave me a look of disgust as if to say, "Where did you find that one?" There were all sorts of people milling around the band members, and just too many hangers on for me. They all went on to party, while I found my way into the bowels of the Cobo underground garage, and made my way home alone.

Daryl Hall and John Oates played the most consecutive dates that early season, but I never got to see them play. The Tubes were the most exciting things that happened in June. They had been playing the bars around Detroit for a while now. I adored their theatrics, and Fee Waybill's platform shoes.

When he cranked out 'She's A Beauty' I about lost it. Great, how am I going to get laid with that kind of negativity around?

Well I got laid plenty. If I wasn't with some musician, I was with some roadie, if I wasn't with some roadie, I was picking up some guy in the bar. I had a case of raging nymphomania. Just trying to make myself fill the void where a heart should be.

My children were 13 and 10 years old by then, so in a desperate attempt not to lose their faith in me, and take a wrong path, I was spending as much time as I possibly could with them. They were both on recreational baseball teams, and I shuttled them around. The world was getting stranger by the minute, and since the Oakland county child killer had scared the hell out of every mother in the area, I was keeping a watchful eye on them, which meant dragging them along to concerts, sometimes against their will.

In the mid-summer heat of July, Jackson Browne came to town, this time without David Lindley or Rosemary Butler singing backup. They were profoundly missed by me. I partied with Russel Kunkel a little bit doing some lines. Russel and I were not sexually attracted to each other, at least he never tried to impose himself upon me. Russel was always just a very nice guy to be around. Someone told me he was the husband of Cass Elliott's sister, Leah, at the time.

The girls and I went out to the show a couple of nights. Jackson started the show with 'She must be somebody's baby' and ended with 'Stay', 'Rosie', 'Doctor My Eyes', and 'For a Rocker', and, of course, I thought he was singing everything directly into my soul.

One night the next week, I was working in the main dining room when who should walk in to be seated at table 24 but the Divine Ms. M. herself, Bette Midler. She was wearing an unpretentious chocolate brown shift dress with no embellishments what so ever. Not the way I had pictured her at all, and very short as well. I still admired her freedom, her passion, and the unabashed way she would present herself in whatever manner she chose. "The Rose" is still one of my favorite songs. One of the waitresses at the service bar said, "What the hell is she wearing, it looks like a potato sack. Do you think she is going to flash the dining room like she did at the concert last year?"

"I think she can wear and do whatever she wants," was my true and strong opinion.

Later, as Bob Seele played his boogie woogie, two very handsome young men sat down. One had flashing blue eyes and wavy brown hair, and a great body. The other was a handsome, coffee-colored, black guy, wearing a black shirt in the button-up military fashion.

I approached their table: "You two have to be part of Bette's group."

"This is Randy the guitar player, and I'm Jim, her drummer," said the white man.

"We are having a party tomorrow following the show would you like to come, maybe bring some of your friends?" they inquired.

"Sure, how many friends can I bring?"

"About four should be good."

"Great, thanks we'll be there."

My fellow waitresses Sue, Norma, Mervi and myself, all managed to get the night off. The performance Bette put onwas superb.

Our seats were half way up center before the mixing board, and we were having the time of our lives. Bette didn't flash that night, but her show was everything I could have wanted or expected.

Dinner following the show was on the golf course side of Pine Knob. The Locchricio's had built a restaurant in the classic fine dining Italian style called LaVerende.

The doors were held open by tuxedo-clad men. We were astonished by the open market atmosphere on either side of the hallway leading to the dining area. There were displays of fresh fruit, a raw bar filled with seafood, a multi-layered three tier display of pastries, and the entire hall was filled with everything delightful, with chefs in their whites, and tall hats keeping proud charge of all of their displays.

Our high-heeled steps could be heard on the burnt sienna clay tiles as we made our way to the dining area. There in the center of the room was a white baby grand piano, and white linens adorned each round table.

We were shown to our table, and flutes of Dom Perignon started to flow. When a tray full of antipasto appetizers arrived, my friend Norma said,

"Who's paying for all of this? We can't afford this," she whispered to me under her breath.

Just then my friends in the band walked in to join us, with Bette herself making a grand entrance. She was wearing white lame, with long strands of pearls, much more her style.

I asked Randy who was footing the bill for all of this, and he answered Bette. Okay I was impressed before, but that lady can throw a party.

We had salads, soups, main courses, and desserts, and all the champagne we desired. Before dessert some of the musicians gathered around the piano, and we all had one big sing along. A little Billy Joel, some Elton John, and just when Bette was coming over to sing with us, panic arose in the dining room.

One of the backup singers had been pushed into the pool by her boyfriend and had lost her diamond earrings. This was equivalent to tragedy, and the entire party traipsed down to the pool to see what all the commotion was about. People were diving in searching for these one karat treasures. Bette demanded the pool be emptied, and needless to say a damper was thrown over the night by this upheaval. Oh don't get me wrong, the cutie pie drummer and I got it on that night, even with everything else happening.

Several days later, during one of Bette's performances at Pine Knob she collapsed on stage from pure exhaustion and was rushed to one of our local hospitals for treatment. That was my close encounter of the divine kind, with the Divine Ms. M. All's well that ends well.

Now my friend Mervi who had been a Tom Jones fan forever had been dragging me along to every nightclub performance he had done for the past year or two. Of course we had to go back stage each time to see what's new pussycat, and I could care less. I thought he was an egotistical, pompous ass, who stuck a sock in his pants to enhance the look of his package, but my friend liked him.

By the time they played Pine Knob, we were great friends with the management and the crew. Mr. Green was Tom Jones' manager and commander of all things Tom.

One night I was hanging with some of the guys in the crew after the show, and they invited Mervi and me to a private party. Very intimate. Tom was slated to make an appearance, and everyone was just sitting around in one of the Hilton suites drinking cocktails from the full service bar and quietly mingling.

"Hey, do you think anyone would mind if I smoked a joint?" I asked of one of the crew guys. Two of them looked back and forth at each other and shook their heads "no" matter-of-factly.

"No it's okay, I don't think anyone cares," was the response I got

CRAZY CHANGING CLIMATE (1983)

as they suspiciously looked around the room.

As I was lighting up Mr. Green came storming into the room, grabbed me by the arm, yanked me out of my chair, and physically threw me out of the suite.

"We don't allow that shit, and you are not welcomed here anymore!" he said, his face turning beet red and his salt and pepper hair standing up.

That was the end of my Tom Jones experience. It was a 360 degree difference between Willie and Tom to be certain. So the following week when Willie came to town it was quite a change. Pooty, Dusty, Rusty and the gang were all still with Willie. They were like a family, a brotherhood if you will, and the feeling conveyed was much more jovial than Tom and company.

They were road weary for certain, but we had a good time. I was once again with Dusty, and we had a quickie and called it a night.

A couple of days later I was working in the main dining room. The room had just opened, and was not filling up quickly. Looking up, I saw a familiar face coming toward me. It was JT. He was with two other men, all casually dressed in summer attire. He would be playing one night only at the Knob the following night.

I pulled the chair out for him to be seated, "Hello James good to see you again," I said.

"Hello there. How do I know you?"

"I used to wait on you at Pine Knob in the lodge, and I know you from David Lindley, and Lee Sklar, and others," I said.

"Oh yeah, good to see you."

He didn't have a clue who I was. They ordered some appetizers and non-alcoholic beverages, and the other two men departed. There was some small talk between James and myself, but nothing earthshattering. After he left, I noticed his room key.

What was that supposed to mean? I thought I knew, but then again I didn't. I marched straight over to the Hilton front desk and told the manager that Mr. Taylor had forgotten his key.

"Are you sure he forgot the key?"

"I don't know what else it could mean."

He looked at me as if to say, sure lady, we both know he wanted you to return the key in person. Well I was busy working. So sweet baby James would just have to be lonely tonight. Besides he didn't even remember me anyway from the previous flirtations. My old dinner partners from Ron's of Japan in Chicago came to town next. Loverboy crew invited me to the show, but alas I could not go. Our little town restaurant was busier than ever.

I had been curious about the New York City music scene ever since I had met Patti Smith. *Rolling Stone* was one of the magazines I subscribed to in order to be in the know on the political scene, but also to read about New York scene musicians. There was no one I was more interested in than David Byrne. As music steered a new course out of the disco era, punk, grunge, funk, underground radical new hybrids began to evolve. The music from CBGB club in New York's east village was where everything new seemed to flow from. Underground clubs and after hours places were the breeding ground for the bee sting of HIV for the next few years. That was the one thing that scared the shit out of me.

When David Byrne walked into Hurley's one night, I knew exactly who he was. I loved the Talking Heads. It was the night before they played and he must have been exploring. Those eyes, those eyes. Not only that, but Tina Weymouth! A bad ass chick with a bass. Joan Jett was the only other one who really made it with an ax, I don't even count Nancy Wilson, but man I loved that band.

There was a young man sitting at the curve in the bar by himself who got up and talked with Mr. Byrne when he came in. Striking up a conversation with him and sharing drinks, he asked if I would like to go to the show the following day. Naturally I agree to go with him, and also agreed to the sex, the sex was good too. Talking Heads were fantastic of course, and that made my week.

In all of my naiveté and ignorance the next show I should have been tuned into, and probably would be in my top five shows ever, was the James Brown Revue with Bo Diddley, Harold Melvin and the

Blue Notes, with Sam and Dave. I love R&B and soul music, so the only thing I can remember scaring me off was that Stephen Stills once told me I should steer clear of Bo Diddley. The bands that were coming up at the Knob really did not lend themselves to good money nights for me, and so I chose to just enjoy the ride. Early August brought one of my all-time favorites the Jefferson Starship to Pine Knob. I would give anything to meet Gracie Slick, my songstress heroine. She was the only singer I couldn't quite copy. I met one of their crew, (let's call him Joe for lack of another name) in Hurley's for a drink, while slowly the rest of the band members trickled in.

"Who's the guy in the pajamas?" I inquired, noticing a guy who resembled my father in the 1950's plotting around the house in the morning.

Laughing he responded,

"That's Grace Slick's husband he does our lighting. That's the latest fashion trend in L.A. by the way," he said.

"Forgive my lack of haute couture knowledge. By the way, I have tomorrow off and I can come out to the show."

Just then Grace walked in looking just as stunning as I thought she would. Joe jumped up and introduced me to Grace while I gushed. She said thank you, took it well, asked if we had seen her husband, and made a hasty exit.

"Come on let's get out of here and find Bill," Joe suggested picking up our tab.

We walked the horseshoe-shaped hallway around the main floor to an interior room with views of the courtyard. Knocking on door 183, a curly haired blond guy with glasses answered and invited us in.

"Christine, this is Bill Thompson, he's the Starship's manager," said Joe with all due respect and intention. He was handsome, blond, a little taller than I was, so my perfect type.

"It's very nice to meet you Bill."

"I am so glad you guys are here....have some lines over there on the table. I got this new game and I need at least four of you to play it," he greeted us with the exuberance of Richard Lewis.

We all gathered on the floor with a white crust on our noses, and drinks in our hands. Bill began explaining the game, with the patience of Job, and some difficulty.

"Ok, this is Trivial Pursuit, and there are four colors and teams, and answer these categories, and move around the board."

"Sure, just start playing and we will follow," suggested Joe.

Well we got going and we were having such a good time that before we knew it the sun was coming up. Bill and I excelled in movies, theatre, movie stars, history and geography, while the crew guys did well in science and sports. We were all geeked and buzzed up and we had nowhere to go.

"You can just stay here," Bill said to me. He did have two beds, but we cuddled and held each other as he pointed to his problem. The man had done so much cocaine that he had to hold himself up with a jock strap and was perhaps forever suffering from erectile dysfunction. That was the first time, no wait, second time, I had seen such physical impairment due to cocaine.

None the les,s he was a wonderful person and we just made out like a couple of teenagers on a first date. The sunlight peeking through the drapery made it impossible for me to get a good long sleep, and so I gingerly made my way out to the car and headed home.

The next day at work was a bit rough to say the least. As I walked up toward the valet area I glanced over at a small patch of grass under a crab apple tree. There was one of the guys from a band down under, 'Men At Work' practicing some form of Tai Chi or Tai Kwan do on the lawn. They must have been playing with some other headliner, but they had arrived a few days early to Troy, Michigan.

"Gooday mate," I greeted him in a phony Aussie accent. He basically ignored me and went on with his exercise.

What was he doing there? Was he trying to get noticed? It was very odd, and an odd patch of grass to be on.

Granted there were no parks in the immediate area, just industrial parks, and business center parks. The people of Troy were deprived. There was White Chapel Park where all of my family is buried, but

I don't think that dancing on graves, or doing Tai Chai would be appreciated.

As summer has a way of doing, it went by too quickly. One of my favorite British performers was coming to Pine Knob the following week. It was Elvis Costello, the guy who penned, 'Oliver's Army' and 'Angels Want to Wear my Red Shoes.' After hearing that one, I raced out and got a pair of red Converse sneakers. 'Pump It Up' always pumped me up. The punk style was undeniable, and the kick and snare quick chops of Pete Thomas help propel Costello to the new level of success they were enjoying.

Sitting in Hurley's one night after work with the usual suspects of Crab crew, a rather tall, lanky, guy with shaggy brown hair came strolling in wearing skin tight jeans, and a white shirt. He sat down next to me, offered to buy me a drink and introduced himself.

"Hey there, my name is Pete, what's yours?" he said in a lovely British accent. We made small talk until the bar was closing, and then some of his friends, and some of my friends, were ravenously hungry.

"Where can we get something to eat at this hour?" Pete asked me. "Well the only place open is Denny's down on Big Beaver."

"Then the big beaver it is, got a car?"

"Sure I can drive," and some five of us piled into my little white Nissan.

Denny's didn't know what hit them. We moved furniture around to our liking, and Pete flirted outrageously with the waitress in order to make certain we had exactly what we wanted.

"We would like to order the entire menu," Pete requested.

"The whole menu is a great deal of food Pete!" I reminded him.

"I have a great big appetite," he said.

We managed to pare it down to three tables filled with food in a veritable buffet of Denny's best. There was breakfast, whole entrees, desserts, cakes and pies. We had the waitress crank up the jukebox music, and we had the entire place to ourselves. We were feasting like kings in a frenzied free-for-all. I don't think I have ever had so much fun in a restaurant.

Afterward Pete and I went back to his room, made "I am too full to fuck" love and crashed out. Of course I made it to the show the following night, and as anticipated Elvis rocked the place down.

Those were the most exciting aspects of 1983 for me. Little Steven and the Disciples of Soul came to play Pine Knob, so that meant no Bruce Springsteen that year, who would have been the only act I would have liked to see, but missed.

CHAPTER 33

Not All Wine and Rosie's

"Greed is the bottomless pit which exhausts the person in an endless effort to satisfy the need without ever reaching satisfaction..." Eric Fromm

How many times had I recited the Lord's Prayer? "And lead us not into temptation, and lead us not into temptation, and lead us not into temptation," endlessly, and apparently mindlessly, babbling, those words as my parents and the world of my childhood demanded.

The fruitless summers had not produced any lasting love, and I was sinking into despair. One autumn evening in the early 1980's, my acquaintances John and his wife Denise, a very nice married couple, who held steady daytime jobs, and on occasion sold cocaine to the bands passing through Detroit, popped into the Crab. The piano man played, and wine glasses chimed above the din, where they were seated in the far end of the lounge.

"Hey Chris, did you hear who is staying next door?" they flagged me over and discretely asked.

"No what's happening?"

"The 'Randy Bachman' of Bachman, Turner, Overdrive is staying over there, he's in town recording something. Would you like to come party with us later?" Denise said.

I trusted them, they had always been honest with me. The one I should not have trusted was myself.

Later that evening when my side work was complete, and my last table was gone, I punched the clock and headed for Hurley's, where we were going to meet. My kids were secure for the night. I had a good baby sitter for once, a college student, who was mature, and didn't mind staying up late since she had studying to do anyway.

We went up to one of the larger suites of the Northfield Hilton, knocked on the door, and a rather stout, tall man, with light brown, longish hair, wearing a red robe as if it were a smoking jacket, like the men would wear in old movies, appeared in the doorway. Only the ascot was missing.

"Hello there, welcome, nice to see you guys again, did you bring the blow?" he queried not even knowing who I was. I was assuming, that he didn't need to be discreet.

"Sure, I can lay out some lines," John responded.

"Good then I can sample the merchandise, there are drinks over there on the table, help yourselves," he offered.

"So 'Randy' this is Christine, she works next door at the Crab," Denise introduced me.

"Yes, I am a fan of BTO, what are you doing in town?"

"Looking at some recording studios."

"I love 'Ain't Seen Nothin' Yet' and 'Let it Ride' those are my favorite tunes of yours," I acknowledged with a lack of anything else to say not knowing too much background on the band. I didn't even know what any of them looked like. I didn't have to, he elaborated on his band background in a bragging sort of manner, talking about himself and verbosely managing my attention.

There was an electric guitar in the room propped on a chair, which validated him, and there were other people present seated in small groups, also an endorsement. By the end of the night he had me in bed, and expressed how much he liked me, wanted to help me, and would I come back the next night.

It was a very difficult time in my life. I had managed to save the most money I had ever socked away in the bank. It was nearly $3000, which I had scrimped and saved for. I denied myself any travel, expensive clothing, I was driving a beater used car, and really struggling to keep my little family together. So the vulnerability could be sniffed out by any dog who wanted to take advantage of me.

The following night as predicted, there was another party in Randy's room, with the same cast of characters as the previous night. After getting us all sufficiently high, he asked that we be left alone.

"I would like to discuss a proposition with you in private," he eluded to something other than sex, which he already had lured me into.

"Sure, what do you have in mind?"

"I need an assistant. Someone to help me choose what to wear on stage and get it ready, someone to make personal plans for me, someone who is a good communicator like you."

"We would go to my offices in Canada, and I could pay you $800 per week to start, with the benefits we all get in the band."

"What about my children?"

"Of course you'll bring your children too. I love that you have children. You can relocate right?"

That should have been the scarlet, crimson, and bright red flag right then and there. No man had ever told me I love that you have children.

"Well I have to talk to them, and my family, and their father, but I don't see why not," my head began to reel with the thoughts of making that kind of money and doing something exciting like being on the road with a prominent band.

The following weeks he worked on convincing me. I went as far as giving notice at work, and planning what to do with my house. I talked to the school about transferring records to Canada. He took me shopping, out for dinner, he was driving around in a Corvette that he said was a rental, and told me about the elite car collection he had at home. For what it is worth, he came off as worldly, wise, and educated.

Several days later, he had met my children, and asked me if it was a good time to look at cars for me. He called me up on my day off, explaining to me that he was staying at a hotel on Woodward Avenue and I was to meet him there, it was close to the Toyota dealership.

"You have to have something nice to drive around in, you can't think of keeping that vehicle you have. There is a huge Toyota dealer down the street here, let's go get you a car."

Packing the girls up in the car with some projects and activities to occupy them, we drove to the shabby motel on Woodward Avenue. Something began to not feel right in the pit of my stomach.

"What's wrong, mom?" one of the girls asked.

"Oh it's nothing, we are meeting my friend Randy, remember him? The guy in the BTO band."

When we reached the Palms motel, rain began coming down in sheets. The half lit sign loomed over the pool blinking ominously. Half an hour had passed by, and the grey, austere, day of rain turned into thunder showers. Parking our car in the front, we ran through the yellow brick open passages to the room number he had given me. There were no other people to be seen.

The "gut feeling" sensation I had been experiencing went away as soon as I saw his face. He had me mesmerized, almost hypnotized in some way. Charming his way around my girls, making them giggle as he kissed me, he said let's go down to the dealership.

"You girls stay here for a little while, watch television and work on your projects, ok?" Randy suggested. We did some lines and took off in his Corvette.

The Toyota dealership was one of the largest in Detroit, and the showroom was impressively well lighted to showcase the cars. The minute we walked in a salesman approached us. "How can I help you folks today?"

"I am buying my girlfriend a car. I think a Camry would be suitable for her," Randy, the hustler, responded.

"Here we are, this is our top of the line model," the man said and he opened the driver's seat door for me.

"Let's go talk price and details at your desk. Honey you stay here and try your new car out," he instructed the salesman and me.

The car was beautiful, gold with a beige interior, and all the bells and whistles. I played the radio, checked out the stereo system, and hit the horn.

"Well thank you Mr. Bachman, you can take delivery on this in a few days," the salesman said shaking the big man's hand.

Back in the car, heading for the motel once again, Randy turned to me and said,

"You know all of my cash right now is tied up in this recording business. You are going to have to pay the taxes on the car, and some of the other things I'm buying you."

I thought long and hard about this statement. My head was flighty like caged butterflies suddenly set free. Over the past two week's, I had witnessed a metamorphosis in him and in me. His appearance was different today though, he had a theme of desperation going on, and a wild sort of Charles Manson air about him.

"How much are we talking?" It came out of my mouth before I could control it.

"I think a couple of thousand should cover it."

"That's almost all I have in the bank."

"We'll get it tomorrow, we have to wrap this up and get back to Canada."

Back in the motel room the girls were watching one of their afternoon "Smurf" shows. When we entered the room they jumped up and hugged me.

"Where have you been, we were getting worried," the oldest one scolded.

"This nice man bought us a new car girls." Upon hearing this, they jumped up and down in celebration. I now had them sucked into the vortex of deception.

"When are we getting it?" the younger one asked.

"It should be ready for delivery by next week, we just need the tax on it to be paid since I am a Canadian, and my currency isn't good here," he said, speaking directly to them in a soft kind manner.

This would never have been possible to pull off in this day and age of course, but in the early 1980's it was believable. We made a plan for the next day while Randy stroked my hair, and massaged my back.

"You are going to love Canada. I have a huge house, you can have your own separate wing to live in. I will take good care of you," he promised with the sincerity of the pope.

"I have to get to work right now, but tomorrow I should be available by 5 or 6 o'clock," I said.

"Good I'll see you then," he said and he bent down and kissed me good-bye.

The following day brought an uncanny sense of uneasiness, and everything that happened was unnerving. I had gone out to get the money from the bank. The teller was skeptical as I withdrew the money. She slowly counted it out without her usual smile. Having arranged for the sitter to come over early, she questioned the unusually early time I needed her services. When I stopped by the corner drug store and paid with a hundred dollar bill, the cashier laughingly snapped it and asked if I had just printed it.

"Is this real? You never have this kind of money, you're usually digging in the bottom of your purse for loose change," she pointed out.

"I know, I just came from the bank."

A block from the condominium, I checked the mailbox, gathered up the bills, and slowly made the turn onto Beechtree Court. The babysitter's car was gone. I ran up the stairs calling out for the girls. No one was there. It was dark by then and fear struck through my heart like a bullet. It was like no pain I had ever felt before. Just then the phone on the kitchen wall loudly rang, startling me. Grabbing the phone with a sense of dread I quickly answered.

"Yes...who is this?"

"Hey sweetheart, it's Randy, where are you?"

"I am where I said I would be, where are my children?"

"They're fine, they're with me, I sent the sitter home and took them out for ice cream," he said.

"Get them back home, right now," I said.

"Sure we're on our way, did you get the money?"

"Get home."

An eternity passed by. He had my children. It was as if he held them for ransom. Nearly an hour later the Corvette pulled up outside, and the girls ran upstairs.

"Mom, Randy bought us ice cream, and got us each a toy."

"Go to your rooms please," I said, trying hard to control my voice.

"What's wrong baby? Everything is all right. I have your car being prepped right now, and I am going to get it tomorrow, I do need that tax money though," he said.

"Fine, here you go, I will see you tomorrow, it's been a very long day, and I just want to spend the evening with my girls, okay?" I said, mustering a slight smile, and handing over, with fear and trepidation, my envelope of life savings.

I woke the following day to the phone ringing in the kitchen. It was John.

"Christine we've been scammed! All of us have been scammed by this Randy guy. He isn't who he says he is."

A long paralyzing silence on my end of the phone made John shout into the receiver,

"Did you hear me?"

"What?"

"This guy's real name is Patrick Wetzel, and he is a scam artist, nationwide scam artist," John repeated.

"How did you find out?"

"The girl who owns the Corvette found me to say he had stolen it and taken her money too. We have called the Oakland County Sheriff. He took me for $500 in cocaine, but of course I can't claim that to the cops," John went on.

"I know where he is. I know where he is right now," I answered.

"Then you had better do something about it right now," he said.

Upon hanging up the phone I called the Oakland County Sheriff. Explaining in great detail all that had happened, they said they would get right on it and call me back. An hour passed by before I heard from them again.

"Ms. Fowler, this is the Oakland County Sheriff's office calling."

"Yes."

"We have apprehended a Patrick Wetzel trying to board a plane at the Pontiac Airport just now. Rest easy, he will not be posting bond, and we will keep you updated. Thank you for the tip. This guy was wanted in 5 states from Utah to Maine. He has several aliases as well," the police officer informed me.

After the scam, I never saw my money again. Attorneys kept me posted about the trial. The prosecuting attorney who handled the trial explained I would not have to appear in court to testify. There were four or five other people who had suffered higher monetary losses than I had, who would be testifying.

The conman spent some quality time in the fair state of Michigan. He was sentenced to 4 years in Marquette prison in the Upper Peninsula. One dreadfully cold place for him to chill out for a while.

CHAPTER 34

Save the Last Dance for Me

"Being deeply loved by someone gives you strength, while loving someone deeply gives you courage..." Lao Tzu

Many exhilarating things had happened to me in a relatively short time, but 1984 was about to be one of the best. Tulips and daffodils were popping out of the ground earlier than usual that year, and the Pine Knob season was beginning earlier than normal. We had a new manager in the restaurant, and although he lacked in personality, he seemed to be a savvy businessman, who, by the way, had a personal dislike of me, and my relationship with Mr. Muer.

Prom dances were still in full swing, boys with their boutonnieres, and girls with their frilly dresses and corsages, filled the restaurant nightly. Then the Beach Boys came to town. Dennis Wilson had died the previous year, so there was no interest for me any longer, members dropping off like flies. May was my favorite month, however, and joy once again filled my heart as we had made it through the doldrums of the winter in Michigan.

Appearances in the restaurant included Waylon Jennings at table 31, that cowboy stands out in a crowd, let me tell you, black on black on black with a black hat, bad ass. David Gilmour of Pink Floyd fame was doing a solo tour, and I met him one night in Hurley's. John Denver and company made their usual walk through the bar, but were having internal problems of some sort, so I stayed away from that show. I made a point of going to see Blue Oyster Cult, simply to see the 30-foot Godzilla display, with smoke billowing from the nostrils and mouth. I had to be back stage for that. Waylon Jennings came back once again for a one-nighter. Huey Lewis and the News played on the Fourth of July and the fireworks were spectacular, one of my favorite new bands of the era.

One of the most impressive shows, and a true departure from anything she had done before, was Linda Ronstadt with Nelson Riddle. They took the audience on a stroll back to a bygone era. It was a soft, romantic, and full on orchestra led by the maestro himself. I really admired her for that, and her voice lent itself very well to that genre of music.

A few days later I received a rather profound phone call.

"Hi Christine this is Travis remember me from the Springsteen tour?"

"Yes I think so, I met you a couple of times in Lansing, and Detroit, when I was with Seger's band, right?"

"Right. We are in town a few days early for the Born in the USA tour, and we would like to invite you to the show, and to the hotel to hang out with us. We are staying at the Dearborn Hyatt."

"That sounds good. I do have several days off of work, and I wanted to catch the show for sure. I bought the new album. It's fantastic, especially Bruce's butt, my favorite," I said and then I sang the chorus to 'Dancing In The Dark'.

"Well, come on down, call me on a house phone when you get here, and I will come down to meet you."

My daughters were 14 and 11 years old by then and could manage by themselves just fine. I told them Bruce Springsteen's manager had called, and invited me to come down to see them.

"Oh mom, you have to go, he's your favorite! We'll be fine, Amy is coming over and we are going to do something with their family, so no problem," Chrisanna exclaimed practically pushing me out of the door.

Summer heat scorched my face when I first turned on the air conditioning in the car. I made my way west across I-94 toward Dearborn, the glass house of the Ford Motor company, and Michigan Avenue.

Sporting a pair of white clam diggers with a buttoned cuff I had made and a white Mackinaw Island shirt with a sailboat on it, I headed down to the Hyatt Regency in the middle of the afternoon.

In a way the Hyatt reminded me of the Northfield Hilton. It shown like a black diamond in the July sun. There was a monorail that shuttled people to and from the Fairlane shopping center. Very George Jetson futuristic.

I parked my car within walking distance to the entry. A wave of nerves shivered down my back as I approached the valet, who was dressed like a New York City doorman.

This was about as high-end as Detroit got back then. It was lavishly decorated, and the luxurious crystal chandeliers led to the bank of elevators. The clamor of pedestrian hotel guests fanned out through the lobby as they made their ways to the restaurants, limousines, and cocktail bar, dressed in their finery. Feelings of incongruity flooded my brain, and I needed to rid myself of this inferior loathing.

The hotel had 933 employees at the time. Somewhat like a small city, in which I felt somewhat subterranean. The palace at Versailles came to mind as I admired the marble floors, the art work, and the vases. I must have appeared very shabby compared to the other patrons in designer suits, and formal attire.

At the elevator I picked up a bronze, old world style house phone perched on a pedestal. The male voice on the other end was familiar, and he said he would be right down.

I was enjoying the people-watching when someone tapped me on the shoulder.

"Hi there good to see you again," he said and gave me a hug. As we entered the elevator, he inserted a special key to the penthouse suites on the 16th floor.

"We have the whole floor. It's very cool," he said as if to impress upon me that no one else was going to bother the band.

We passed Nils Lofgren in the hallway wearing those "LA style" pajamas that Gracie Slick's husband had worn. He and Travis exchanged a few syllables. He introduced me to Nils, and they bantered back and forth. We reached his suite.

He took my hand and led me into what was apparently his room, his half unpacked suitcase, his supplies in the bathroom, his unmade queen-sized bed. So this was the way into the world of Bruce Springsteen. This is what I had to do to be accepted. This was the wormhole. Only it was Travis' worm in my hole. My availability was advertised.

Usually unaccustomed to making love in a bright room, I reached for the bedside lamp, and took it down a notch. We got undressed, he shoved me down on the bed, and I pulled him down next to me. Passionately I proceeded to make love to his very stiff organ with my mouth. Just before getting him off, I stopped and rolled him over to be on top for a ride. That didn't last very much longer. We were spent.

"I don't even know your first name," I announced post coitus.

"George, it's George," he managed breathlessly."

"Is there anything to drink in this place?" I said, seeking a beverage container in the other room.

"Sure, but come back and get dressed, the guys are coming over here soon."

I went into the bathroom to freshen up, and clean the black circles of mascara that had formed under my eyes. Several minutes later when I walked back into the formal area of the suite, there was Bruce, Gary Tallant, and another man I didn't recognize standing in the shadows of the vestibule. Elton John's 'Tiny Dancer' played in the background from the canned music overhead. I found a chaise lounge to lay upon Cleopatra style. My back to all of them, sipping on a Heineken beer. They were standing in the doorway vestibule. I could still see them in my peripheral vision. Bruce kept glancing over at me, they were all doing a great deal of whispering, and then Bruce walked over to me.

"Hello I'm Bruce," he said, holding out his hand to me.

"I am Christine," I said, which was the last thing I ever spoke to him. Time stood still, I was flashing back to my childhood visualizing a little girl with brown curly hair pulling her red wagon, and a boy with a striped shirt and a sideways baseball cap. I was as paralyzed as Deborah Kerr in 'An Affair to Remember' without the blanket to hide under. Wanting desperately to stand up and tell him that his song 'Born to Run' was the reason I left my husband, that he had had a profound impact on my life, and that I wanted to have his children. Bruce said nothing else to me either.

I must have come off as smug, somnolent, and an absolute idiot. Of course, it can all be chalked up to my lifelong theme of not being able to speak to people I truly loved.

Somehow that afternoon I ended up with David, Bruce's trainer. Bruce had taken up a regimen of exercise that was transforming him from beanpole to hunk, all with the help of his good friend and trainer from New Jersey.

"Let's go to dinner," David suggested.

"I'm not exactly dressed for dinner. I wish I had brought some other clothes with me, but I was not planning on all of this happening."

"You look just fine, we're only going to Benihana next door."

Out in the hallway, the entire band was gathering. That was the first time I saw Patti Scialfa. She was very tall, and looked like my cousin Nancy with red hair. She could have been my sister. It was apparent to me that she and Bruce were not a couple at the time, she wasn't walking with him, and she was just part of the band.

We got on the elevators, and when we got off, I discovered what it was like to be famous. All the people in the lobby stopped to stare and point at us. There were several waiting limousines. Max, Bruce, Patti, and a couple of other people got into the limos.

"I thought we were all going to dinner," I said to David.

"Some of the band is going to see the Cars at Pine Knob."

My heart sank. I fell into deep rejection and despair. Of all the things that I would have loved to be doing in that moment it was going out to my "home away from home" to be with Bruce and see one of my favorite bands.

Little Steven showed up at Benihana, and several other band members, none of whom sat with us. The smell of the shrimp on the hot steaming black grill filled the air. The familiar chef with his tall white hat approached our group and started to entertain us flipping shrimp into his pocket. Seeing Ric Ocasek flip his guitar singing 'Just What I Needed' would have been more entertaining. Gulping down glasses of white wine as quickly as the waitress could bring them, I plied myself with alcohol to forget where I wanted to be.

"Who's the chick singing with Bruce?"

"That's Patti Scialfa, she sings with a local Jersey band, and he wanted a backup singer for this tour, so that's all there is to it," David offered.

"So they aren't a couple?" curiosity overwhelming me.

"Not that I know of, just friends. He's so busy working out whenever he is not on stage that he probably doesn't have time for a romance, trust me, I know."

"So you will be at the shows the next two nights, right? You have to come back," David said.

"Sure I'll come back down tomorrow afternoon for sound check. I'll give Travis a call."

"No just call me up when you're leaving and I'll meet you, okay?" David gave me his room phone number, his home phone, and address in New Jersey as well.

After dinner, back to the room for a quickie in the dark, I could feel that he was fairly well built, but not like a trainer would be. He had a hairy chest. Then it was time for Cinderella to run away home to check on her girls. On the way back to Lake Orion I felt very sorry for myself.

The next morning I made certain the Chrisanna and Damian were staying with friends for the night, and packed them up. Putting on my best face, looking as good as Stevie Nicks ever did, I throttled up the sewing machine and made a full flouncy, midi length, scarlet red skirt, with a ruffle around the bottom, a bright yellow gauze blouse held up only by a band of elastic, and a poufy sleeve, natural white cotton shirt with tiny buttons and a collarless, scoop, neck. Red scarf in my hair, and full on make-up I made my way back to the Hyatt.

Greeting me with open arms, David took me up to the penthouse for a gathering of band members to make certain we all had the agenda. Jon Landau was running through the happenings of the day. We all piled into white vans and off we went for Detroit and Cobo Hall on the Detroit River.

The penetrating heat was only felt momentarily as we disembarked in the garage and made our way into the dressing room area. I must say I was greatly surprised that someone like Bruce Springsteen would travel around in a white van. The most inconspicuous vehicle ever made.

Sound check was fabulous of course and I got to meet Clarence Clemens, "the big man" finally. They gave me a seat at the side of the stage, eye level view, and I had brought my Canon AE-1 with a telephoto lens to grab some shots. I could even see the hole in Bruce's t-shirt clearly as I went through the evening, singing, screaming, and picture taking. Now ripped clothing is the trend, maybe he started it. During 'Dancing in the Dark' he brought a blushing, pubescent girl onstage to dance with him. What a thrill that must have been for her, something to talk about for the rest of your life.

The afterglow backstage was cloistered in several rooms. I assume Bob Seger was there with his people, and maybe the pope or Rabi Rosin, who knows. I hung out with the crew, as usual, they were much more fun anyway.

The concert the following night was just as great, and again I rode to the concert in the white vans with the band. To this day, the 'Born in the USA' album remains one of my favorites. I also enjoyed the musical departure 'Nebraska', and the album with Pete Seeger. Just a down to earth, hometown guy, trying to make his mark on the world, and leaving a mark on my heart.

Other highlights of that mid-summer nights dream were Steve

Lawrence and Eydie Gorme sitting at table 41 in the Farragut dining room. They looked exactly like they do on television, in full make-up, and sprayed pompadour haircut. They were peaches and cream sweet whenever I came up to the table, then they would go back to bickering. It was hilarious. One of my all-time favorite guests came into Charley's the following week. Johnny Mathis, by himself, at table 51, ordered his Gazpacho soup, as 'Chances Are' dreamily swooshed through my brain.

Here is a very strange thing. Neil Diamond came into town mid-August that year. My fellow groupie Doris (clitoris) was staying with him in one of the Northfield Hilton suites. She came into the Crab, and asked me to come up for Neil's surprise birthday party.

When my work for the night was complete, I went up to the party room on the second floor. Still wearing my black and whites, and smelling like a fish, because I hadn't prepared for an evening out. The commotion could be heard out in the hallway. I knocked loudly on the door. No answer. I knocked again. No answer, and I turned to walk away. Just then the door flew open and it was skinny, mousy Doris.

"Hi Chris, come on in," she yelled down the hall. The doors of the hotel were very heavy, and recessed, so if you walked away from it for any reason, it would slam closed behind you. So it did on us, but Doris had the room key.

"Look what I got for Neil," she said as she dragged me through the gathered guests to a tall table holding a one layer cake of Neil's head. His own music filled the background, as Doris stood there gloating over her cleverness.

"That is so cool, you even got the hair black and the nose right," I complimented.

Just then Neil entered the party room from an adjacent room and greeted everyone. Of course all the party people rushed to say hello and tell him how much they loved the show that night.

"Neil, this is my friend Chris," Doris shoved me toward him ignoring the others.

He managed a deep sexy voice and said, "It is a pleasure meeting you. You look very familiar." "I used to work at Pine Knob, and several years ago, gosh, nine years ago now, I worked your private press conference in the downstairs of the ski lodge," I offered.

He was kind and acknowledged that he remembered, although I am certain he did not. At any rate, he loved the cake Doris had gotten him, and she sang happy birthday, as we all joined in, much to a perplexed looking Neil.

"It is your birthday right?" I said.

"Ah no not really, it is in January, she just misses it every year, so she does this," he laughed in an endearing way.

Following a few champagne toasts I said my farewells. After a very crazy night at work, and looking the way I did, my party zest got up and went. As I drove home, I thought of all the old ladies who would probably kill to be in my black, greasy, work shoes that night.

A few shows filled my nights the rest of that summer. Jefferson Starship was in town, and of course Mickey Thomas, in true form, was partying hardy, up to his old tricks.

I caught Billy Squier at the Knob, promoting his 'Signs of Life' album. He had everyone up and yelling "stroke me stroke me" at the tops of their lungs. Very fun show, very handsome man, with that shock of long, black, curly hair flying.

Closing out the season was our old pal Willie. He and his band of merry men, and family, spent a week hunkered down at the Hilton. My friend Mervi and I went to a couple of shows, and hung out with Dusty, and Pootie, slightly more subdued these days than the original tequila, twisted, tarantulas they used to be. We just smoked a whole lot of weed.

At the end of it all I was still dancing alone. In my living room, with only the street lamp light streaming through a window, I twirled around and around in my night gown, while my favorite Bruce song, 'Drive All Night' played on my little stereo turntable.

CHAPTER 35

1985

"The world as we have created it is a process of our think-
ing. It cannot be changed without changing our thinking..."
Albert Einstein

Change was definitely called for. The AIDS epidemic had rocked New
York City and people were dying. It was afflicting mostly white males,
which was exactly the demographic I was attracted to. Although it
was the male to male gay community who was suffering the most. My
mindset was developing new strategies, and I was being much more
careful, closely scrutinizing my partners. As this happened I began
thinking of ending my long time association with the restaurant business. It had always gone hand in hand with my personal promiscuity.

The new season at the Knob brought my old friends who had
finally busted out of the local club circuit in Detroit to opening and
headlining. Fee Waybill and the Tubes opened for one night in 1985.
They were still doing 'White Punks On Dope' and really had not had
another hit to promote, 'She's a Beauty' which smacked of how most
musicians must feel about aloof groupies.

Summer began with an unusually cold start. The disco era was an
old man hobbling around with a walker, there was some good rock

and roll still around, but Pine Knob, and the Nederlanders were hard pressed to find any good new acts to play their venue. It was all very tired. The old Mountain band, Dan Fogelberg, Iron Maiden were some of the bands of the week.

By the end of the week when Santana came through town, it was only 70 degrees, so no festivities on the lake that year. There was no friendly get together at all. Carlos and his wife came into the lounge briefly and said "hello" that was it, my thrill for the week. Then some Brit named Howard Jones followed Santana, who the heck was that?

Restaurant business was still a money maker however, and we were turning out the bouillabaisse and paella like crazy. We were still attracting the local who's who of Detroit, and the businessmen from all the world headquarters finding a home in Troy. Nothing had changed in terms of the décor of the restaurant, sometimes Chuck would bring in a new work of art he had acquired on his travels, but the main dining room was still high back upholstered chairs with brass nail head trim, and brown linen rolled over stylish flatware. We would place large brandy snifters on the table with fresh flowers inside each day.

In the Farragut, the tables were much less formal with a printed oil cloth, and the wooden bench booths enhanced with padded cushions for comfort. Bare wooden floors made the room a noisier place as Windsor backed colonial style chairs scraped in and out. No jacket required.

I walked into the kitchen in the middle of our rush to pick up some salads for my table, when the expeditor flagged me over.

"Please take this order out to table 40, Kathy isn't picking up right away," he instructed me.

I read the ticket that had been stuck underneath the platter, gathered the necessary side dishes, and loaded up my little three-tiered wooden cart with the plates. Easing my way down the ramp, (things would go flying easily even though the carpeting helped to slow the inertia a bit), I made the turn to the hidden away table.

As I looked at the smiling faces staring back at me, I recognized Phil Collins.

"Oh hello, big fan here, I loved the Genesis band." On and on I gushed as I passed out the pasta, the salmon, and filleted a Dover sole tableside, jabbering away, dousing it with a buttery almandine.

Phil was cordial and thanked me, and after dinner he sent his friend from the table to inquire whether or not I would like to attend his concert the following night. Of course, I said yes, and he explained there would be tickets and passes at the trailer for me. Maybe this wouldn't be such a bad summer after all.

At home the next night, I got ready for the show and decided this would be something the girls would enjoy too, so we all got our big hair ready and sprayed, very Farrah Fawcett, and away we went. The drive was only about ten minutes from where we lived in Lake Orion. Arriving early, we found our seats, got refreshments and anxiously awaited the performance.

Phil Collins band came out to rapturous applause, then a long pause, then Phil sauntered across the stage to the microphone. He tried to sing a few notes, but nothing was forthcoming. He stopped the band and began again. He sang, 'I Don't Care Anymore.' His voice was cracking, and he turned right around, stormed off the stage, and did not return. They announced he had cancelled the show. My disappointment was enormous, as well as that of my children, and the rest of the concert goers. That was unprecedented, I had never seen that happen before, except the night Kris Kristofferson passed out, and Rita had to finish the show herself.

Collins was fined thousands of dollars for not playing. There was no back stage, and no music. That was the night the music died. Nothing else came close to intriguing me the rest of that summer. Several nights later, Don Henley walked through the restaurant with a stunningly beautiful redhead on his arm, and that didn't phase me. I did not attempt to go to his show. Eric Clapton, REO Speedwagon, the Beach Boys, none of them were inspirational. Crosby, Stills, and Nash were playing in July. I was invited to the show and given tickets, only to have Stephen blatantly snub me during the show by pointing out a blond standing next to me jumping up and down, having a crew member go out into the audience, and bring her back stage.

There was one last hurrah for me when Foreigner and Joe Walsh played together in September. Foreigner had a runaway successful hit with 'I Wanna Know What Love Is' and each time they would visit a city they would have a local choir come out in full robes and regalia and perform with them. Being a guest of Joe Walsh and company instead of the headliner we were sequestered to the side of the stage where the choir warmed up. This could not have been a sweeter experience for me. They were a nearly all black choir from inner city Detroit, I believe it was New Bethel Baptist Church, and they were remarkable. I chimed right in with them. When it came time for them to go onto the stage I went right along with them, standing off to the wings, but you couldn't miss me hitting some high notes.

Following that Pine Knob season I met a local man, and decided to give up my wild groupie life and settle down. Give the monogamy game a shot. That was in some respects heartbreaking, but in a way, cathartic, and in yet another way necessary.

CHAPTER 36

Final Curtain

"Happiness equals reality minus expectations..." Tom Magliozzi

Ayn Rand once said, "You can avoid reality, but you can't avoid the consequences of avoiding reality."

Coming face to face with my reality meant leaving behind my fantasy world of rock and roll. I was entering a new phase of checking my reality, raising my now teenage daughters, and finding a career for myself that was sustainable.

There are a few words of wisdom I would like to impart to any "would be" groupies. As the last vestiges of the "old boys club" crumble and die, let us not reflect, but go forward with courage and pride. We should tell our stories and live our best lives. Being your own true self will save you from indignation and humiliation. Famous people are, in the end, just as naked and human as the rest of us. They shouldn't be worshipped, or put up on some pedestal. Simply because they were the ugly kid in school who happened to pick up a guitar in order to pick up girls does not make them worldly wise, kind, or sincere in their intentions. Sometimes there are dreadful gaps between what they sing, and how they conduct themselves in reality.

Some were kind, some I didn't mind, some were bad, and some were blind.

At the time, I didn't have the ability to be introspective or to contemplate the consequences of my actions and I suppose that was the worst part. Unintentionally, I am certain that there were men that I hurt, and vice versa. Plenty of men hurt me too.

In the end was it worth the denigration of my soul?

In the end and after all, I did have the time of my life.

Several weeks ago I drove past the old Northfield Hilton and Charley's Crab building. They were grown over with brambles and weeds, everything of any value had been stripped away. The building sat on its acreage like the Titanic at the bottom of the ocean, a barren hulk of what used to be. As I slowly drove my car around the perimeter of the parking lot, tears filled my eyes, and it was like the beginning of the movie when the maître d' opens the doors to the dining room of Titanic and it suddenly comes back to life, all the glamour, glitz, sounds, lights, music, wine glasses ringing out their crystalline charms, and people laughing, above all, the laughter. At least we have our memories, where once there was a more congenial spot for "happy ever aftering" called Charley's Crab.

March 13, 1993 a cell phone signal came into the 911 reception of Palm Beach. Chuck and Betty Muer along with their friends Mr. and Mrs. Drummy were sailing back from the Bahamas to Florida a day earlier than expected. Chuck was a long time avid sailor and had weathered many storms in his day.

I will never forget him telling me one story about being hit by a rogue wave in the Bermuda Triangle, his youngest son Paul washed overboard. God was with them that day as they circled for miles again and again, and finally after several hours found him floundering in the ocean. That experience had aged him terribly, he had deeper lines in his face, and his hair had turned from blond to whitish blond. I said he looked like a man who had been through a presidency.

The forty-foot ketch, Charley's Crab, was no match for the storm of the century as it caught them by surprise in the early morning hours with 30 foot waves, and 70 mile per hour winds. They would have been rendered mast less and motor less in a storm of that magnitude. They were all lost at sea. God rest their souls, and hold them in the palm of your loving hand, for they were kind and giving people.

In the end we survived all my craziness. Chrisanna excelled in her classes, the mathematical genius was bored with anything junior colleges had to offer and education in general. Damian and I went to college at the same time, she graduated with a business degree, and after nine years of school one class at a time I became a registered nurse with a bachelor's in science degree.

CPSIA information can be obtained
at www.ICGtesting.com
Printed in the USA
LVHW042008290419
616026LV00002B/187